RAMA'S LATER HISTORY

OR

UTTARA-RAMA-CHARITA

AN ANCIENT HINDU DRAMA BY BHAVABHUTI

CRITICALLY EDITED IN THE ORIGINAL SANSKRIT AND PRAKRIT
WITH AN INTRODUCTION AND ENGLISH TRANSLATION
AND NOTES AND VARIANTS, ETC., BY

SHRIPAD KRISHNA BELVALKAR

GRADUATE STUDENT OF HARVARD UNIVERSITY
ASSISTANT TO THE PROFESSOR OF SANSKRIT AT DECCAN COLLEGE
POONA, INDIA

PART 1: INTRODUCTION AND TRANSLATION

CAMBRIDGE, MASSACHUSETTS
Harvard University Press
1915

The volumes of this Series may be had, in America, by addressing Messrs. GINN AND COMPANY, at New York or Chicago or San Francisco, or at the home-office, 29 Beacon Street, Boston, Mass.; in England, by addressing Messrs. GINN & Co., 9 St. Martin's Street, Leicester Square, London, W.C.; and in Continental Europe, by addressing Mr. Otto Harrassowitz, Leipzig.—For the titles and descriptions and prices, see the List at the end of this volume.

PRINTED FROM TYPE AT THE
UNIVERSITY PRESS, OXFORD, ENGLAND
BY HORACE HART, M.A.
PRINTER TO THE UNIVERSITY

First edition, 1915, One Thousand Copies

महाकविश्रीभवभूतिप्रणीतम्

उत्तररामचरितम्

तत्र

उपोद्धातानुवादादिसंवलितम्

प्रथमं दलम्

बिल्वावलिकरोपनाम्ना कृष्णात्मजेन श्रीपादाह्वेन

हारवर्डविश्वविद्यालयनिदेशेन

प्रकाशतां नीतम्

संवत् १९७१

TRANSLATION OF THE DEDICATORY STANZA

That nectar of learning which [by your favour] I drank day after day for two years in succession—to make for it an adequate return is not indeed my part nor have I the power; and yet, this wreath of the three-petaled *bilva*-leaves your pupil Bilvāvalikara lays here at your feet in loyal regard.

Bilvāvalikara is a Sanskritization of the name Belvalkar, literally, one who has in his hand a wreath of *bilva*. The *bilva* is a ternate or a compound leaf of three leaflets (*dala*), to which the three parts (*dala*) of this work (Translation, Text, Notes) are here likened in poetic word-play. The floret on the Sanskrit title-page is meant to represent the *bilva*.

TO

CHARLES ROCKWELL LANMAN

MY HONOURED TEACHER

निपीतं यद्विद्यामृतमनुदिवं वर्षयुगलं
न तत् कामं प्रत्यर्पयितुमधिकारो न विभवः ।
तथापि त्वद्भक्त्या त्रिदलयुतबिल्वावलिमिमां
निधत्तेऽन्तेवासी पुरत इह बिल्वावलिकरः ॥

The three parts of this work upon Rāma's Later History form volumes 21 and 22 and 23 of the Harvard Oriental Series. The contents of the three parts are distributed as follows:

Part 1: Introduction and English Translation.

Part 2: Text in Sanskrit and Prākrit; Indexes of stanzas, metres, &c.; Parallel passages; Extracts from sources; Prākrit glossary.

Part 3: Critical account of the critical apparatus; Notes, exegetic, critical, aesthetic, &c.; Variants; Appendixes.

Part 1 was printed at the University Press, Oxford, England.

Part 2 was printed at the Nirṇaya Sāgara Press of Bombay, India. A number of copies of the Text alone, for use in the colleges and universities of India, will be published at a nominal price. Applications may be made to Professor Belvalkar, Deccan College, Poona, India.

The work upon Part 3 was far advanced at the time of Dr. Belvalkar's departure from Harvard in June, 1914, on his way home to India. His manuscript material for Part 3 and his books were dispatched by the steamship *Fangturm*, which is now (June, 1915) interned at a port of the Balearic Islands. That material included his collation-sheets, which give the readings of the various codices of this drama. On account of the great difficulty of getting those codices together again, it seems best to await the release of the steamship.

CONTENTS

NOTE BY THE GENERAL EDITOR OF THIS SERIES

WITHIN the last decade, the West and the Far East have become virtually near neighbours. From the responsibilities of such neighbourhood there is no escape. We must have to do with the East, and as members of the world-family of nations we must treat the East aright. To treat the people of the East aright, we must respect them; and to respect them, we must know them. And in order that we may know them, competent scholars must study their history and make it accessible to the Occident. The business of the Orientalist is something that is in vital relation with the practical and political needs of to-day.

It is a fact of happy augury that scholars of the East are joining hands with those of the West in the great work of helping each to understand the other. The work calls for just such co-operation, and above all things else for co-operation in a spirit of mutual sympathy and teachableness. There is much of great moment that America may learn, for example, from the history of the peoples of India, and much again that the Hindus may learn from us. But the lessons will indeed be of no avail, unless the spirit of arrogant self-sufficiency give way to the spirit of docility, and the spirit of unfriendly criticism to that of mutually helpful constructive effort. The relation of teacher and taught is here, in an eminent degree, a reciprocal one, for both East and West must be at once both teacher and taught.

The whole spiritual and material background of the life of the East differs so completely from that of the West that neither can ever understand the other from a mere study of the other's literary monuments. Such study is indeed inexorably necessary, and it must be fortified by broad and rigorous training in the many-sided methods of to-day. But that is not enough. An Occidental who would faithfully interpret the East to the West must also know the life of the East from actual observation and experience, and must look at it from the Eastern angle of vision. Accordingly, for example, the Sanskrit professor of the next generation must have resided in India, have mixed (so far as possible) with its people, and have mastered at least one of the great modern vernaculars, such as Marāṭhī or Bengālī. And, on the other hand, since the Hindus themselves are already actively engaged in interpreting the East to the West, it is needful also that they visit us, not merely to learn our way of doing things, but also to look at life as we look at it, and thus to find out what things—such, let us say, as repose of spirit or the simple life—the West most needs to learn of the East.

Sir William Jones and Henry Thomas Colebrooke, illustrious pioneers of Indic philology, are ideal examples of the spirit and methods that were and are and must ever remain exemplary. They went to India and learned of the Hindus, and to the work of making the East known to the West they gave, with heroic devotion, all that they had to give. And ever since their day, the business of the East India Company or of the Imperial Government has taken men to India who have proved to be not only faithful officials, but also Indianists of large achievement. With the spread of Sanskrit studies upon the Continent in the second third of the last century, there arose men who, like Eugène Burnouf or the lexicographers Böhtlingk and Roth, accomplished great things without ever visiting the Land of the Rose-apple. More recently, the ease and speed of ocean-travel have brought it about that the Indianists who have not visited India are few indeed. They feel that they must go; for thus, as so often in modern life, do greater opportunities make obligations greater.

But it is not only for a better understanding of each other's hopes and aspirations that the Indianists of the two hemispheres must join forces. They must realize, far better than they now do, the importance of turning to account the modern methods of organization and business efficiency, and the modern progress of the graphic arts. The value of organization, and of combining the labours of isolated scholars for well-considered ends, is illustrated by the Kāvya-Mālā of Bombay and the Ānandāçrama Series of Poona. Moreover, as regards wide circulation and usefulness, complete works issued in such large groups or series as those, and in such form as only an adequate printing establishment can give them, have an enormous advantage over works issued singly or in incomplete parts, and at some obscure press, and in a small edition. Let me add that the work of eminent printers, such as the late Jāvajī Dādājī of Bombay, seems to me to be a very real service to science, and as such to deserve generous recognition from scholars.

His Excellency the Prime Minister of Nepal sent lately to Oxford, to be copied photographically for the use of scholars, seventy manuscripts of the Nepal Durbar Library. Such enlightened co-operation between East and West deserves mention, not only by way of grateful acknowledgement, but also as an admirable example which—let us hope—may be followed by others. It suggests the establishment, perhaps at the Nirṇaya Sāgara Press in Bombay, of a central agency to which Hindu Librarians may safely entrust manuscripts for mechanical reproduction, without sending them to Europe. The requirements for such an establishment are by no means too hard to provide. They are (1) a safe place of storage, (2) the photographic apparatus, and (3) a competent operator.—See Postscript on the next page.

It is with hope and with gladness that I lay before students of the history of the East the work of Doctor Belvalkar. I am glad that a Hindu, well versed in the learning of his native land, should think it worth while to learn of the West. And I hope that his residence in America may make his Eastern learning vastly more fruitful for us Occidentals than it ever could be, if he had not come hither to find out (as I said) what lessons from his country's past may best be taught to us. And I hope again that many in the coming years may follow his example, establishing thus most valuable relations of personal friendship and co-operation between Indianists of the Orient and the Occident.

Aeschylus—as Athenaeus[1] reports—said that his dramas were fragments of the great banquet of Homer's table. And so of Sophocles: his Ajax, for example, is essentially the Ajax of the Iliad. In like manner, the material of the greatest Hindu dramatists, Bhāsa and Kālidāsa and Bhavabhūti, is in large measure taken from the Hindu epics.[2] Thus the play before us, Rāma's Later History, is, as appears from its title, a dramatization of the Rāmāyaṇa. Its author, Bhavabhūti, for knowledge

[1] viii. 39 . . . *Αἰσχύλου, ὃς τὰς αὑτοῦ τραγῳδίας τεμάχη εἶναι ἔλεγε τῶν Ὁμήρου μεγάλων δείπνων.*

[2] The Mahā-Bhārata itself, using the very same metaphor as Aeschylus, declares (i. 2. 389) that 'all the best poets live upon this story' of the Bhāratans. And it adds (385, 388) that 'the inspiration of the poets comes from this incomparable narrative', and that 'there is not a story in the world that does not go back to the Bhārata'.

इदं कविवरैः सर्वैराख्यानमुपजीव्यते ।
इतिहासोत्तमादस्माज्जायन्ते कविबुद्धयः ।
अनाश्रित्यैतदाख्यानं कथा भुवि न विद्यते ॥

of what was to him the classics, and for his use of that knowledge, may justly be compared with John Milton; and for the exquisite finish of his diction, we might call him the Thomas Gray of India. For the student of comparative literature, in particular of literary genetics and the history of the drama, this play has many aspects of interest which I hope the editor has not failed to put in a clear light. But it is for the student of the history of religions that the Rāma-legend is especially instructive: its hero has become a pattern, often quite divine, of all that is good and noble; Sītā is wifely fidelity incarnate; and the Rāmāyaṇa—translated from Sanskrit into the great vernaculars, Bengālī, Hindī, Marāṭhī, and so on, and especially the Rāmāyan of Tulsīdās—has become to untold millions literally a Bible to which they look for examples of virtue and for inspiration to righteous living.

Our drama is accordingly one of the many forms into which the Indian genius has cast the story of its greatest popular hero, its deified hero; one of the many expressions of its loftiest ideals. May the knowledge of those ideals so enlarge our minds and our sympathies that, when we pass judgements on the East, we shall realize the truth of the Sanskrit proverb, 'The whole world is one family'.

C. R. LANMAN.

HARVARD UNIVERSITY,
December, 1914.

Postscript.—The prism-process was described by K. Krumbacher in an article entitled 'Die Photographie im Dienste der Geisteswissenschaften'. This appeared in 1906 in the *Neue Jahrbücher für das klassische Altertum*, 17. 601–659, and was also published separately by Teubner, price marks 3.60. For further articles on the photographic reproduction of manuscripts, see *The Nation*, of New York, for March 5, 1908 (procédé Graffin), for March 19, 1908 (excellence of 'good ordinary photographs', and ease of making them), and for December 30, 1909 (apparatus of Carl von Arnhard of Munich).

The Photostat, manufactured by the Eastman Kodak Co., is sold by the Commercial Camera Co. of Rochester, New York, for $500 or $750 or $1,100 according to the size. The Camera Co. issues a pamphlet entitled 'The Photostat and its operation'. 'The photostat is a simple and practical apparatus for the rapid photographing of printed or written documents . . . directly upon the surface of sensitized paper with the image in correct position. . . . No previous knowledge of photography is necessary.' For a great library or scientific society which is not too painfully hampered by lack of funds, and in which the apparatus will be much used, the photostat is unquestionably the best and in the long run the cheapest apparatus.

A METHOD FOR CITING SANSKRIT DRAMAS

PROPOSED BY THE GENERAL EDITOR OF THIS SERIES

Method of citing the metrical parts of a play.—These are cited by act, and by stanza as numbered from the beginning of that act, and by quarter or pāda, the pāda being indicated by a or b or c or d.

Method of citing the prose parts of a play.—The prose lines between any two consecutive stanzas are numbered from the prior to the latter stanza, starting always anew from the prior stanza. A given line is cited by number of act and by number of prior stanza (counted as above) and by number of line as counted from said prior stanza.—If there is no prior stanza (that is, if the act begins with prose), a zero is put in place of the stanza number.

Examples of the use of this method.—Thus, for this play, the Uttara-Rāma-charita, the citation iii. 2^{c} means quarter or pāda 3 of stanza 2 of act iii, *mohe mohe Rāmabhadrasya jīvam.* Thus again iii. 2^{3} means prose-line 3 as counted from stanza 2 of act iii, *Muralā—Katham iva.* And iii. 0^{3} means prose-line 3 at the beginning of act iii, *Muralā—Bhagavati Tamase,* &c.

Appeal to future editors to use this method.—We might suppose a method of citation to be a matter wholly unworthy of the serious consideration of a great scholar, if we judge by the way in which such great scholars as Böhtlingk or Pischel have failed to consider it. And from the brevity of the foregoing three paragraphs, one might suppose the matter of a method of citation to be so simple as to call for no elaborate discussion. It *is* simple, but the simplicity is the outcome of a laborious consideration of complexities arising from bad methods or lack of method, which complexities are a constant annoyance to the scholar and a hindrance to his progress. The essentials of a good method are discussed on the following pages, and the need of a good method is made clear by showing the faults of some bad ones. A bad method puts the student to a deal of worse than useless trouble, and wastes his time, just as a good method saves it. A good method should be so good as to commend itself to general acceptance by scholars and future editors, since uniformity is in itself highly desirable.

For these reasons I earnestly hope that this system will be widely accepted and followed by scholars of India and the Occident.

Importance of a good method of citation.—'A simple and sufficient means of citation is absolutely indispensable for any text of mingled verse and prose that is of consequence enough to be studied and cited at all. The editor who fails to provide such means is guilty of flagrant neglect of plain duty and of gross disregard for the time and convenience of students and of his colleagues. By way of punishment he may count upon the seriously circumscribed usefulness of his book and the silent maledictions of those who are forced to use it.'—This was my plea, in 1900, before the court of intending editors, on behalf of a good method of citation, and made in the preface of the translator of Konow's Karpūra-mañjarī, Harvard Oriental Series, vol. 4, p. xvi. The system tried by me in 1900 proved unsatisfactory in one particular, the method of citing the prose-passages. The one now proposed is substantially the same as that of 1900, excepting the feature which concerns the prose-passages.

Two aspects of the method: its logical character and its typographical expression.—A good method must be good in that it is logical and therefore easy to understand and to remember, and good also in that the typographical devices for its expression are simple and are easily and quickly caught by the eye. These general requirements are so obvious as to need no argument. Nobody disputes them—chiefly (I fear) because nobody stops to think of them. Hence the need of bringing them to the attention of future editors.

The excellences of a good method appeal in part to the mind and in part to the sense of sight, and the means for securing them will accordingly be treated under two heads (which, however, cannot be wholly separated in discussion), namely, The logically essential features of a good method, and (p. xxiv) Typographical devices for making this method usable.

Logically essential features of a good method.—A good method should utilize the native divisions of the text so far as these are natural or logical or generally accepted.—To illustrate. For the English Bible we have the generally accepted divisions into books and chapters and verses. These are always accordant among the innumerable editions, while the pagination (unless by some strange chance) is always discordant. To cite the English Bible by pages, ignoring those divisions, would be futile folly. And it is no less wrong in principle to ignore the natural divisions of a Sanskrit play. Hence

Canon 1. A good method should utilize the logical divisions of the text—that is, the divisions of the play into acts, and the divisions of the acts into stanzas and prose-passages. Canon 1 forbids us to cite the play by pages, since this ignores the division into acts, and results in endless discord as between different editions. Again, it forbids us to number either the speeches or the lines from the beginning of the act, since this ignores the division of the act into prose and verse, and results in the very undesirable possibility of citing the same verse in more than one way (by stanza-number or speech-number or line-number).

Canon 2 (corollary to canon 1). The numbering should start anew with each division.—The numbering of stanzas should start afresh at the beginning of each act; and the numbering of prose-lines should start afresh from the last stanza preceding the prose-passage.

Discord from numbering stanzas in one sequence for entire play.—The numbering of all stanzas in one sequence from beginning to end of the play has this result: that any differences in the number of stanzas in prior acts as between different editions become operative or even cumulative for any later act or acts. The serious disadvantages of this bad practice are strikingly illustrated by four European editions of the Śākuntala, namely Böhtlingk's of 1846, Williams's of 1876, Pischel's of 1877, and Cappeller's of 1909. In all these four editions act vii has thirty-five stanzas (no more and no less), and these stanzas (apart from mere variants) are identical. In Böhtlingk they are numbered from 160 to 194; in Williams, from 165 to 199; in Pischel, from 187 to 221; and in Cappeller, from 155 to 189. This is confusion worse confounded, and (with all deference to these honoured names) it is the more inexcusable because it is wholly needless.

The discord results primarily from the fact that the numbering of stanzas goes in one sequence from the beginning of the play to the end, and secondarily from the fact that, for example, act iii contains twenty-four stanzas in one text (so Böhtlingk, Cappeller) and forty-one in another (so Pischel). This wholly wrong method of numeration continues the discord of act iii through all the remaining four acts. If only the numeration began anew with each act, the stanza-numbers of act vii would be wholly accordant in all four editions, and the same references would have been precisely correct for each and all. The discord in the other acts is on the whole so slight as to cause little trouble, and even that little is avoidable (see below, p. xx).

Canon 3. The citations should be precise.—A citation which makes it necessary to search an entire page or long prose-passage is not precise. It should be so precise that you can instantly find the exact word intended.

It should therefore consist of three elements, and, if possible, of not more than three. A citation consisting of two elements only (act-number and stanza-number) may be used to designate an entire stanza, but not to designate a prose-passage.

Canon 4. They should apply at one and the same time to text and translation and notes.—The system should be such that the same citation will serve equally well for finding either a passage in the text or the corresponding passage of the translation or of an appurtenant native commentary or the corresponding exegetical or critical notes. Thus a given matter may be found by the same reference in any one of three or four different places. The method here proposed by me is usable at once in these three or four ways, and this is a very great convenience.

Canon 5. The system should be such that the citations will need little change for new editions.—That is, it should be applicable to edition after edition of the same play with the very least possible change and inconvenience. This requirement also is met by the system here proposed. First as to the stanzas. If a stanza rejected from the text of an earlier editor is to be inserted in the text of a later editor, let the later editor insert it in its place and (without changing the number of all the subsequent stanzas) assign to it the number of the preceding stanza and distinguish the repeated number by a star. On the other hand, if a stanza inserted by an earlier editor is to be rejected by a later editor, then let the later editor leave out not only the stanza but also the number.

For example, act ii of the Śākuntala has, in each of the four above-named editions, the same eighteen stanzas, all numbered with the utmost possible discord. Next after the stanza *śamapradhāneshu* (ii. 7) some MSS. give a stanza *nirākṛita-*, &c. Böhtlingk and Williams give this in their notes, while Pischel receives it into his text, and Cappeller rejects it. If the stanza-numbering had begun anew with each act, Pischel might have inserted *nirākṛita-* with the numbering ii. 7*; or, if Pischel's edition had been the editio princeps and he had numbered *nirākṛita-* as ii. 8, Cappeller might have left the stanza out and have numbered *śamapradhāneshu* as ii. 7, and (skipping ii. 8) have numbered his next stanza as ii. 9. In this way, even in spite of the difference in the total number of stanzas, the numbering of them could very easily have been kept entirely harmonious.

As to the prose-passages, this may be added. Although the prose-passages are occasionally long, they are for the most part short. As between different editions of the same play, the numbering of the prose-lines will not correspond exactly; but since the numbering starts anew with each new prose-passage, the discordances will never be cumulative and thus they will usually be so slight as to cause very little inconvenience.

At this point a word in defence of Mr. Belvalkar's procedure in giving, immediately after a Prākrit passage, its explanation in Sanskrit (or chhāyā), set off by double verticals and by a difference of type. It is true that this increases the length of the prose-passages, and consequently the possible discord in the line-numbers as between one edition and another. But this disadvantage is seldom considerable, and it is more than offset by the convenience of always having the explanation just where it is needed, instead of having to search for it at the bottom of the page or the end of the volume. Moreover the breaking up of one printed page into two or three or four typographically varying parts for text and chhāyā and variants and comments is very unsightly.

The elements of the citations.—These may now be discussed in systematic order. It is only the second and third elements of the citations for the prose-passages that occasion doubts or difficulties.

For metrical and prose-passages alike, the first element of the citation should of course be the act-number, as canon 1 requires.

For metrical passages, the second element should of course be the stanza-number as counted from the beginning of the act. The stanzas are short, and of a length (two or four printed lines) which is uniform as compared with that of the prose-passages, so that stanzas are precisely indicated and easily found by a single number.

For metrical passages, the third element should indicate the natural subdivisions of the stanza. A Sanskrit stanza consists of four quarters or pādas. A quarter of a stanza may therefore be indicated by a letter (a, b, c, d). If an entire stanza is intended, the third element, the letter, should be omitted. In this edition, anushṭubh and āryā stanzas are printed as two lines, each line consisting of two undivided pādas; and in referring to such a line, the letters ab are used together without any comma[1] between them, or else cd.

Metrical passages containing interjected prose.—Prose-lines sometimes intervene between parts of a stanza. This complication is met in a manner so logical and natural as hardly to need description: namely, the stanza-number and pāda-letter together are treated as *one* element of the citation, that is, as the second element, and the letter is not set as a 'superior'. Thus between iv. 24^{b} and iv. 24^{c} of Uttara-Rāma-charita a prose-passage of two lines and a complete stanza (iv. 25) intervene. The prose-lines are cited as iv. 24 b^{1} and iv. 24 b^{2}. The prose-lines following iv. 24^{d} are cited as iv. 24 d^{1}, iv. 24 d^{2}, and so on (although iv. 25 precedes them!).

[1] If there *is* a comma (e. g. ii. $25^{a, b}$), the punctuation indicates that the pādas referred to are not printed in the same line (are not anushṭubh or āryā).

It even happens that a bit of prose intervenes[1] between two fractions of a pāda: so between the first and second words of pāda d of Mahāvīra-charita vi. 7 (*durgo*, &c.). Here the line of prose may be cited as vi. 7^{d1}.

For prose-passages, the second element of the citation should be the number of the stanza immediately preceding.—This solution of the matter is not obvious, and that is the reason why different editors use so perplexingly different methods.—The indication of the prose-passage ought to be logically parallel with the indication of the stanza. This rule requires that each prose-passage, like each stanza, be regarded as a unit and be numbered from the beginning of the act. Editors have not usually treated each prose-passage as a unit,—apparently for the entirely invalid reason that a prose-passage unit often consists of two or more speech-units, and perhaps also because they did not see how to indicate typographically the numbering of units so complex and of such irregular length.

Act i of the Śākuntala begins with a stanza. This is followed by a prose-passage unit consisting of several speeches; but there is no difficulty in citing them all as 'act i, prose-passage 1'. And since each one of stanzas 1–9 of act i is followed by a prose-passage, it is evident that each of these nine prose-passages may be cited by the number of the stanza immediately preceding it. The like is true of the remaining twenty-three prose-passages which follow stanzas 11-33 (st. 33 is the last of act. i in Pischel's posthumous ed.). There is no prose-passage immediately following stanza 10. But it is not necessary on this account to give to the twenty-three prose-passages which follow stanzas 11–33 the numbering 10–32 just for the sake of a strict arithmetical sequence, since this produces a discord through most of the act. It is simpler to number them as 11–33, that is, to skip the number 10. In this way there is no need of any special or separate typographical indication of the number of a prose-passage. In short, it suffices to give to any prose-passage the number of the stanza immediately preceding.

For prose-passages, the citation should always contain a third element, an Arabic numeral, that is, an element which will distinguish a prose-citation from a stanza-citation. A stanza-citation consists of an act-numeral (Roman) and stanza-numeral (Arabic), followed, if necessary by a letter (a, b, c, or d) to indicate the quarter or pāda. The distinguishing element of a prose-citation should therefore be an Arabic number (1, 2, 3, 4, 5, &c.). Thus i. 5 means act i, stanza 5; and i. 5^{d} means act i, stanza 5,

[1] Since the citations of the system here proposed are intended to show on their face whether they refer to prose or to verse, it is necessary that an editor should rigorously exclude all prose (except the bare name of a dramatis persona) from a line which contains a verse-portion. Thus the stage-direction after iii. 39 of this play should not be printed in the same line with iii. 39^{d}.

pāda 4. But i. 5[4] means act i, prose-passage immediately following stanza 5, subdivision 4.—It will be observed that this method has the incidental advantage (a very considerable one) of showing on its face whether a line of poetry or a line of prose is intended.—The prose-passages vary in length from a single word to several pages. Examples of long prose-passages (forty to sixty lines) in the Śākuntala are those following i. 24, vi. 1, vi. 24, vii. 20. Precision of reference (and not alone the need of distinguishing prose-citations from stanza-citations) requires a third element indicating the subdivision.—What then shall this subdivision of the prose-passage be?

The subdivision of the prose-passage should be the printed line.—The natural subdivisions of a prose-passage are the single speeches. But these are very uneven in length, and the numbers employed to indicate them would come at *such irregular intervals and places on the page as not to be readily caught by the eye* (a grave disadvantage). Moreover, a single speech is sometimes so long that a single number would not show precisely enough where a word or phrase is. In the case of prose-passages, therefore, it is best to use the printed line as the basis of subdivision, and to place the line-numbers at brief and regular intervals, and always in the same relative position on the page, that is, in the left-hand margin, and never in the right-hand margin. The numbering of the lines of the prose-passage must of course start anew with each new passage (canon 2, p. xix). The numbering of the lines or of the speeches from the beginning of the act is ruled out as wholly illogical and as a source of confusion (canon 1).[1]

In Konow's Karpūra-mañjarī, Cambridge, 1901, the numbers of the act, and of the stanza as counted from the beginning of the act, are clearly shown. For the prose between two consecutive stanzas, I have numbered *each clause* (not speech and not line) of prose, counting from the prior stanza. The disadvantage of this method is that the numbers have to be put at irregular intervals and in irregular positions, and are therefore not easily caught by the eye. The disadvantage is so serious as to condemn this my former method.

[1] The Mālavikāgnimitra of Mr. S. P. Pandit, Bombay, 1889, numbers the stanzas from the beginning of the act. But it also numbers the speeches from the beginning of the act, without distinction of prose and verse or of Sanskrit and Prākrit. Mr. Pandit makes a great gain in simplicity by using the same numbers (many, of course, are skipped) for reference to his chhāyā and his variants on the lower part of the page and to his notes at the end of the volume. His speech-numbers are very easily caught by the eye because they are always in the same relative position, a free vertical column on the left-hand edge of the page, no matter whether it is a right-hand page or a left-hand page. So far as convenience goes, I have long deemed this to be the best edition of its time among Sanskrit plays. Only the speeches are sometimes too long for a precise citation, and the numbering of speeches from the beginning of the act is wrong in principle.

Typographical devices for making the present system usable.—No matter how easy the system is for the mind, it will be a failure unless it is easy also for the eyes. That is, the system must not only be well thought out, but there must also be adequate typographic devices for its expression.—**Device 1.** The number of the act should be clearly stated in the headline of the right-hand page.—**Device 2.** The number of the stanza *as counted from the beginning of the act* should be given at the end of each stanza.—**Device 3.** The number of every third prose-line *as counted from the last preceding stanza* should be shown by a figure close to the beginning (not the end) of that line, but nevertheless standing free in the left-hand margin, and thus very readily caught by the eye. The number should be placed exactly opposite the middle of the type-line. The numbering by threes is far more convenient than the numbering by fives. The reason why the marginal number should be on the left and not on the right is that many prose-lines contain only a word or two, so that the eye has to travel a long distance over blank paper to find the number. Any one may convince himself that this is a real inconvenience by examining the line-numbers of a wide-paged book (for example, p. 70 of Hertel's Tantrākhyāyika, Berlin, 1910). If the marginal numbers for prose-lines in all editions were uniformly put on the left-hand side, the gain of convenience would be very great. Any one may assure himself of this by looking at Mr. S. P. Pandit's Mālavikāgnimitra, where the speech-numbers are thus given (see above, p. xxiii, note). The eye catches them with wonderful ease.

Additional device for making this method easy: corner-citations.—In the outer upper corner of the left-hand page is given the citation of the line with which that page *begins*; and in the outer upper corner of the right-hand page is given the citation of the line with which that page *ends*. A dash and square bracket are placed after the left-hand citation, and a square bracket and dash are placed before the right-hand citation, and the two citations are intended to be read together. Thus the two corner-citations

vii. 31^5—] [—vii. 35^b

are to be read as follows: 'From vii. 31^5 to vii. 35^b.' The purpose of the corner-citations is to show just what parts of the text are to be found included on any two pages which face each other at an 'opening' of the book (beim Aufschlagen des Buches, à l'ouverture du livre). The object of putting the citations in the outer corners is to enable the reader, when 'thumbing' the volume, to find any passage with the least possible opening of the leaves, and therefore with the minimum of time and trouble. If they were put, as they often are, on the inner corners, the reader would have to open the leaves almost completely in order to make use of the corner-citations.—The page-numbers are relegated to the inconvenient inner corners in order to discourage as far as possible the employment of them for citation. (The page-numbers have their use for the printer and book-binder.)

Minor typographic details.—As to the corner-citations: The numerals and letters and dashes should be set close together, without spacing, to the left or right of the single square bracket. The act-numerals should be Roman numerals (not Arabic), and lower-case (not capitals). The stanza-numbers should be Arabic. The letters which indicate the verse of the stanza should be 'superiors' (that is, be set higher than the rest of the type-line) and Roman (not Italic). The same holds for the figures which indicate the prose-line. The corner-citations should be set thus:

vii.31^{5}—] [—vii.35^{b}

They should not be set as follows: not thus, [—vii. 35. b; nor thus, [—VII. 35. b; nor thus, [—VII. 35.^{b}

I have no quarrel with one who insists on using Arabic figures for the number of a maṇḍala of the Rigveda, of a parvan of the Mahā-Bhārata, or of a kāṇḍa of the Rāmāyaṇa. But for an act of a play, the Roman numeral has undoubted advantages. And if the Roman numeral *is* used, let it be in lower-case, not in capitals. As eminent printers have observed (so Bänsch-Drugulin, De Vinne), the use of many capitals on a page 'stört die Ruhe des Satzbildes', 'spots the page', gives it an unrestful look.

For punctuating the elements of one citation, moreover, periods are much better than commas: thus, iii. 1^{1}, iv. 2^{c}, v. 6^{1}, vii. 35^{b}. In a mass of references, the overworked commas give the line a serrated or very ragged effect: thus, III, 1, 1; IV, 2, c; V, 6, 1; VII, 35, b. The contrast between the serrated style and the restful style is so great as to make comment needless.

Inconveniences resulting from lack of system or from a bad system.—These might well be adduced by way of comment on the foregoing principles and canons and devices, or to serve as arguments therefor. Their relevance is clear.

Lack of system, good or bad.—As an example may be cited the old edition of Uttara-Rāma-charita, of Calcutta, 1831. This gives the number of the page, but not the line of the page, nor any stanza-numbering (good or bad), nor even the number of the act except at the beginning and end of each act. Since the edition is long out of print and the page-numbers of later editions have no determinable relation with the page-numbers of the old one, all references made to the old one by writers on the drama and by lexicographers and grammarians and others have of course become worthless.

Citation by pages and multiple sequences of pagination.—An extreme example of the futility of citing by pages is seen in Ghāṭe's edition of this play (Nagpur, 1895). Here the pagination begins anew in one and the same volume no less than seven times: namely, for preface (1–2), introduction (1–12), text (1–192), translation (1–60), notes (1–51), glossary (1–8), and corrections (1–3), to say nothing of two sequences without pagination. Thus for example there are (if we disregard the differences of Arabic, Roman, and Nāgarī numbers) two pages for every page numbered '60' or less, three pages numbered '51', four pages numbered '12', five pages numbered '8', and seven pages numbered '2'. In Kāḷe's Śākuntala, Bombay, 1898, there are no less than ten different sequences of pages! two sequences are without pagination, and eight sequences begin with page 1. Multiple sequences of pagination are very frequently found in books printed in India, and I call upon Hindu editors to recognize the inconvenience thereby occasioned, and to exclude such sequences from the works which they edit.

Combinations of bad system and systemlessness.—These need hardly be described except to show the bewildering perplexities that result. Of these an example or two.

The Mṛichchhakaṭika of Calcutta, 1829, gives in the headlines the name of the play (343 times repeated, but with no indication of the act!) and the page-numbers. There is no numbering of the stanzas and none of the prose-lines. Stenzler's edition of Bonn, 1847, gives in the headlines the number of the act and the page-numbers, and every fifth page-line is indicated by a marginal number. Lassen's Prākrit grammar refers to the Calcutta edition. In order that students may use Lassen's book with Stenzler's text, Stenzler puts the Calcutta page-numbers in his margins. The general effect is confusing, and the confusion is aggravated by the numbers at the end of every speech (not line) in Prākrit (not Sanskrit) counted from the top of the page! Böhtlingk's translation of this play gives no help for finding a desired passage except the number of the act at the beginning of each act. In order to use it with reasonable facility, I had to write the number of the act on the outer corner of the uneven pages, and the number of the stanza in the margin.

Goḍabole's Mṛichchhakaṭika of Bombay, 1896, gives the act-number in the headlines. It numbers the stanzas from the beginning of each act, and gives these numbers between double verticals at the end of each stanza. But it also gives a number between European parentheses at the end of each speech in Prākrit (not Sanskrit) for reference to the explanation at the foot of the page. This double numbering is, to use an English *nyāya*, like having a big hole for the big cat and a little hole for the kitten. Moreover, it gives a marginal numbering of the lines counted (without distinction of prose and verse or of Prākrit and Sanskrit) from the beginning of the act.—Now observe the result. A prose-passage may be cited, if in Sanskrit, by page and by line (the line you must count for yourself), or by act and marginal line-number; if in Prākrit, by either of these methods or else by act and Prākrit speech-number. For metrical passages take the words *kukkehiṁ kukkīhiṁ a bukkaante* as an example. These may be cited as Mṛichchhakaṭika, ed. Goḍabole, Bombay, 1896, p. 62, l. 3; or as ditto, act i, line 556; or as ditto, act i, stanza 52ᶜ. But this stanza is actually numbered as '**(**46**)** ‖ 52 ‖', because, being a Prākrit speech, the number 46 is given for reference to the explanation. And even the number 46 is an abbreviation (the common one) for 146, so that stanza 41 on page 48 (an earlier page!) is numbered as '**(**91**)** ‖ 41 ‖'. The general appearance of the text is further marred by excessively frequent Nāgarī numbers referring to the variants.

No one can comprehend all these complexities at a glance. They require careful study. But needless complexities are not worth careful study. Moreover, one writer will cite a line in one way and another writer in another. The upshot of it all is—baffling confusion! In closing, I beg the reader to remember that these inconveniences are mentioned, not in order to discredit the past work of honoured scholars, but rather in order to persuade scholars to avoid them in their future work.

C. R. LANMAN.

HARVARD UNIVERSITY,
June 18, 1914.

PREFACE

It is now just a century and a quarter since Sir William Jones published, in 1789, his translation of Kālidāsa's Śākuntala, and thereby gave to the western world its first knowledge of the dramatic literature of the Hindus. During these hundred and twenty-five years the Śākuntala has been edited some thirty times, and there are over fifty translations in as many as thirteen European tongues, to say nothing of translations into the vernaculars of India. Its own intrinsic merits have won for it, in the land of its birth, the title of a masterpiece, not only of Kālidāsa's plays, but even of the Indian literature. And on the strength of these merits, and in part perhaps on account of Goethe's lavish praise, this title has been recognized in the Occident, and without demur.

The Hindus, on other hand, hold that our present play, Rama's Later History or Uttara-Rāma-charita, the masterpiece of Bhavabhūti, surpasses in some respects even the Śākuntala. Almost a hundred years ago, in 1827, Horace Hayman Wilson introduced it to western readers by giving a very free version of it in his *Hindu Theatre*. But strangely enough, in all this time, not a single edition of the play has appeared in the Occident, nor even a translation that is both adequate and now obtainable. Félix Nève's French version, long out of print, was issued in 1880. The English version of Charles H. Tawney was twice printed, in 1871 and 1874, but in distant Calcutta and in scant supply.

In India the Uttara-Rāma-charita is placed in the hands of almost every college student, and he admires it and loves it ever after. It becomes a part of his experience, 'revealing new and newer charms every moment.'[1] So at least it has been with me ever since 1899, when I made my first acquaintance with the play. And it is as a partial return for the many happy hours that I passed in the company of Bhavabhūti that I here undertake to make the real genius of the author, his greatness as a dramatic poet, known beyond the little band of zealous Indianists in Europe and America who can study the play in the original. For there are many, in the West as elsewhere, who are eager for an intelligent general knowledge of the great literatures of the world, such as is accessible, however, to no human being in the originals, so numerous are the languages in which veritable masterpieces have been written.

[1] *Kshaṇe kshaṇe yan navatām upaiti tad eva rūpaṁ ramaṇīyatāyāḥ.*—Śiśupālavadha, iv. 17.

Moreover, the history and technique of the drama in general have now become a recognized university study; and as a specimen of what India, independently, has achieved in the way of dramatic literature, the present play will not fail to be interesting. To Indianists, to students of comparative literature, and to students of drama, accordingly, this edition makes its appeal.

But it is one thing to read a book and feel its beauties for oneself, and a very different thing to help others to feel them. And the difficulty is all the greater when that help has to be rendered through the medium of a language which is not one's mother tongue. In that case the translator can never be quite certain that the English word which he is using will convey the exact shade of meaning which the original Sanskrit word has for him; or that the English word may not have, for an English reader, some unpoetical connotation or lurking suggestion due to facts in his social environment which the translator may not fairly be expected to know. The kind criticism of Professor Lanman has saved me from some of these pitfalls; but it is too much to hope that I have always done full justice to the poet.

To translate a narrative work, or a work which interests us only by reason of the facts which it tells us, is fairly easy. For a scientific or philosophical treatise one has only to choose suitable technical terms and define them precisely and use them consistently; and what is obscure or unduly terse you can explain and expand. But in translating poetry we are called upon not only to give the meaning correctly, but also to reproduce the subtle literary qualities of the original. Rhythm, word-order, figures of speech, compactness or diffuseness of expression—in short, almost every literary device of the original ought, in theory, to reappear in the translation. But since the genius of one language differs radically from that of another, an ideal translation is, as von Wilamowitz-Moellendorff observes, a travesty or perhaps a metempsychosis: in other words, a wellnigh impossible task. Some things must be sacrificed. But it is far better, wherever possible, to keep close to the original and show the author *in his true native colours*, rather than, under the pretext of giving a literary finish to the translation, to make him say things which he did not say and would never dream of saying.

A few words then as to certain principles, mostly limitations, that have governed me in my translation. First, whereas the original play is mingled prose and verse, the translation is all in prose. The translation of the stanzas is set in narrow measure (that is, with an indentation on both sides) and with the stanza-number at the end in bold-face type, and it is thus distinguished typographically from the translation of the prose. There are in the play nineteen kinds of metre, having from eight to nineteen syllables to the line. Bhavabhūti uses these metres with consummate skill, as I have tried to show in the Notes, and especially in Appendix 1. The succession of light and heavy syllables and the rhythmic pauses which break the line at irregular intervals give to each of these metres an emotional effect which a Hindu at least can feel and perhaps describe, but which it is absolutely impossible to reproduce in a language where the system of verse-accent is wholly different. The use of prose in translation carries with it, of course, the giving up of rhyme. Both rhyme and metre are apt to lead to useless padding or unwarranted curtailing. Bentley's familiar comment on Pope's *Iliad* is worth repeating: 'A very pretty poem, but he must not call it Homer.' There have been, no doubt, a few ideal translations made by men gifted with true poetic inspiration, but unless the translator is sure that he has this gift, let him beware.

Secondly, as to literalness. An attempt, on linguistic or other grounds, to render words radically akin in Sanskrit by words radically akin in English, or to render the same word or phrase in just the same way at every occurrence, is apt to defeat its own end. The word *saṁskṛita* is indeed equal to *con-fectus*; but *confection* as a version of *saṁskāra* is absurd. Again, the exigencies of the situation sometimes move the translator to render noun by adjective, adjective by adverb, adverb by verb, and so on. In such cases, for the sake of those who are reading the original also, the literal version or the analysis of the compound will be given in the Notes. Once more, it may happen that the ever-varying context shows that the same word has a dozen finely differenced shades of meaning in as many different places. The particle *kila*, for example, is here rendered in perhaps a dozen different ways. The like holds true for the forms of address. In all this I have tried to heed von Wilamowitz-Moellendorff's precept (*Reden und Vorträge*[3], p. 5): 'To give free and original expression to the thoughts and feelings and moods of the poet because you [the translator] have yourself fully comprehended and experienced them: that—no more, but also no less—is translating.'

Thirdly, as to word-order. It was Bhavabhūti's boast (i. 2) that upon him the Goddess of Speech and Eloquence waited as a submissive handmaid. And so, we may not assume that with him 'rhyme was the rudder to sense', in other words that his diction was determined by exigencies of metre or the like. On the contrary, his word-order is deliberate and almost always artistic; and in the stanzas especially he likes to create a sort of suspense by withholding the principal word, or putting it in only towards the end. In a highly inflected tongue like Sanskrit, the resultant suspending of the sense or the resultant inversion is easily possible and even natural, and I have often tried to reproduce it. But in English the inflections are nearly all lost, and for this very reason the sense is so dependent on the word-order as to leave little freedom in the arrangement of words, save at the cost of unclearness or extreme harshness. And since a translation, whatever else it pretends to be, *must* be intelligible, I have had, yet oftener and against my will, to sacrifice the effects of the original in the interest of ready intelligibility.

The alliterative effects of the original are often very striking. Bhavabhūti uses smooth liquid sounds for the softer emotions and harsh guttural combinations to express the sturdier ones. To reproduce these effects in English is in some cases not feasible, and in others not advisable, and in most cases I had to give up the attempt.

Finally, as to exotic colour. If East and West are ever to understand each other, then each must bring to the other a sympathetic hearing. On either side a top-lofty condemnation of the peculiarities of the other quite defeats the purposes of a book like this. Accordingly, I have not tried to avoid an idea or an expression peculiar to the Hindus and easily understood by them, just because it may seem 'queer' to a foreigner, and I venture to hope that my attitude will be taken as the best compliment that I could pay, not only to the author or to his native country, but also to the fair-mindedness of my foreign readers. An instance or two. An older person in addressing a younger, says *āyushman*. This I have rendered by long-lived one', meaning thereby not 'one who *has* lived long', but 'one who, it is hoped, *may* live long'. My version is un-English; but the prayer for long life or the benediction (if indeed the speaker is conscious of it at all) is an implicit one, and to render it always as if it were an explicit one, by the phrase 'may thy days be long', or the like, is wholly wrong. The synonymous (Marāṭhī) *chirañjīva* is still current in India, and is almost equivalent to 'my son' as used by an older man (not necessarily the father) to the younger. Like comment might be made on the phrases 'my father's feet', 'lotus-feet', 'vitals of my heart', 'valiant monkeys', 'shampooing', and others.

A few minor matters. Certain words, like *yathā* or *iti* (as marking the beginning or the end of a quotation), or like *iti* or *abhinīya* with a stage-direction, are sufficiently rendered by the italics in which those directions are printed or by marks of punctuation. Sometimes, where my version seemed too free, the original word is given in parentheses, although it is not to be regarded as the precise equivalent of the adjacent English word. Words inserted to complete the sense or to bring out more fully the exact force of the original are put in square brackets. Most of the other devices are self-explaining. In all these matters I have tried to follow the dictates of common sense.

The foot-notes to the translation are meant to give the help that a non-Hindu reader may need for understanding the play, but no more. The play bristles with proper names as familiar to a Hindu as is the name of Achilles to a Greek or of St. Paul to a Christian. These Sanskrit names are hard for the Occidental. Moreover, he is confused as to the identity of a character, partly because the same person is called by so many different names. I have therefore given a brief foot-note every time a new name appears in the translation. And to show the relation of the several characters in the action, I have (on the advice of Professor Lanman) given in the Introduction a summary of Vālmīki's Rāmāyaṇa, a poem which (strange as it may seem to a Hindu) is very little known outside of India. More elaborate verbal or aesthetic comments are reserved for the Notes proper.

The conclusion of a preface, the grateful acknowledgement of kind counsel and friendly services, is, to the author at least, a most delightful task. It is right and it is pleasant to say 'Thank you'. And it is pleasanter still to think that the names of men who share your enthusiasms are to be permanently associated with your work, and that the turning of its pages will always remind you of those who have toiled and are toiling with you to reach a common goal.

The names of those who have edited or translated this play before me are given in Appendix 12, and need not be repeated here.

Dr. Frederick W. Thomas, Librarian of the India Office in London, has procured for me the loan of manuscripts from the India Office Library, the Deccan College Manuscripts Library and the Ānandāśrama Library of Poona, and the Sanskrit College Library of Calcutta—and all with a zeal and kindness that go far beyond the perfunctory discharge of official duty. Dr. Otto Schrader of the Adyar Library at Madras did me the valued favour of sending to the Harvard Library for my use some palm-leaf manuscripts. And I am indebted to Mr. S. P. V. Ranganāthaswāmi, Āryavaraguru, of Vizagapatam, for a similar favour, and also for providing me with some early editions of the play, now out of print.

The Prime Minister of Nepal, with a liberality and insight that deserve all praise, sent seventy manuscripts of the Durbar Library to Oxford for photographic reproduction under the supervision of Professor Macdonell, among them the old and important Nevārī manuscript (dated 1196) of this play, and of it the Harvard College Library generously procured for me a rotograph copy. To His Excellency, to Dr. Macdonell, and to the College, my hearty thanks.

Shreemant Babasaheb Ghorpade, the talented Chief of Inchalkaranji, has laid me under considerable obligation. It is to his kindness that

I owe the loan of the important Old Javanese version of the Rāmāyaṇa which he had secured from Java. Professor H. Kern of Utrecht, the editor of that version, very kindly supplied me with certain items of information about it. My college friend, Mr. R. D. Ranade of Poona, and my brother-in-law, Dr. N. G. Sardesai, have kept me constantly supplied with books and information of all kinds, which, but for them and at such a distance from India, I should not have been able to obtain.

The suggestion to edit this play for the Harvard Oriental Series came first from Professor James Haughton Woods of Harvard University, whose acquaintance I made while he was studying philosophy in India, and who, both at the inception of the work and in its progress, has given me his help and his whole-hearted sympathy.

To the Controller of the Oxford University Press, Mr. Horace Hart, M.A., my thanks are due not only for the typographic excellence of the work, but also for the promptness with which he printed it.

This work, while yet incomplete, was submitted in partial fulfilment of the requirements for the degree of Doctor of Philosophy at Harvard University.

There is yet one more name which I must mention, and which I have purposely kept to the last. It is impossible to express adequately all that this edition owes to the sympathy, the assistance, the almost fatherly care that it has received from my honoured teacher, Professor C. R. Lanman, the editor of this series. When in India, I had made some sort of a plan for bringing out an annotated edition of the Uttara-Rāma-charita. I cannot say what that edition would have been like; but if the present form of the work is in any way an improvement on my earlier plan, as it undoubtedly is, the difference is all to the credit of Professor Lanman. He assisted me in my work most unselfishly. There was no detail too slight to escape his attention, and on every point he would bring to bear all the mature results of his wide experience as a scholar and an editor. His criticisms were always judicious and sympathetic; and I have profited as much by what he taught me expressly in the way of western scientific methods of research as by the indirect inspiration that I derived while observing him at work upon the Visuddhimagga. As the work was born and has grown, so it is natural that it should also go forth into the world under Professor Lanman's guidance, and I congratulate myself upon having succeeded in overcoming his reluctance to have this work dedicated to him.

S. K. BELVALKAR.

HARVARD UNIVERSITY,
April, 1914.

INTRODUCTION

Bhavabhūti, his life, and his date

1. Bhavabhūti's account of himself.—Bhavabhūti, the author of the Uttara-Rāma-charita, gives in the prologues to his three plays various items of information about himself and his family. This information is fullest in the Mahāvīra-charita,[1] which is probably the poet's earliest work. In his second work, the Mālatī-Mādhava,[2] there is, in addition to this information, an attempt to glorify his family (i. 7) and his own attainments (i. 10). There is also a note of defiance or of discontent (i. 8) at the reception accorded to his earlier work. His latest work, the Uttara-Rāma-charita, is most meagre and also modest in the biographical matter. These items may be put together as follows:

In the country to the south there is a city called Padma-pura. In it live certain Brahmans surnamed Udumbara, who trace their lineage to the saint Kaśyapa. They follow the Taittirīya branch of the Black Yajur Veda, are well versed in the Brahma-lore, and have performed the Soma sacrifice.[3] They are pious householders, heads of their school, revered of all men, and duly maintain the five Sacred Fires. It was to this family of the Udumbaras that that famous performer of the Vājapeya sacrifice, he who was called Mahā-Kavi (Great Poet), belonged. Fifth in descent from him is our Bhavabhūti, Bhaṭṭa Gopāla of blessed name being his grandfather, and Nīlakaṇṭha of hallowed memory being his father. His mother's name is Jatukarṇī. Bhavabhūti's original name is Śrīkaṇṭha;[4]

[1] Mahāvīra-charita is cited from the Nirṇaya Sāgara edition of 1901 with Vīrarāghava's commentary. From v. 46[1] to the end, I cite the version given in that edition without the comm., on the pages following 247 (first sequence).

[2] The Mālatī-Mādhava is cited from the Nirṇaya Sāgara ed. of 1900 with the comm.'s of Tripurāri and Nānyadeva, and of Jagaddhara. The various Nirṇaya Sāgara editions of the two plays do not differ much as to pagination.

[3] See Dr. A. B. Keith, Bhavabhūti and the Veda, *JRAS.*, July, 1914, p. 729. [Added in proof-sheets.]

[4] 'In whose throat—upon whose lips—resides the Goddess of Wealth and Eloquence.' This probably was the name given him by his parents. His full name would accordingly be Śrīkaṇṭha Nīlakaṇṭha Udumbara. He was called Bhava-bhūti, say some, because God Śiva (Bhava) gave him 'luck' or 'holy ashes' (bhūti); others say, because he wrote a stanza containing either the line *Sāmbā punātu Bhava-bhūti-pavitra-mūrtiḥ* or *Girijāyāḥ kuchau vande Bhava-bhūti-sitānanau.*

he has mastered the sciences of grammar and rhetoric and logic,[1] and has studied the Vedas and the Upanishads, the Sāñkhya and the Yoga. His preceptor was Jñāna-nidhi,[2] rightly so called, a pious ascetic, and, like Añgiras, pre-eminent among the sages. Bhavabhūti is a poet and, as is natural, is in friendly relations with the actors, into whose hands he gave his dramatic works.

2. His family-home, Padmapura in the Berars.—Some manuscripts of the Mālatī-Mādhava distinctly say that Padmapura was 'in the Berars', *Vidarbheshu.*[3] In the prologue, the stage-manager speaks of the play as enacted on the occasion of the 'fair of Lord Kālapriya'. If the usual assumption is correct that Lord Kālapriya is the same as Mahākāleśvara, whose famous shrine at Ujjain in Mālva is mentioned by Kālidāsa and Bāṇa and others,[4] and if we are justified in inferring that the Mālatī-Mādhava was therefore enacted at Ujjain,—then the stage-manager's mention of Padmapura as 'in the country to the south' or as 'in the Dekkan' (Dakshiṇāpathe) would be entirely in harmony with the datum of the manuscripts which specify Padmapura as 'in the Berars'; for Vidarbha is in fact to the south (and a little east) of Ujjain. In fairness, however, we must add that the oldest extant manuscript[5] of the Mālatī-Mādhava, dated Nevārī Saṁvat 276=A.D. 1156, does not mention the province in which Padmapura was situated, nor does the prologue to the Mahāvīra-charita.

3. Identity of Padmapura with Padmāvatī of the Mālatī-Mādhava unproved.—The scene of the Mālatī-Mādhava is laid in a city named Padmāvatī. This city and its surroundings are so minutely described in that play, especially at the end of act iv and the beginning of act ix, that Mr. M. V. Lele[6] believes he has succeeded in identifying its exact site with that of what is now a small village called Pavāyā or Polā-Pavāyā, near which remains of a considerable city are discernible. Pavāyā is a little to the north-east of Narvār. Narvār is near the centre of Gwalior state, and is almost due south of Agra, and just 100 miles from it; and it is 220 miles from Ujjain, about north-east by north.

If Bhavabhūti's ancestral home, Padmapura, is to be identified with the

[1] 'Science of words and of sentences and of syllogisms.'

[2] 'Store of knowledge.'

[3] See Dr. Bhandarkar's 2nd edition, p. 11 of the Text, end.

[4] See Raghuvaṁśa, vi. 34; Meghadūta 37 (stanza *Bhartuḥ kaṇṭha-*, &c.) and 38; also Kādambarī, p. 53, ed. of the Bombay Skt. Series.

[5] The Nepal Durbar Library MS., no. 1473 ṭ of the Catalogue (Calcutta, 1905), a palm-leaf MS. I used a rotograph copy of it made for the Harvard College Library.

[6] See his book (in Marāṭhī) entitled *Mālatī-Mādhava, Sāra va Vichāra*, p. 5 a. Also Cunningham, Archaeological Report for 1862–5, vol. ii, pp. 307–8, where, however, Padmāvatī is identified with Narvār itself.

Padmāvatī described in the Mālatī-Mādhava (as is sometimes done), we must find some shrine of Lord Kālapriya with reference to which Padmāvatī may be said to be 'on the road to the south', and Mr. Lele suggests [1] that Kālpi on the Jumna (about fifty miles south-west of Cawnpur) does meet this requirement. According to this view, the play was first enacted at the fair at Kālpi (=Kālapriya), and the poet's family seat, Padmapura (=Padmāvatī, near Narvār), would indeed have been 'on the road to the south' from Kālpi. The arguments for this view concern 1. the names, and 2. the preciseness of the description of Padmāvatī. As to the names, Padmapura and Padmāvatī do indeed mean the same thing, Lotus-ville, but neither of them is a distinctive name (there are twenty-nine Green-villes in the United States); and the surface similarity between Kālpi and Kālapriya is not by itself convincing. As for the argument that Bhavabhūti's description of Padmāvatī could only have been written by one familiar with the place from birth, it is quite devoid of cogency. His description of the Daṇḍakā forest would prove just as well that he was born there also! It proves his keenness of observation, not his birthplace.

Moreover in describing the region of Padmāvatī, Bhavabhūti says: 'These hills and forests remind me of the Godāvarī and the southern mountains.' The word 'remind' (*smārayanti*, M. M. ix. 3²) clearly marks his acquaintance with Padmāvatī as the later experience and his familiarity with the south as the earlier one. Pending the discovery of new data, then, we may assume that Bhavabhūti's ancestral home, Padmapura, was in the Berars,[2] and not near the site of Narvār in Gwalior state.

This would not of course necessarily involve the further assumption, which it is usual to make, of the identity of the shrine of Lord Kālapriya with that of Mahākaleśvara of Ujjain. That is possible, but it is better to leave the question open.

4. Further biographical details.—It would thus seem that, like the hero in his Mālatī-Mādhava, Bhavabhūti quite early in life left his native country of the Berars and went to Ujjain in Mālva, or perhaps to Padmāvatī, there to complete his studies under his preceptor Jñānanidhi. Bhavabhūti here not only grounded himself in the various sciences,[3] but also, like his older contemporary or immediate predecessor, Bāṇa,[4] stood

[1] In his book just cited, pp. 4 b, 84 a.

[2] Dr. Bhandarkar (in his M.M., 2nd ed., note to act i, line 31) observes that there are still many Brahman families in the region around Chandā who follow the Taittirīya branch of the Black Yajur Veda, the branch to which Bhavabhūti's family belonged (above, § 1). Chandā is in Nagpur, near the border of the Berars, and not far from the Godāvarī.

[3] He likes to show off his knowledge: cp. Glossary 1, Technical terms from the three plays.

[4] Cp. Harsha-charita, p. 47 f, Nir. Sāg. ed. For the chronological relation cp. below, § 8.

on friendly terms with all sorts and conditions of men. Especially intimate was his friendship with the actors. The Mahāvīra-charita and Mālatī-Mādhava actually mention this friendship in the prologue; in the Uttara-Rāma-charita it is hinted at in the account given by Lava of Vālmīki's play-within-the-play (act iv. 22^{27-35}), which we may well believe to be autobiographical. We should very much like to have some details about this relation between the actors and the would-be dramatist, but all is left to imagination. It is possible that Bhavabhūti began by writing for his actor-friends prologues for other people's plays.[1] He may even at times have modified an earlier play. Possibly again he may have actually taken parts in the plays.[2] Certain it is that he soon persuaded the actors to stage his own plays, and though he did not immediately succeed as a playwright, he soon got recognition, and was perhaps even able (below, § 13) to secure royal patronage.

5. Bhavabhūti's personality as inferred from his writings.—Regarding Bhavabhūti's private life, the impression which the perusal of his plays leaves upon us is of the most favourable kind. He was by no means Fortune's favourite. His was an uphill fight for fame, may be for even food and the daily necessities of the family; and he complains very bitterly (Māl. Mādh. i. 8) against the proverbially fickle judgements of the people. Even his latest play (Uttara-Rāma, i. 5) is not without this pessimistic note. It would thus seem that our poet had experienced many a reverse of fortune[3] and had emerged triumphant from them all. What gave him the strength to fight his unequal fight with the world, what sustained his courage and infused a new enthusiasm in him, was the consolation of an ideal family life such as, we must believe, was his. Love was not to him a mere sensuous affair, as it often is with poets Sanskrit or non-Sanskrit; it was with him a spiritual communion of souls. Of such a love he has left us many an idealized picture which may well bear comparison with those of other literatures. Thus he says:

> Uniform in happiness and in sorrow—conformable to all the conditions of life—in which the heart finds solace—the flavour of which age cannot stint—which, with time, as the veil of reserve drops away, abides as a perfect and ripened affection,—that one supreme blessing only the fortunate among mankind, and after a sore trial, attain. (Uttara-Rāma-charita, i. 39.)

And it is not only in the Uttara-Rāma-charita, where the theme was exalted, and the personages ideal, that we find such lofty sentiments. We have similar ones in the Mālatī-Mādhava: for example, vi. 18:

[1] See Appendix 8.

[2] Cp. note to English Translation, act vii. 19^{9}.

[3] Cp. Mālatī-Mādhava, viii. 14; Uttara-Rāma-charita, vii. $4^{c,d}$.

> Know ye, my dear children, that for the man his lawfully wedded wife and for the wife her lord are, the one to the other, the dearest of friends, the sum-total, I should say, of all relations, the consummation of all desires, a priceless treasure, the very life and all.

And when children come, this affection between man and wife reaches its utmost perfection (Uttara-Rāma, iii. 18):

> As being the common meeting-ground of the father's and the mother's affection, in a child we, so to say, tie in a common knot of joy the several strands of their hearts.

Bhavabhūti's conception of friendship was also equally lofty. Compare, for instance, Mahāvīra-charita, v. 59:

> To guard thy friend's interests even at the sacrifice of thy own life; in thy dealings with him to avoid all malice, all guile; and to strive for his weal as thou wouldst for thy own: such is the course of noble friendship.

Other instances of this are the relation between Mādhava and Makaranda (Mālatī-Mādhava, ix. 40) and that between Janaka and Daśaratha (Uttara-Rāma, iv. 13, 14). These extracts from Bhavabhūti's works will help to make the otherwise shadowy figure of the poet somewhat life-like and real. We now proceed to the more difficult task of determining his date.

6. Bhavabhūti's date: traditional story about Kālidāsa and Bhavabhūti.—Tradition couples Bhavabhūti's name with that of Kālidāsa, grouping them with seven others as the 'nine gems' of the court of king Vikrama or Vikramāditya of Ujjain. The story goes that, when Kālidāsa was already a recognized 'gem' in the court of Vikramāditya, there came to him one day a Brahman poet, and begged him to intercede with the king and secure the royal patronage. This poet was no other than our Bhavabhūti. He read aloud his Uttara-Rāma-charita while Kālidāsa was half listening to him and half engaged in playing a game of *sāra's* (a kind of chess). When Bhavabhūti had finished, Kālidāsa praised the work very highly, and agreed to use his influence for the poet if he would but drop a *bindu* (nasal) in the last line of one of the stanzas (i. 27. See Notes). Bhavabhūti accepted the improvement, and became an acknowledged 'gem'.

The stanza about the 'nine gems' is late, and we do not even know from it who is meant by 'Vikramāditya', since that is a title assumed by several kings. The Saṁvat era which is still current in many parts of

India is supposed to have been founded by a Vikramāditya (57 B.C.), and some scholars place Kālidāsa in the court of this Vikramāditya. But the best modern opinion[1] makes the Golden Age of the classical Sanskrit literature coincident with the bloom of the Gupta dynasty, several kings of which had assumed the title of Vikramāditya. This brings Kālidāsa somewhere between 375 and 475 A.D.

7. Bhavabhūti's works certainly influenced by those of Kālidāsa.—The matter of Kālidāsa's Śākuntala is an old epic legend which we find in the Mahā-Bhārata; and the matter of his Urvaśī may be traced through the Brāhmaṇas back to the hymns of the Ṛigveda itself. Accordingly, the fact that Bhavabhūti alludes in his Mālatī-Mādhava (see ii. 7^{10}, iii. 3) to the familiar tales of Śakuntalā and Dushyanta, and of Purūravas and Urvaśī, has of course not an atom's weight towards proving that he knew the tales from Kālidāsa's plays. On the other hand, the dénouement of the Uttara-Rāma-charita resembles that of the Śākuntala enough to suggest that Bhavabhūti was familiar with Kālidāsa's technique. Again, the parallelisms in thought and expression as between Bhavabhūti and Kālidāsa (they have been put together for study in appendix 4) present further cumulative evidence looking in the same direction. Thirdly, the parallelism between act ix of Mālatī and act iv of Urvaśī is even yet more weighty as proof. In the one we have the love-lorn Mādhava wandering in quest of his Mālatī, and in the other the distracted Purūravas seeking in vain for Urvaśī. Here again, as between Bhavabhūti and Kālidāsa, the dramatic situation and its poetic treatment bear such striking similarity as to suggest direct and conscious imitation. Fourthly, Bhavabhūti's dramatic device (at M. M. ix. 25, 26) of making the desperate Mādhava send a cloud as messenger to his beloved, is so clearly an imitation of Kālidāsa's Cloud-messenger or Megha-dūta that there can be scarcely a doubt that Bhavabhūti (perhaps its earliest imitator) here had that famous and much-imitated poem distinctly in mind,—so complete is the correspondence of the stanzas concerned not only in situation but also in the words and even in the characteristic metre. Indeed, as concerns points three and four, we may say that Bhavabhūti has deliberately set himself to use Kālidāsa's motifs, and if possible, in so doing, to surpass him.

So much then seems certain, that Bhavabhūti studied and imitated Kālidāsa. Accordingly he may have been either a somewhat younger

[1] See B. Liebich, Das Datum des Kālidāsa, Indogermanische Forschungen, Band xxxi (1912), pp. 198–203. This paper gives a convenient statement of the various older views and arguments with the needed references to previous discussions. Compare also Professor Pathak's paper on Kālidāsa and the Hūṇas of the Oxus valley, Ind. Ant. for Nov. 1912, pp. 265–267.

contemporary of Kālidāsa, or else he may (so far as this evidence goes) be later than Kālidāsa by any amount of time. To try to determine the interval between them as small or great by differences of style small or great is a futile task such as has often been tried, and in vain.

8. Bhavabhūti probably later than Bāṇa, about A.D. 610.—The emperor Harsha of Kanauj reigned from 606 to 648, and the illustrious Chinese pilgrim Hiuen Tsang has made for us many interesting records of that memorable reign. Bāṇa was Harsha's court-poet, and wrote a 'History of Harsha' or Harsha-charita to glorify his imperial patron. The date of the book may be set at A.D. 610. In the introduction Bāṇa mentions Bhāsa and Kālidāsa and other famous poets, but not Bhavabhūti.

The argumentum ex silentio is indeed a dangerous one. In this same introduction Bāṇa omits all mention of Vālmīki, although Bāṇa certainly knew about the Rāmāyaṇa and its author (cp. Kādambarī, ed. Peterson, pp. 51, 91, &c.). Nevertheless, if Bhavabhūti preceded Bāṇa or was contemporaneous with him, it is very unlikely that Bāṇa, as an eminent man of letters, should not have known Bhavabhūti, an eminent man of letters. True, Bāṇa and Bhavabhūti did not belong to the same court, and in old times news did not travel fast; or it may be that Bhavabhūti did not attain eminence until after the Harsha-charita was finished. But otherwise it is hard to see why Bāṇa—when mentioning the dramatists Bhāsa and Kālidāsa—did not mention the dramatist Bhavabhūti also, except on the assumption that Bhavabhūti was somewhat later than Bāṇa.

9. Identity of Bhavabhūti with 'a pupil of Kumārila' (say 700–750) unproved.—There is a manuscript of the Mālatī-Mādhava, in appearance about 400 years old, which in the colophons to acts iii and vi assigns the play to 'a pupil of Kumārila', but elsewhere assigns it to Bhavabhūti. According to this evidence,[1] Bhavabhūti was a pupil of the great Mīmāṅsā teacher, Kumārila, of about A.D. 700. Unfortunately, the colophon to act vi complicates the matter by giving the name of that pupil as Uṁvekāchārya. It follows either 1. that this was an alias of Bhavabhūti, or else 2. that the Mālatī-Mādhava is a composite work, and that, while the other eight acts are by Bhavabhūti, acts iii and vi are by Uṁvekāchārya, perhaps a substitution (like that of Subrahmaṇya in the Mahāvīra-charita[2]) of his own version of these two acts in place of Bhavabhūti's original version which this 'pupil of Kumārila' did not like.

Obviously we are giving undue weight to the testimony of a single

[1] First brought out by Mr. Lele, p. 84 of his book cited above at p. xxxvi; further discussed by Mr. S. P. Pandit, introd. to Gaüḍavaho, pp. ccv ff. See also preface to Dr. Bhandarkar's M. M, 2nd ed., p. viii.

[2] See Nirṇaya Sāgara ed. of the play, p. 213 n.

manuscript. A solitary manuscript, Bd, of the Uttara-Rāma gives Bhavabhūti's original name as Śīlakaṇṭha instead of Śrīkaṇṭha; and the oldest extant manuscript of the Mālatī-Mādhava (of A.D. 1156; cp. p. xxxvi, above) says, after the colophon to act x, *kṛitir iyam mahāva(ka)ver Bhūgarbhasya.* Is Bhūgarbha still another alias of Bhavabhūti? Perhaps all this confusion means merely that the name of our poet was not so well and so widely known as we might like to think.[1]

Bhavabhūti and Kumārila were both Southerners or Dākshiṇātyas. It is probable that they were nearly contemporaries (Kumārila's time is put as 700–750[2]). And Bhavabhūti does use a technical term or two of the Mīmāṅsā (so *arthavāda* at Uttara-Rāma, i. 39[5]). But there do not seem to be any cogent reasons for an inference that Bhavabhūti was a direct pupil of the famous Mīmāṅsā teacher Kumārila.

10. Bhavabhūti certainly earlier than Rājaśekhara (about 900).—The earliest *unmistakable* reference to Bhavabhūti[3] occurs in Rājaśekhara. In his play, the Bāla-Rāmāyaṇa, i. 16, he pays a handsome compliment to Bhavabhūti, and incidentally to himself, as follows:

> He who was formerly known as the poet Vālmīki, and who subsequently assumed on earth the form of Bhartṛimeṇṭha, and who appeared once again in the person of Bhavabhūti,—that same [Vālmīki] is existing now as Rājaśekhara.[4]

The whole tenor of the stanza makes it certain that Rājaśekhara has in mind no other Bhavabhūti than the one who dramatized the Rāmāyaṇa, that is to say, our Bhavabhūti. And in order that the reincarnation may be poetically plausible, we must of course assume that Bhavabhūti had been dead for some time before Rājaśekhara was born.

But there are further data confirming Bhavabhūti's priority to Rājaśekhara. That the latter imitated Bhavabhūti is shown by Professor V. S. Apte.[5] And among his dramatic devices derived from Bhavabhūti are pictures (Bāla-Rāmāyaṇa, act iv), play-within-play (ibid., act iii), a pupil wandering in search of instruction (ibid., interlude to act iv), and so on. In the Bāla-Rāmayaṇa, iv. 41[7], Rājaśekhara actually mentions, though with a skilful double meaning, Bhavabhūti's Mahāvīra-charita.

In all his four extant plays Rājaśekhara mentions the fact that he was

[1] And it is in this way perhaps that we have to explain the reference *Mālatīmādhavasya* in Jalhaṇa's anthology; see below, § 15.

[2] See Professor Pathak's paper in the JBBRAS, vol. xviii, pp. 213–38.

[3] Of later references there are many. The more important ones may be found together in Appendix 2.

[4] See Konow and Lanman's Karpūra-mañjarī, Harvard Oriental Series, vol. iv, p. 187.

[5] In an extremely rare tract. See Konow, *l. c.*, p. 187.

the spiritual teacher or *guru* of Mahendrapāla of Kanauj; and this monarch is mentioned in the Siyadoni inscription[1] with the dates 903–4 and 907–8. The date of Rājaśekhara is accordingly put at about A. D. 900. So far as these facts may determine it therefore, the latest limit for Bhavabhūti would be about 850 to 875.

11. Date of Yaśovarman of Kanauj as determining that of Vākpatirāja.—Kalhaṇa's Chronicle of the kings of Kaśmir or Rājataraṅgiṇī, written 1148–9, states at iv. 134 that the king of Kaśmir, Lalitāditya-Muktāpīḍa (Mu-to-pi of the Chinese Annals), subdued king Yaśovarman of Kānyakubja or Kanauj. From the Chronicle, the limits of Lalitāditya's reign appear to be 699 to 735 A. D.; but Stein is of opinion that the humiliation of Yaśovarman by Lalitāditya was subsequent[2] to a certain embassy sent by the latter to the Chinese emperor, which embassy, according to the Annals, cannot have been earlier than 736.

12. Date of Vākpatirāja's Gaüḍavaho not far from 736.—Yaśovarman's court-poet during some part of his reign (presumably the later) was a man called in Sanskrit Vākpatirāja, or in Prākrit, Bappairāa. He wrote a Prākrit poem entitled Gaüḍavaho (Sanskrit Gāuḍavadhaḥ). This means 'Slaughter of the Gauḍian [king]'. It is a long poem of over 1200 stanzas, devoted ostensibly to the glorification of his Royal patron Yaśovarman. It was evidently planned on an 'enormous' (viyaḍa=vikaṭa) scale; for, long as it is, it is in fact only a prelude, and does not even give the name of the 'Gauḍian king', much less any details about his 'slaughter'. It was edited by Shankar Pandurang Pandit (Bombay, 1887), with an elaborate introduction, discussing Yaśovarman (pp. xvii ff.), his date (lxvii), Vākpatirāja's personal history (xxxiii and lxiv), and the date of the writing of the poem (xcvi). Other pertinent discussions are: Bühler's paper in WZKM, Band ii, pp. 328–40; Jacobi's, in the Göttinger Gel. Anzeigen of 1888, no. 2, p. 68; Stein's notes to his translation (1900) of Kalhaṇa; and Bhandarkar's 2nd ed. (1905) of Mālatī-Mādhava, preface, p. xiii.

In determining the date of the writing of the Gaüḍavaho, no question could be more pertinent than this: Why does the poem, planned upon an 'enormous' scale, stop short with the prelude, and not even take up the slaughter of the Gauḍian king,[3] that is, the very subject which, to judge from the title of the poem, should form its main substance? The most natural answer is that Vākpatirāja began his panegyric in the days of Yaśovarman's greatest successes, and that, after writing his prelude of

[1] See Kielhorn, *Epigraphia Indica*, i. 171; or Konow, *l. c.*, pp. 178–9.

[2] See Stein's *Translation of the Chronicle*, Introduction, § 85, and cp. his notes on iv. 134 and iv. 126, and § 66.

[3] For meagre and incidental mentions of him, see Mr. S. P. Pandit, Introd. p. xlii.

1200 stanzas, he was moved to abandon the subject proper by reason of some great disaster or humiliation[1] that befell his patron—presumably the humiliation experienced at the hands of Lalitāditya. If this is as certain as it is plausible, the composition of the Gaüḍavaho would be not very far from A.D. 736.

13. Bhavabhūti probably a little earlier than Vākpatirāja.—We are now in a position to consider the bearing of Vākpatirāja's date upon the date of Bhavabhūti. For the chronological relation of these two men we have two important texts. The first is in Kalhaṇa's Chronicle, iv. 144, and reads as follows:

kaviVākpatirāja-śrīBhavabhūty-ādi-sevitaḥ
jito yayau Yaśovarmā tadguṇastutivanditām.

'Yaśovarman, on whom attended the poet Vākpatirāja, the illustrious Bhavabhūti, and other [poets], became by his defeat [at the hands of Lalitāditya] a panegyrist of his [Lalitāditya's] virtues.' There is not the smallest reason to doubt that this Vākpatirāja is the same as the author of the Gaüḍavaho; and the complete reversal of fortune which explains so well the author's leaving the main part of his poem unwritten, is here most clearly set forth. And it would seem extremely improbable that, when speaking of 'illustrious Bhavabhūti', Kalhaṇa had any other poet in mind than the great dramatist who now engages our attention. In short, it is a safe inference that both Bhavabhūti and Vākpatirāja,—the latter officially, the former we know not how,—were connected with the court of Yaśovarman.

As making against the inference that Bhavabhūti was connected with the court of Yaśovarman we must in fairness mention two facts: 1. from none of Bhavabhūti's extant works do we get the impression that he was at any time basking in royal favour; and 2. still less do we find any direct statement that he was ever in attendance upon Yaśovarman. But these facts are not perhaps of much consequence. In spite of his silence, Bhavabhūti may have received occasional gifts from that king.

Secondly, as making against the assumption that 'the illustrious Bhavabhūti' mentioned by Kalhaṇa is the same as our Bhavabhūti, we must mention the circumstance that, in the dvandva compound contained in the stanza above cited, Kalhaṇa places 'śrī-Bhavabhūti' *after* 'Vākpatirāja', whereas, *if* Kalhaṇa knew that the *dramatist* Bhavabhūti was older than Vākpatirāja (see below) and *if* he was scrupulous as to a point of grammar like this, he should have placed 'śrī-Bhavabhūti' *before* 'Vākpatirāja', since vārtika 3 to Pāṇini ii. 2. 34 requires that what is prior in order

[1] Cp. Mr. S. P. Pandit, *l. c.*, pp. lxxii, lxxiii.

of time or nature should come earlier in a dvandva compound. This objection can be met by supposing that 'Vākpatirāja', the first member of the compound, was in Kalhaṇa's view the more important one, *abhyarhita* (vār. 4 to Pāṇ. ii. 2. 34), the one more intimately connected with the court of Yaśovarman, and so he could be placed before 'śrī-Bhavabhūti'.

As a matter of fact, however, we should not attempt to make much out of a subtle point of grammar like the present. Compounds which seem to violate one rule are often justifiable by another. Thus the compound *grahītṛi-grahaṇa-grāhyeshu* (Yoga-sūtra, i. 41) may seem to go against Pāṇini ii. 2. 34, but it would be perfectly correct if the author of the Yoga-sūtra considered *grahītṛi*, the percipient, as more important than *grāhya*, the object perceived. Or it may be that the Sūtrakara is here following a traditional order of words, as he certainly is in the compound *śraddhā-vīrya-smṛiti-samādhi-prajñā*[1] in i. 20. I do not think, therefore, that Professor Jacobi (JAOS., December, 1910, pp. 26–7) has succeeded in establishing, on the strength of two 'incorrect' dvandva compounds, the existence of a Yoga-Patañjali as distinct from Vyākaraṇa-Patañjali, seeing that the latter himself does not quarrel with Kātyāyana's 'incorrect' dvandva compounds in vār. 1 to ii. 2. 35, vār. 1 to ii. 2. 36, vār. 6 to ii. 1. 51, &c. But this is by the way.

The second relevant text is a passage of eight stanzas (797–804) found in the Gaüḍavaho itself. In it Vākpatirāja is speaking about himself, and the gist of it is as follows: Vākpatirāja was a favourite friend of Yaśovarman and bore the title of Head-poet or Kavirāja [797]. Although not naturally gifted as a poet, he yet came to honour through [the teaching (?) or the favour (?) of] Kamalāyudha [798]. And in his enormous (viyaḍa) narrative-structures even now there flash excellences, like drops of the nectar of poetry from the ocean of Bhavabhūti [literal version of 799]. And his delight is in the works of Bhāsa, Jvalanamitra, Kālidāsa, Subandhu, &c. [800]. He is versed in logic, &c. &c. [801–804].

Taking the passage as a whole, and especially the mention of the great dramatists Bhāsa and Kālidāsa, there is no good reason for doubt as to who is meant by 'Bhavabhūti'. It must be the dramatist Bhavabhūti. Next, it is clear that in stanza 799 Vākpatirāja is modestly acknowledging an indebtedness to the influence of Bhavabhūti. Was that influence exerted personally, that is, was Vākpatirāja a pupil of Bhavabhūti? or was it exerted through Bhavabhūti's writings which Vākpatirāja read and studied? Apart from the phrase 'even now', the general wording of the stanza seems to favour the latter view. The phrase 'even now' does not decide

[1] Compare also the compounds in Yoga-sūtra, i. 6; ii. 3, 15, 18, 29, 30, 32; iii. 53; iv. 1.

the matter either way. A man of to-day, and fifty years old, may say 'The influence of Bacon appears even now in my style'. But you cannot decide from the words 'even now' whether it was the reading of Francis Bacon's *Essays* in the man's college days or the personal influence of a teacher of English named Bacon that he has in mind. The phrase merely implies the lapse of an interval of time. Accordingly, admitting the influence without trying to decide whether it was by the spoken or the written word, and admitting the interval without trying to determine its length,—we are probably justified in concluding that Bhavabhūti's connexion with the court of Yaśovarman fell in the earlier part of that monarch's reign, and that the dramatist was somewhat earlier than Vākpatirāja.

14. Bhavabhūti probably flourished near the close of the seventh century.—The considerations recited above point to the following conclusions. Bhavabhūti's activity is *certainly* later than that of Kālidāsa, and for Kālidāsa the middle of the fifth century is most probable. We can also say that Bhavabhūti is *probably* later than even Bāṇa, who flourished about 610. Bhavabhūti appears to have lived, if not at the court of Yaśovarman of Kanauj, at least during the reign of that king, and before the date of Vākpatirāja's Gaüḍavaho, which we set at about 736. Accordingly we may conclude with some confidence that Bhavabhūti flourished in the closing years of the seventh century.

Bhavabhūti's Works

15. Lost works of Bhavabhūti.—The first question that presents itself is, did Bhavabhūti write anything besides the three plays that we at present know to be his? Stanzas ascribed to Bhavabhūti are found in various anthologies dating from the twelfth century onwards, and among them are a number of stanzas which do not occur in any one of the three plays of our poet. The natural inference is that Bhavabhūti wrote some other works, perhaps dramas, perhaps *kāvyas* (poems), which have not come down to us. Dr. Bhandarkar, however, on the basis of a distinction which Jalhaṇa, one of the anthologists, makes between an *author* called Mālatīmādhava, and Bhavabhūti the author of the *play* called Mālatī-Mādhava, comes to the conclusion that the stray verses in the anthologies belong not to Bhavabhūti but to the author Mālatīmādhava. But there is no valid ground for this distinction, which is unknown to other anthologists earlier as well as later. And even according to Jalhaṇa's Sūktimuktāvali, Bhavabhūti wrote at least one stanza (*Yadaivārabhyāntaḥ*, &c.: see Dr. Bhandarkar's Report for

1887–91, p. xxxv) which does not occur in any of his three extant plays. By Jalhaṇa's own showing, therefore, Bhavabhūti presumably wrote some other work or works; and that is the main point.—Furthermore, compare § 38 below.

The anthologies together have preserved for us about a dozen stanzas. As is to be expected, they are not consistent in the ascription of a particular stanza to a particular author, and a stanza ascribed by one anthology to Bhavabhūti is not infrequently given anonymously in another. All that we can do then is merely to put the various stanzas together (see Appendix 2). Almost all of them are of such a colourless nature that from them we cannot make any inference regarding the nature of the original work or works, now lost to us, from which they were extracted.

16. Bhavabhūti's extant works.—Only three plays belonging to Bhavabhūti have come down to us: 1. Mahāvīra-charita, which deals with the early history and adventures of Rāma down to the battle of Laṅkā and Rāma's coronation; 2. Mālatī-Mādhava, a love-story of the romantic type, the plot of which was probably the poet's own invention; 3. the present play called Uttara-Rāma-charita, which continues the history of Rāma from his coronation to the banishment of his wife and their final reunion. Seeing that in two of his plays Bhavabhūti has thus dramatized the entire Rāma-story, it will be useful at this point to make a digression and survey this story in the various forms in which it existed before and after the celebrated epic of Vālmīki.

Excursus: History of the Rāma-story

17. Vālmīki's Rāmāyaṇa: its present form.—Vālmīki's Rāmāyaṇa has come down to us in three or four distinct recensions:[1] 1. The Northern recension or the recension of the commentators; 2. the Bengali recension; 3. the so-called West-Indian recension; and 4. the recently (1905) published South-Indian recension. These recensions agree in essential particulars, but each gives a number of stanzas peculiar to itself, and the sequence of cantos varies. We are not yet in a position to say which of these recensions is the oldest. Moreover, whatever recension we follow, we meet therein a number of repetitions and inconsistencies and peculiarities of diction and metre, which go to prove that the epic has been submitted to a process of enlargement by more than one hand; so that it is almost impossible to say what parts of the epic are Vālmīki's own and what are later interpolations, although in most cases the interpolators have been so simple or so honest as to leave traces of their working more or less clearly visible.

[1] We ignore here the forms of the Rāmāyaṇa that are known to exist outside India.

We are not here concerned with the problem, important and even urgent as it is, of sifting the new from the old. The Rāmāyaṇa as Bhavabhūti knew it differs very little from the present form of the Rāmāyaṇa—so far, that is to say, as the mere story goes. We will therefore summarize the story as given in the first of these recensions, which we will call the Bombay recension.

18, A. Rāma-story as given in Vālmīki's Rāmāyaṇa.—Formerly there ruled over the kingdom of Kosala (capital Ayodhyā) a king called Daśaratha. He belonged to the Solar race, and counted among his ancestors such famous names as Manu, Ikshvāku (first king of Ayodhyā), Sagara, Bhagīratha (who brought the Ganges down from heaven), Kakutstha, and Raghu. He had three wives: Kausalyā, Sumitrā, and Kaikeyī; the first was the eldest, the last the most beloved. Daśaratha ruled long and prosperously, but had only one daughter,[1] Śāntā, and no sons, though he was getting old. Following the advice of Vasishṭha, his family preceptor, Daśaratha offered a sacrifice in which his son-in-law, Ṛishyaśṛiṅga, officiated as head-priest. As a consequence, the king got four sons: 1. Rāma, the eldest, born of Kausalyā; 2. Bharata, born of Kaikeyī; 3. Lakshmaṇa and 4. Śatrughna, both born of Sumitrā.

18, B.—The kingdom of Videha (capital Mithilā) was to the east of the kingdom of Kosala. It was at this time ruled by the saintly king Janaka, who, as he was once for a holy sacrifice preparing the ground with a plough, came upon an infant, and brought her up as his own daughter. This was Sītā thus miraculously sprung from the Earth. The girl grew up in the company of Ūrmilā, another daughter of Janaka, and of Māṇḍavī and Śrutakīrti, daughters of Janaka's brother Kuśadhvaja. As Sītā became of an age to be married, Janaka instituted a *svayaṁvara*: whoever should succeed in bending a mighty bow (which Janaka had received from God Śiva) was to marry the princess. Many attempted, but none succeeded.

18, C.—One day there came to the court of Daśaratha the royal sage[2] Viśvāmitra who, finding the demons frequently molesting his penances, requested the king to send two of his sons, Rāma and Lakshmaṇa, with him to his penance-grove. Since a person of Viśvāmitra's position could not be denied anything, Daśaratha reluctantly agreed to give over his sons, though yet in tender years. Viśvāmitra resumed his holy rites, and when the molestors came, Rāma, at Viśvāmitra's behest, killed the demon Subāhu

[1] The epic does not say who the mother of Śāntā was. Daśaratha gave his daughter in adoption to Lomapāda, and he married her to Ṛishyaśṛiṅga; cp. Vishṇu-Purāṇa, iv. 18.

[2] This title is used of one who, formerly a king, had now taken to the practice of austerities. As a sage he was expected to forgo all activities proper to a warrior, and so the royal sage Viśvāmitra had to apply to Daśaratha for help.

and the terrible she-demon Tāṭakā. Pleased at the prince's valour, Viśvāmitra thereupon taught him the mystic formulae relating to all the missiles that he knew, and particularly the *jṛimbhaka* missile, which had the power of producing instantaneous stupor or paralysis in the ranks of the assailants. After the conclusion of the sacrifice, Viśvāmitra took Rāma and Lakshmaṇa with him to Mithilā, the capital of Janaka. Janaka was very favourably impressed by the princes; and Viśvāmitra called upon Rāma to try his hand at the mighty bow. Young though he was, Rāma not only succeeded in bending it, but even in breaking it in twain, and thus winning him a wife. Viśvāmitra now proposed that, along with Sītā's marriage to Rāma, there be celebrated the marriages of Sītā's sister Ūrmilā and her cousins Māṇḍavī and Śrutakīrti to the three brothers of Rāma, Lakshmaṇa and Bharata and Śatrughna respectively. The following table (in which *m.* stands for *married*) makes these relations clear:

Daśaratha: *m.*	Kausalyā: son,	Rāma: *m.* Sītā, born of the Earth, reared by Janaka Twins, Kuśa and Lava		
	Sumitrā: sons,	Lakshmaṇa: *m.* Ūrmilā, daughter of Janaka Chandraketu		
		Śatrughna: *m.* Śrutakīrti,		daughters of Janaka's brother, Kuśadhvaja
	Kaikeyī: son,	Bharata: *m.* Māṇḍavī,		

The proposal was agreed to. Daśaratha was called from Ayodhyā, and the marriages were celebrated with due pomp.

18, D.—The nuptial joys, however, were interrupted by the arrival of Paraśurāma, son of Jamadagni. Paraśurāma was a fiery Brahman, sage and warrior, who had twenty-one times rid the earth of all Kshatriyas. He was a devotee of God Śiva, and was incensed to learn that Rāma had not only bent but broken the bow of his favourite Divinity. As nothing short of a fight with the young prince would satisfy him, Rāma managed to reduce him to terms, and sent him away humbled and abashed. The four princes then returned to Ayodhyā with their brides. Here they passed some twelve years.[1] End of Bāla-Kāṇḍa.

18, E.—Daśaratha, finding his eldest son Rāma now arrived at a proper age, resolves to crown him heir-apparent. Preparations were accordingly set on foot. But Kaikeyī, the youngest queen, following the advice of Mantharā, her nurse and confidante, calls upon her husband to

[1] In the present form of the Rāmāyaṇa there is some inconsistency here; according to one version the exile and the events leading to it follow immediately after the marriages. From the Uttara-Rāma-charita (i.19, 20; vi. 33–35) it is clear that Bhavabhūti assumes such an interval between the marriages and the exile. Compare also Padma-Purāṇa, iv. 36^{15-17}.

fulfil immediately the two boons which on an earlier occasion he had granted her. Daśaratha consents, but is sorely grieved to learn that the boons are: 1. That Bharata, Kaikeyī's son, be appointed heir-apparent; 2. that Rāma be forthwith sent away into exile for fourteen years. As the king could not belie his words, Rāma had to submit to the wishes of his step-mother, which he cheerfully does. His wife Sītā and his brother Lakshmaṇa[1] refuse to be left behind, and they are all three accordingly carried away through the weeping multitudes. The old king was so much afflicted by this great blow that he barely lived to hear the news of the exiles being taken over safe beyond the boundaries of his kingdom.

18, F.—Bharata, who all this while was in utter ignorance of the happenings at Ayodhyā, is now sent for in order to perform the obsequies of his father and assume the sovereignty thus devolved upon him. He returns; but discovering the mean conduct of his mother, he reproves her bitterly, and refuses to take charge of the kingdom and thus give his consent to the base intrigue. He resolves immediately to start in search of Rāma, and to implore him to return. On the other side of the Ganges, near the mountain called Chitrakūṭa, close by the saint Bharadvāja's hermitage, Bharata finds Rāma leading a forester's life in the company of his wife and brother. Rāma is struck by Bharata's magnanimity, but insists upon carrying out his father's command to the letter, and is unwilling to return before the completion of the full term of fourteen years. Bharata thereupon resolves to keep company with Rāma; the latter, however, reminds him of the duty they all owed to their subjects, and persuades him to return, which Bharata does, only on the condition that Rāma will come back at the appointed time, himself in the meanwhile conducting the affairs of the state only as Rāma's agent. END OF AYODHYĀ-KĀṆḌA.

18, G.—Rāma now resolves to withdraw farther away from his kingdom, and learning that the regions on the other side of the Vindhya mountains were infested with wild demons and cannibals, he sets forth in that direction. At his entrance into the Vindhya forests he meets the demon Virādha, whom he kills. He then meets a number of sages and ascetics, in whose company he is said to have passed no less than ten years.[2] Going

[1] The two brothers, Bharata and Śatrughna, were at this time absent in the kingdom of their maternal uncle.

[2] These seem to be quite uneventful years; and it is rather strange that Rāma should, for the sake of a few months, think of building a hut at Pañchavaṭī (see below), and do nothing of the kind here, where he stayed so long. Evidently something is wrong with the text of the epic. We may add that the Padma-Purāṇa (vi. 269^{226}) says that it was in Pañchavaṭī that Rāma stayed so many years; and this appears more probable.

further south into the Daṇḍakā forests he reaches the river Godāvarī, and there, in the part of the country known as Janasthāna,[1] comes upon the hermitage of Agastya and his wife Lopāmudrā. The holy pair heartily welcome the newcomers, and here at the foot of a mountain called Prasravaṇa, and in a region known as Pañchavaṭī, Rāma resolves to build a small hut and to pass the rest of his exile peacefully in the company of the saint Agastya and the vulture-king Jaṭāyus.[2]

18, H.—Peace, however, was not vouchsafed to him long. At this time there ruled in the island of Laṅkā (identified with modern Ceylon) a demon king, Rāvaṇa. He was called 'ten-headed' and was a terror to the world. Having established his power in Laṅkā proper, Rāvaṇa crossed over to the mainland and overran the whole of Southern India, subduing everything that came in his way. Rāvaṇa, however, found more than his match in Vālin, king of the Monkeys, whose kingdom comprised the part of South India then known as Kishkindhā. An agreement was entered into whereby, except for a narrow strip of land along the coast, the bulk of the peninsula came into the possession of Vālin. Rāvaṇa's territory touched the Janasthāna, and here he left a large army of demons under the command of Khara (Rāvaṇa's younger brother) and Dūshaṇa and Triśiras.

18, I.—Once Śūrpaṇakhā,[3] a widowed sister of Rāvaṇa, came upon Rāma in the Pañchavaṭī, and smitten with his graceful form made him frank overtures of love, promising to eat up Sītā and thus put her out of the way, if Rāma would but consent. Rāma in jest sent her to Lakshmaṇa, who rewarded her insistence by cutting off her nose and ears. Śūrpaṇakhā went weeping and bleeding to her brother Khara, who in anger dispatched fourteen picked men to capture Rāma. As they did not return, Khara marched with his whole army, 14,000 demons strong, and engaged Rāma in a close fight. Rāma stepped back a few paces so as to gain room for working with his bow, and then, one after another, he killed the entire army of demons, as also its three leaders.

18, J.—Śūrpaṇakhā vows revenge. She now repairs to Rāvaṇa in Laṅkā and inflames his mind with a passion for Sītā, whose charms she praises loudly. Rāvaṇa resolves to capture her. He asks Mārīcha, another demon, to assume the form of a golden deer, and to lure Rāma in chase away from his cottage. Mārīcha does this and is mortally wounded by Rāma's arrow. Before he dies, however, imitating the voice of Rāma, he

[1] 'Abode of men' or 'the habitable portion of the Daṇḍakā'. Agastya is said to be the earliest Aryan colonizer of Southern India.

[2] He had his nest on the top of the mountain Prasravaṇa (cp. U. R. C. ii. 25). He was very old, of superhuman strength, and a friend of Rāma's father.

[3] 'Whose nails are large as a winnowing-basket.'

calls upon Lakshmaṇa for help. Lakshmaṇa was left behind to guard Sītā in the cottage; but upon hearing the cry, which she mistook for her husband's, Sītā urges and even commands Lakshmaṇa to go, which he does reluctantly. Utilizing the favourable moment, Rāvaṇa now pounces upon the forlorn Sītā and flies away with her, striking down on his way the vulture-king Jaṭāyus, who from his mountain peak had watched this daring act and attempted to intercept the abductor. Jaṭāyus falls down to die, surviving just long enough to inform Rāma and Lakshmaṇa (already returned from the deer-chase and amazed at not finding Sītā in the cottage) of what had happened. Rāma's grief was unbounded. END OF ARAṆYA-KĀṆḌA.

18, K.—Wandering further onward, the princes at last reach the lake called Pampā. Here they come upon Sugrīva and his trusty friend and minister Hanūmant, alias Māruti. Sugrīva was the brother of Vālin, king of the Monkeys, and had been dispossessed by him both of his kingdom and his wife. Rāma and Sugrīva enter into an alliance whereby Rāma agrees to restore Sugrīva to his kingdom, and in return the latter promises to send out search-parties and help Rāma to punish the abductor and recover his lost wife. Rāma accordingly asks Sugrīva to challenge Vālin to a duel, and as the two brothers join in combat, Rāma wounds Vālin mortally with an arrow. For this unprovoked wrong and treachery Vālin reproaches Rāma severely; the latter simply replies that as an agent of the sovereign king of Ayodhyā he took upon himself the duty of inflicting proper punishment upon malefactors who, like Vālin, had usurped a brother's throne and wife. The death of Vālin leaves Sugrīva master of the kingdom of Kishkindhā; and in gratitude he now sends, under proper leaders, parties of Monkeys in search of Sītā. The most important of these was the one sent to the south under the command of Māruti. This party presses forward and southward until it gains the sea-coast. END OF KISHKINDHĀ-KĀṆḌA.

18, L.—The waters seemed to offer an impassable barrier, for the island of Laṅkā stood on the other side of the ocean; but Māruti undertakes to clear it by a leap. This he does and enters Laṅkā. Here he was fortunate enough to meet Sītā, sorrowing in Rāvaṇa's garden under the shade of an *aśoka* tree, she-demons of hideous and terrible looks keeping watch over her day and night. In glowing terms they describe to her the glory and the greatness of Rāvaṇa, and work alternately upon her hopes and her fears to the end that she consent to have Rāvaṇa. Sītā refuses to listen, and Rāvaṇa is too proud to stoop to force.[1] Māruti soon finds

[1] The epic gives yet another motive. As the heavenly nymph Rambhā was once upon a time going to the house of her lover Nalakūbara, she was forcibly intercepted by Rāvaṇa, who thereupon was cursed by the lover to the effect that if ever

opportunity to console Sītā and assure her of a speedy deliverance. Having thus achieved the chief object of his journey, Māruti now leaves Laṅkā, not without meeting sundry adventures, in the course of which he succeeds in killing a few hundred demons and setting the whole city on fire. Once more he leaps over the ocean and returns to Kishkindhā with the glad news. END OF SUNDARA-KĀṆḌA.

18, M.—Rāma immediately resolves to invade Laṅkā. Sugrīva with his army of Monkeys and Jāmbavant with his army of Bears offer their assistance, and the whole army soon gains the Southern Ocean. Here they are joined by Vibhīshaṇa, the youngest brother of Rāvaṇa. Vibhīshaṇa had tried to remonstrate with his eldest brother against the evil course of conduct he was pursuing, and being rewarded with contempt, he now came over to Rāma's side. Rāma receives him well and promises him the kingdom of Laṅkā after Rāvaṇa's death. To make it possible for the army to cross over, Rāma now resolves to construct a stone bridge over the ocean, and in this he is helped by the engineering genius of Nala.[1] Having gained the island he next lays siege to the capital. The battle which follows lasts, according to the several inconsistent time-indications, for four or fifteen or thirty-nine or eighty-eight days; Rāvaṇa together with his brothers and sons and the entire army of demons is put to death; and Rāma, in accordance with his promise, installs Vibhīshaṇa as king of Laṅkā.

18, N.—Having thus vanquished the enemy and wiped out the insult, Rāma now meets Sītā. He is, however, unwilling, for fear of public scandal, to take his wife back until she has proved her purity. Pierced to the quick by Rāma's suspicion, Sītā proposes the fire-ordeal. A huge pyre is kindled and with a firm tread she walks towards it and is engulfed by the flames. Immediately, however, she reappears, led forth by the Fire-god himself, who in the hearing of all proclaims her innocence. Rāma now accepts her, saying that he never doubted her innocence, but had to do what he did for the sake of the people. The fourteen-year period of exile having now almost expired, Rāma, along with his wife, brother, friends, and allies, makes the journey northwards, utilizing for the purpose an aerial car called *Pushpaka* which belonged to Rāvaṇa. They reach their home, where they meet Bharata and the Queen-mothers anxiously awaiting the return of the exiles. Rāma's coronation is now celebrated with due pomp and there is rejoicing everywhere. END OF YUDDHA-KĀṆḌA.

Rāvaṇa should again touch a woman against her free will he would instantaneously meet his death. An exactly similar story is told also in connexion with another maiden, Vedavatī.

[1] He was the son of the Architect of the Gods. Traces of this bridge, on the maps called Adam's Bridge, are still pointed out.

18, O.—The epic should naturally end here; but there is one more book or kāṇḍa, dealing with the history of Rāma from his coronation to his death. Here we are told how a few months after the coronation rumours regarding Sītā began to be circulated amongst the people, who did not like that Rāma should have received his wife back after she had been nearly a year in the house of Rāvaṇa. Through his spies Rāma comes to know of this, and resolves to abandon Sītā, although at this time she was in a state of advanced pregnancy. Rāma charges his brother Lakshmaṇa with the carrying out of this plan. Lakshmaṇa obeys, places Sītā in a chariot, takes her into a forest on the other side of the Ganges, and there leaves her, after communicating to her the actual state of things. Thereupon Sītā sends back to Rāma a spirited reply [1] and patiently succumbs to the inevitable. In her forlorn condition she fortunately chances upon the saint Vālmīki, whose hermitage was near by. Vālmīki receives the exiled queen under his protection. In his hermitage she gives birth to twin sons, Kuśa and Lava, whom Vālmīki brings up and educates along with his other pupils.

18, P.—Meanwhile in Ayodhyā Rāma is not at peace. From a mere sense of duty he discharges his manifold functions as a king, but is always haunted by the image of her whom he had treated so unjustly. Years go by, and at last he resolves to perform a horse-sacrifice.[2] For the festivities attending the completion of the sacrifice there came Vālmīki bringing with him the twins, Kuśa and Lava, whom he had taught to sing the Rāmāyaṇa, a panegyric poem on Rāma which Vālmīki had composed. With great applause the boys recite the poem in the presence of Rāma and the whole assembly. Rāma inquires about the boys and is pleasantly surprised to learn from Vālmīki that they are Rāma's own sons. Understanding that Sītā is still alive, he sends for her. Sītā comes. Rāma asks her to give further evidence of her innocence and purity. 'If it is true', exclaims Sītā, 'that in mind and deed and word I have never been unfaithful to Rāma, may Mother Earth receive me into her bosom!' Just as she utters these words the Earth gapes open and a divine form stretches forth her hands to Sītā, who enters the abyss and there finds eternal rest.

[1] This (vii. 48) is one of the most touching passages in the epic. Even Kālidāsa's Raghu, xiv. 59–68, is but a faint echo of it.

[2] Only kings of eminence could aspire to perform the horse-sacrifice. In this sacrifice a horse is let loose, and a guard of three hundred follows his track. Should any one hinder the horse's progress, he has to fight. When the horse completes a victorious circuit of the earth and returns to the capital, he is offered as a sacrifice, and the sacrificing king thereupon assumes the title of Sovereign Emperor.

18, Q.—Soon after the disappearance of Sītā, Rāma feels his own end drawing near. The kingdom is divided amongst the four brothers, who in turn settle it upon their children. In the meantime the aged Queen-mothers die. Thereafter Lakshmaṇa, whom Rāma, for no fault of his own, was compelled to send away from him, gives up the ghost. Finally Rāma himself enters the waters of the river Sarayū, and his other brothers, and the whole city of Ayodhyā in fact, follow after him to heaven. END OF UTTARA-KĀṆḌA.

19. Vālmīki's Rāmāyaṇa not the sole source of our play.—Professor Jacobi (in his book entitled Das Rāmāyaṇa, Geschichte und Inhalt, nebst Concordanz, Bonn, 1893, p. 111), upon linguistic, geographical, astronomical, and various other grounds, assigns the Rāmāyaṇa to the period between 800 and 500 B.C. By this he means of course the oldest strata of the epic. Additions and interpolations came to be made from time to time even down to the beginning of the Christian era. Besides the few cantos here and there which carry the marks of spuriousness on their face, it is almost certain that the major part of the Bāla-kāṇḍa (where for the first time we find an attempt to treat Rāma as a divine Avatar) and the whole of the Uttara-kāṇḍa (which deals with the later history of Rāma) are relatively late additions. The present play, as its title shows, deals with the later history of Rāma; and since it differs in many essential respects from the account given in the last book of the Rāmāyaṇa, the question arises whether Bhavabhūti used for his plot other sources than Vālmīki's epic.

The Mahā-Bhārata contains, at iii. 273 ff., a 'Rāma-episode' or Rāmopākhyāna; but this text does not carry the story beyond Rāma's coronation. In this fact some see a reason for considering the Rāmāyaṇa (at least in its present form) as later than the Mahā-Bhārata. This does not follow; for, considering that Mārkaṇḍeya relates the episode to illustrate how good people, fallen in misfortune, do in turn gain happiness, there is no motive for him to carry the story beyond the return to Ayodhyā, even if he knew it. Further, the Mahā-Bhārata does elsewhere (vii. 59) narrate the story of Rāma's death; but it is very short, and is of no significance for the present problem.

The Rāma-story is given with more or less detail in the various Purāṇas such as the Brahma-Purāṇa (of which the Adhyātma Rāmāyaṇa forms a part), the Bhāgavata, Garuḍa, Skanda, Agni, Kūrma, and so on. But in discussing the sources of Bhavabhūti's plays, and particularly of the present play, the most important text is the Padma-Purāṇa.

20. Three forms of the Rāma-story in the Padma-Purāṇa.—The Padma gives the Rāma-story in three different places, each time with significant variations. These differing versions could not of course have been introduced into the Purāṇa at one and the same time, as will be evident upon a brief consideration of them.

First form.—This is a summary of the Rāmāyaṇa, and occupies three chapters, 269–271, of the fifth or Sṛishṭi-khaṇḍa. This part of the Padma seems to be relatively late. The summary corresponds exactly to the story as we have it in the Bombay recension of Vālmīki's Rāmāyaṇa, except in the following six points: 1. Rāma, after the marriage, is expressly said to have lived for twelve years at Ayodhyā (chap. 269, stanza 181); 2. the story of the crow, which is given in that recension in a spurious canto coming after ii. 95, is here given as a genuine part of the epic (ch. 269, st. 194); 3. Rāma stays for thirteen years in Pañchavaṭī itself before he encounters Śūrpaṇakhā (ch. 269, st. 226); 4. Rāma himself, and not his brother, cuts off the nose and ears of Śūrpaṇakhā; 5. after the coronation Rāma rules with his queen Sītā for a thousand years (cp. also ch. 6, st. 45): it is only then that the rumour comes to his ears and he abandons his wife; 6. the god-like character of Rāma intrudes itself too frequently in the course of the Padma narration.

Second form.—Chapter 112 of the fourth or Pātāla-khaṇḍa gives what is expressly said to be the ancient or *purātana* Rāmāyaṇa. No authority is, however, given for the statement, and elsewhere (stanza 12) it is even called fictitious or *kalpita*; and this in fact it seems to be. What is more, it is not even good fiction, as any one may easily see.

Third form.—A brief passage of the fourth or Pātāla-khaṇḍa, stanzas 164–184 of chapter 66, gives not a form of the Rāma-story as such, but a statement as to the original form of Vālmīki's Rāmāyaṇa. According to this, Vālmīki's poem had six (not seven) kāṇḍas: 1. Bāla-kāṇḍa, which was equal to the present Bāla and Ayodhyā kāṇḍas taken together; 2. Araṇya-kāṇḍa, 3. Kishkindhā-kāṇḍa, 4. Sundara-kāṇḍa, 5. Yuddha-kāṇḍa,—all these not differing from the similarly named present kāṇḍas; and 6. Uttara-kāṇḍa, giving Rāma's conversations with Agastya and other sages, and describing the commencement of the horse-sacrifice, and including presumably the account of the abandonment of Sītā.

Sītā's ultimate ordeal and disappearance, the death of Lakshmaṇa and Rāma and others, and whatever else occurred after Vālmīki's appearance with the twins at Rāma's court,—all these things the Padma ignores as elements of the original Rāmāyaṇa, as of course it was bound to do, since the twins could not be expected to sing of events yet to be. We also find here a statement as to the original extent of the poem, 24,000 stanzas. This agrees with Vālmīki's statement in Bāla-kāṇḍa i. 4[2], except that the Padma does not state the number of cantos (500). This account of the original form of Vālmīki's Rāmāyaṇa seems to be a statement made in good faith by the author of the Padma.

21. The later history of Rāma as given by the Padma-Purāṇa.—If we accept the above statement as to the original form of Vālmīki's Rāmāyaṇa, who was it that completed it and gave to it its present tragic ending? Bhavabhūti (U. R. C. iv. 22[43]) tells us that Vālmīki's poem, at least the first form of it, ended with the abandonment of Sītā soon after the coronation. He also tells us that it was Vālmīki himself who later added to it a supplement, which ended happily with the reunion of Rāma and Sītā. But here Bhavabhūti is purposely vague. In some passages (U. R. C. vii. 15[12]) he seems to betray a consciousness of the fact that this supplement ended tragically; and it is quite conceivable that owing to the usual reluctance[1] of Hindu dramatists to write tragedies, Bhavabhūti may have deliberately modified his source and made the Uttara-Rāma-charita end happily.

More probably, however, Bhavabhūti derived his material from the first sixty-eight chapters of the Pātāla-khaṇḍa of the Padma-Purāṇa. Here we get an account of Rāma's life after his coronation, and more particularly of the horse-sacrifice which he performed. We are told how in the course of its wanderings the horse was captured by several kings and how bloody fights—always ending with a victory for Rāma—ensued in consequence, until finally, on its return journey, the horse arrives in Vālmīki's penance-grove. Lava, one of the twins, seizes the horse and a battle follows, in the first part of which Lava is the victor. Then he is made captive. His brother Kuśa now appears on the scene. He puts the whole army to flight and takes all the leaders captive. Sītā, however, intercedes for the prisoners, and these as well as the horse are let loose. The sacrifice then concludes as mentioned in § 18, P above. When Rāma comes to know of the valorous deeds of the two youths, he inquires of Vālmīki, who had come for the sacrifice, and learns the truth. Sītā is now sent for, and in the meantime the twins recite the Rāmāyaṇa as they had learnt it from Vālmīki. Rāma finally takes Sītā back, on the solemn testimony of Vālmīki and Śatrughna and others. There is no appeal to the Earth-

[1] It is not correct to say that no tragically-ending play was written in ancient India. The Ūrubhaṅga, a newly-discovered play of Bhāsa, comes as a welcome proof to the contrary. And in the Nāṭya-śāstra (i. 73 ff.) Bharata expressly says: 'Drama is a representation of all the happenings of the world, of all the moods of the people, happy or unhappy. Here you have, now a religious rite (*dharma*), now some festivity or even frivolity, now peaceful serenity; then again laughter, or a fight, or a love-making, or a *death*.' True, the Hindus liked to have all their plays end happily, and hence the ruling of later works on dramaturgy against any form of tragedy.

goddess or any other ordeal. Thereafter Rāma and Sītā rule in peace for many a year.

Since we have no reason to suppose that this Rāmāśvamedha-prakaraṇa in the Padma-Purāṇa was posterior to Bhavabhūti, there is just the possibility that in Bhavabhūti's days two forms of the supplement to the Rāmāyaṇa were current, one ending with a happy reunion as above, and the other, in the genuine Purāṇa fashion, carrying the story right up to the death of the hero. Bhavabhūti's source for the incidents in acts iv–vi of the Uttara-Rāma-charita must undoubtedly have been some account like that in the Padma-Purāṇa.

The variations of Bhavabhūti from the Padma-Purāṇa are: 1. According to the Padma, the leader of the army guarding the horse is Pushkala, son of Bharata; according to Bhavabhūti, it is Chandraketu, son of Lakshmaṇa. 2. The boy's age is sixteen years in the Purāṇa (ch. 65, st. 73), while it is twelve in the Uttara-Rāma-charita. 3. Vālmīki himself teaches the twins the science of archery and fighting; contrast with this U. R. C. v. 14^{1-3}. 4. In the Purāṇa, Rāma does not appear personally on the battlefield; Sītā intercedes for the horse, and the recognition of the princes takes place only at Ayodhyā. 5. Sītā does not have to submit to a second ordeal.

Before taking up the consideration of Bhavabhūti's plays, we shall now briefly discuss the sources (§§ 22–23) of the Rāmāyaṇa itself, and some of the modifications (§§ 24–26) which were introduced into the story by later writers.

22. Sources of the Rāmāyaṇa: historical element.—The main story of the Rāmāyaṇa seems to have a basis in fact. Had it been otherwise, Vālmīki might very easily have omitted or altered the two or three compromising actions of his hero, such as the unprovoked killing of Vālin (see U. R. C. v. 35). The poem, except in the battle-portion, seems to have such a semblance of truth that it is hard to imagine that Vālmīki invented it all. It may well be that the Rāmāyaṇa is a composite of two distinct stories, the first ending with the palace-intrigue and exile, and the second dealing with the adventures of some early semi-mythical Aryan explorer of Southern India; and Vālmīki may have assigned both these stories to the same hero. Vālmīki was a northerner,[1] and we need not expect to find in his work any very accurate geographical description of Southern India, the absence of which is sometimes pointed out as an argument to prove the entirely imaginative character of the poem.[2] Vālmīki's geography is

[1] His hermitage is said to have been on the Tamasā, a tributary of the Ganges. See Rāmāyaṇa, i. 2^{3}, vii. 45^{17}; cp. also vii. 66^{15}.

[2] If immediately after the return of Columbus

confused, and scholars are still disputing as to the precise road which Rāma took, and the precise position of Pañchavaṭī, Ṛishyamūka, and Pampā. Nevertheless, the main threads of the story may well be considered historical. So at least Vālmīki seems to have regarded them.

23. The Rāmāyaṇa a blending of history and allegory.—It is also conceivable that the Rāmāyaṇa is a blending of history and some form of primitive nature-allegory. Thus in the Ṛigveda (iv. 57[6,7], i. 140[4]) the word 'sítā' means furrow, and is not a proper name. Sītā's birth from the Earth as narrated in the epic, the names of her twin sons ('kuśa' is a kind of grass, and 'lava' means reaping [1]), and Sītā's final disappearance into the bosom of the Earth,—all this appears to be the mythology of some agricultural deity. If it were safe to think of Rāma as answering to the Vedic Rain-god Indra, the coincidence would harmonize well with the fact that the son of Rāvaṇa, who carries off Sītā, is called 'Vanquisher of Indra' or Indrajit, and also with the fact that Māruti, who like a rain-cloud in the monsoons, flies over the ocean and brings Rāma the comforting news about Sītā, means the 'Son of the Wind-god'. All these things point to a possible commingling of history and certain features of agricultural mythology. The mythology, however, belongs to Vedic times. In Vālmīki's days it must almost have ceased to be regarded as such.

Thus the ultimate sources for the Rāmāyaṇa may have been threefold: 1. a real historical account about the palace-intrigue and exile; 2. another account also historical but more vague and uncertain about the experience of some early Aryan explorer (as distinguished from a colonizer and a permanent settler) of the south; and 3. the mythical account of Indra and his fight with the Enemy of the Harvest, an account which probably had lost most of its significance as nature-allegory, and had come to be regarded as genuine history dealing with persons as real as any legendary heroes are expected to be.

It is no longer necessary to discuss the theory that Vālmīki derived the matter of his epic from the Iliad of Homer. The theory originated with Weber, and has been thoroughly answered by K. T. Telang (Indian Antiquary, 1872, pp. 143–7; 1873, pp. 123 ff.) and Professor Jacobi (Das Rāmāyaṇa, pp. 94–9). It is now no more than a literary curiosity.[2]

from the West Indies, and on the basis of statements made by him and his sailors, an epic had been written describing the discovery and exploration of America, could we have reasonably impugned the truth of its main story merely because the geography was wrong?

[1] Otherwise explained at Raghuvaṁśa, xv. 32.

[2] Per contra, Arthur Lillie (among others) maintains that Homer took his themes from the Indian Epics: see 'Rāma and Homer', London, 1912.

24. Later modifications of the Rāma-story: 1. Buddhistic form.—The Buddhistic form of the Rāma-story is to be found in the 'Dasaratha-Jātaka' (Faüsboll, iv. pp. 124 ff.). The story is as follows. Daśaratha, king of Benares, had three children: Rāma, Lakshmaṇa, and Sītā, all born from his first wife, after whose death he marries a second, and has by her a fourth child, a son named Bharata. Overjoyed at having another son born to him, Daśaratha grants a boon to his wife. After seven or eight years the wife remembers the boon and asks Daśaratha to fulfil it by giving the throne to her son. The king refuses to grant her request; but fearing the machinations of the woman, he advises the three children by his first wife to stay away from the court for twelve years. He makes it twelve years, because astrologers had told him that he would live so long. Rāma, with his brother Lakshmaṇa and his *sister* Sītā, repairs to the Himalayas. Contrary to the prophecy of the astrologers Daśaratha dies in the ninth year. The widowed queen tries to secure the throne for Bharata, but he sternly refuses and goes to seek his eldest brother, to whom the throne by right belonged. Rāma, however, is unwilling to come immediately, seeing that the period of twelve years assigned to him by his father was not yet over. He stays away another three years and then returns, marries Sītā, and rules in peace.

This feeble, distorted, unmotivated story was once regarded as a possible source of Vālmīki's Rāmāyaṇa. Professor Jacobi (Das Rāmāyaṇa, pp. 84–93) has already shown the utter untenability of such a view. And now we have definite evidence to prove that the Rāma-Rāvaṇa story was already well known[1] before 300 B.C.

25. Later modifications of the Rāma-story: 2. Jain forms.—The Jain forms of the Rāma-story are to be found in works like the Padma-Purāṇa of Ravisheṇa, the Dharma-parīkshā of Amitagati, and the Trishashṭhiśalākāpurushacharita (chap. vii) of Hemachandra. The story in the main follows Vālmīki's Rāmāyaṇa, and the evident object of these works must be to utilize an already existing story for preaching the special doctrines of the cult. Thus they make Rāma a pious Jain, a total abstainer from meat. This of course involved the omission of the golden deer incident (see § 18, J); Rāvaṇa abducts Sītā while Rāma is engaged in the battle with the fourteen thousand. Similarly Rāma kills Vālin in a fair fight (contrast § 18, K). Years after her abandonment, when Rāma meets Sītā once more, it was not through the instrumentality of Vālmīki, or through the incidents attending

[1] See Kauṭilīya, p. 11, line 3 from the bottom. As Bhāsa's date is uncertain, the fact of his having written two Rāma-plays and the reference to the Rāmāyaṇa in one of his plays (Avimāraka, p. 16, line 2) cannot have much significance chronologically.

the horse-sacrifice (a Jain could not perform a sacrifice involving the death of any living animal), but merely and simply because people told him about her forlorn state; and he finally loses her again, not because Sītā disappears into the earth, but because, after her purity is attested anew by the fire-ordeal, she is convinced of the vanity of the world and becomes a Jain nun, tearing out her hair with her own hand. Rāma himself takes the mendicant vow soon after. We may note in passing that the Jain accounts tell us that the monkeys and bears and demons who took part in the battle at Lañkā were not really monkeys or bears or demons. They were human beings who carried the images of a monkey or a bear or a demon on their banners.

26. Later modifications of the Rāma-story: 3. Hindu forms.—A whole treatise could be written discussing the various forms which the Rāma-story assumed in the later Hindu tellings of it, either in Sanskrit or in the different vernaculars of the country. And the special interest of such a treatise would lie in the attempt to show how the story came to be modified in accordance with changing beliefs and varying standards of judgement. We shall content ourselves with indicating merely the several tendencies that are discernible in the process.

26, A. Exaggeration.—In these later tellings of the story mere exaggerations are what we naturally expect. Thus, even in the present form of the Rāmāyaṇa, the battle at Lañkā is spun out and made to last for months, the intervals being filled in with one superhuman deed after another on both sides. There is a good deal of repetition. The same applies to some of the later descriptions of the battle of the twins with the army attending the sacrificial horse of Rāma. The twins are made to defeat all the great heroes who fought by Rāma's side at Lañkā, including Māruti, Lakshmaṇa, and even Rāma himself. Or, to take another instance which is significant in connexion with Bhavabhūti's treatment of the theme, Rāvaṇa himself is represented as having been present at Sītā's *svayaṁvara,* but unable to bend the bow (see § 18, C), which Rāma alone did.

26, B. Deification.—The beginnings of this process are already observable in the later portions of the Rāmāyaṇa, especially books i and vii, where Rāma is exalted into an Avatar of Vishṇu or the Supreme Spirit. This tendency was in course of time so much exaggerated that it eventually defeated its own purpose. Rāvaṇa also came to be considered as a regular devotee of Rāma; for, works on devotion admit intense enmity as a form of worship no less efficacious than friendship or service. So Rāvaṇa longs to be killed by Rāma and thereby to attain salvation (see U.R.C. ii. 11).

If he robs Sītā, it is simply to hasten the wished-for end, and without any sinful designs against Sītā, whom he revered as his mother.

26, C. Idealization.—Attempts were made quite early to clear the character of the intriguing queen Kaikeyī. Thus her nurse Mantharā (see § 18, E) becomes a special messenger sent by the Gods to secure Rāma's exile, and, as a necessary consequence, Rāvaṇa's death. Mantharā is the spirit of *Kali* (Quarrel), and she possesses Kaikeyī's soul, and makes her say and do what she, a paragon of virtue and kindness, would never otherwise have said and done. Similarly in regard to the episode of Sītā's residence at Laṅkā, the capital of the demon Rāvaṇa. The point was to establish her purity beyond the possibility of a suspicion. To effect this we found that the Uttara-kāṇḍa brought in the story of the curse (see § 18, L, note). Even that apparently did not suffice. The Adhyātma Rāmāyaṇa (iii. 7) goes farther and says that Rāvaṇa did not abduct Sītā at all: only her shadow. When the golden deer appeared, Rāma, being an omniscient God, knew that it was a trick of the demon, and he rather welcomed it as it would give him a pretext to kill Rāvaṇa. So he tells Sītā to remain invisible for a while, himself creating in her place an illusory Sītā, which Rāvaṇa carries away. At the time of the fire-ordeal, this illusion is consumed and the real Sītā, untouched by the hand of the demon, shows herself. It is not necessary to mention the other fantastic devices adopted for the same purpose.

26, D. Curse-motif.—Curse as a motif in explaining conduct and fate came to be increasingly applied. Thus Daśaratha dies of grief for separation from his son Rāma, because Daśaratha had himself been the unwitting instrument of causing separation between a father and his son (see Rāmāyaṇa, ii. 63–64), and so had been cursed to that effect. Similarly almost every demon whom Rāma in his wanderings meets and kills, was represented as a God or a superhuman being who had been, for one fault or another, cursed to assume the form of that particular demon, the release from the curse following immediately after his being killed by Rāma's hand. Quite a number of these additions also resulted from the attempt to describe the earlier lives of the characters that figure in the Rāmāyaṇa, the object being to explain their conduct in this birth by the influence of a previous birth.

26, E. Philosophizing.—Nor, we may be sure, were the interests of philosophy neglected. The Yoga-Vāsishṭha, a philosophical poem even larger than the Rāmāyaṇa, and attributed to Vālmīki himself, is in form a dialogue which takes place between Vasishṭha and Rāma on the occasion of Viśvāmitra's visit (§ 18, C) to Daśaratha's court. This work is in substance a huge discursive treatise on the Vedānta philosophy. Adhyātma-Rāmāyaṇa, vii. 5, is popularly known as Rāma-gītā, and is in fact a condensed statement of the Vedānta doctrine after the fashion of the Bhagavad-gītā. And there are any number of lesser treatises exhibiting a tendency to philosophize in and out of season.

26, F. Invention and poetic embellishment.—Finally, single episodes from the Rāmāyaṇa, such as the marriage of Sītā, or the embassy of Aṅgada to Rāvaṇa just before the commencement of the battle, came to be embellished and enlarged, while a few other episodes not actually in the Rāmāyaṇa were invented and treated with much poetic feeling.

The number of writers who have in these and various other ways treated the story of the Rāmāyaṇa can be easily counted by hundreds, among them some exceptionally gifted female authors; and their works are even to the present day read by hundreds of thousands of people throughout India; and those who cannot read, go to hear other people—the *Kathakas* or the *Purāṇikas*—read and explain them. The Rāmāyaṇa in India is not—and never will be, let us hope—a dead mythology. It is full of the noblest examples of virtue and truth, of devotion and self-sacrifice. Its characters have been for centuries, and still are, living forces moulding the actions and aspirations of the men and women of India.

Bhavabhūti's early plays: Mahāvīra-charita, Mālatī-Mādhava

27. The Mahāvīra-charita.—Such was the Rāma-story, with a past so glorious and a future so vast and promising, that fascinated our poet and was in fact his first love (M. V. C. i. 7). In the Mahāvīra-charita Bhavabhūti dramatizes the early history of Rāma, beginning shortly before his marriage and taking up the story of his exile and the abduction of his wife and her recovery, and ending with the return from Laṅkā and the coronation.

Now here Bhavabhūti's most immediate problem was to give dramatic unity to a vast number of actions and incidents which extended over a period of fourteen years or more, and which had no intrinsic unity except in so far as they all concerned one person, Rāma. The poet might have introduced the various characters which figure in this part of Rāma's history;—Paraśurāma, Mantharā, Śūrpaṇakhā, Khara and the army of the fourteen thousand, Mārīcha, Jaṭāyus, Sugrīva, Vālin, Hanūmant, Śramaṇā, Vibhīshaṇa, Kumbhakarṇa, Rāvaṇa, and so on,—like a series of moving pictures, and then dismissed them as quickly as they appeared. The result would have been a panoramic procession and not a play with a unified plot.

It is likely that the earliest dramatizations of the Rāma-story were of this kind. The first step in the evolution of these 'epic plays' or 'chronicle plays', as we might call them, was perhaps the division of the story as a whole into minor episodes of inherent dramatic unity, and the employment of one of these units as the material for a play. This step may well have been taken by Bhāsa, who comes at least a century or two before Kālidāsa. Two of Bhāsa's plays—'The Coronation of Rāma' or Abhisheka-nāṭaka and 'The Image' or Pratimā—are based upon books iv–vi of the Rāmāyaṇa. We should expect a third Rāma-play by Bhāsa covering books i–iii, if not also a fourth covering book vii. At any rate Bhāsa treated the Mahā-Bhārata story in this fashion, dividing it into a number of separate episodes, each forming the subject of a single play.

In most of these earlier plays, however, there was presumably no attempt made to show that the incidents were inevitable. They followed in a definite sequence, because the epic narrated them in that sequence.

28. Bhavabhūti's departure from the Rāmāyaṇa.—Now consider what Bhavabhūti does in order to bring about the desired unity of plot and adequate motivation. When Janaka proclaims his daughter Sītā's *svayaṁvara*, then Rāvaṇa, king of the demons, offers himself as a candidate for her hand. He does not indeed come personally, as suitors were expected to do: he is too proud for that. He sends a messenger who was to ask or rather demand Sītā in marriage. His suit is not only refused, but, even in the presence of his messenger, the girl is betrothed to Rāma—a mere mortal. This was an insult to Rāvaṇa's valour and prowess, and he is further incensed and mortified to learn that Rāma had killed Tāṭakā and Subāhu, and a number of other demons. Rāvaṇa is naturally burning for revenge (act i).

However, Mālyavant, Rāvaṇa's trusted minister and adviser, tries to pacify him, and promises to secure his ends by gentler means: by diplomacy. The minister accordingly meets Paraśurāma and instigates him against Rāma (act ii, interlude). Unexpectedly, Paraśurāma is himself vanquished (act iii). This was a great blow to Mālyavant's scheme; the old diplomat does not, however, despair. He sends Rāvaṇa's sister, Śūrpaṇakhā, with instructions that she was to assume the form of the nurse Mantharā and, before Rāma returned to Ayodhyā from his marriage, give him the message (as if coming from his step-mother Kaikeyī) to withdraw into exile for fourteen years. By this plan Mālyavant hoped to draw Rāma and his wife undefended into the forest, where with the army of demons that Khara had under command, it would not have been very difficult to overpower Rāma and abduct his wife. The ruse succeeds.[1] Rāma dutifully accepts his exile, and Lakshmaṇa and Sītā accompany him (act iv).

The abduction of Sītā now follows as a matter of course (act v, interlude). Since, however, Mālyavant did not succeed in crushing Rāma by the help of the army of the fourteen thousand, he prevails upon the very reluctant Vālin to undertake that task. The fight between Vālin and Rāma which follows is a fair one, and at its end Vālin dies, commending his son and his brother Sugrīva to Rāma's care[2] (act v). This is the real climax of the play. Mālyavant has been using one means after another to secure his desired end, but all things work against him. Diplomacy had been tried and in vain. Nothing now remained but to risk one last united effort to overpower the enemy by force. This also succeeds no better. Rāvaṇa is killed (act vi) and Vibhīshaṇa installed in his place. Rāma thereupon recovers his wife, returns to Ayodhyā, and is crowned king (act vii).

29. Technical significance of these changes.—Now it is quite clear that even from the start Bhavabhūti has here taken great liberties with his sources. His changes are deliberate, well-advised. He seems to have had a clear conception of just what he wanted to do, and what to avoid. He was not satisfied with a mere reproduction in dramatic form of what the epic gave in a narrative form. He wanted to establish, as far as feasible, a necessary sequence between the various experiences and adventures through which his hero passes. But this is not all. He so selects the incidents, and, where there was no choice for him, so modifies them as to bring out, by contrast, all the fine points in Rāma's character. Bhavabhūti represents Rāma as an embodiment of duty, patience, truthfulness, valour, and chivalry. And to set these qualities in high relief, he brings Rāma into contact with Paraśurāma, who has indeed valour, but valour marred by a fiery temper; with Vālin, who is chivalrous, but lacks strength of conviction, and so is easily beguiled by diplomacy; with

[1] Notice how by this one stroke Bhavabhūti secures three distinct objects. 1. He saves the character of Kaikeyī entirely. 2. By bringing Śūrpaṇakhā thus early into contact with Rāma he gains adequate motivation for her later conduct; for, if Rāma could not see through Śūrpaṇakhā's disguise as a nurse, no more was he expected to see through her disguise as a beautiful woman (which disguise she could, as a she-demon, easily assume). 3. Bhavabhūti also gains further opportunity for heightening Rāma's character.

[2] Thus the poet skilfully avoids 1. Rāma's compromising conduct in relation to Vālin, and 2. the spectacle of the unrighteous quarrel between the brothers Vālin and Sugrīva.

Mālyavant, whose misfortune it is to know the better and follow the worse; and finally with Rāvaṇa, whose great qualities of mind and of body (and they are great) are rendered futile by the adulterous passion that dominates and ruins him. In fact, it would not be incorrect to say that the whole play is a struggle between a noble, sincere, straightforward policy and a crooked, underhand, unscrupulous diplomacy, ending in an utter discomfiture of the latter.

30. Merits of the Mahāvīra-charita.—In addition to a unified plot the play affords us some attempts at genuine characterization. The poet has taken great pains to make Rāma an ideal of chivalry. He has no malice against his enemies (i. 31, i. 32[1]), generously recognizes their valour (ii. 35, 36, and *passim*), and is considerate in his treatment of them after their defeat (iv. 21, v. 56). At the same time he is fully confident of his prowess (ii. 33[2]), and scorns to receive from his enemies any sympathy or advantage that goes beyond the strict code of chivalry (ii. 46[1], v. 50). He is generous and devoted to those whom he has once called his friends (v. 58[17], v. 60), and has a supreme sense of his duty as a pupil (i. 38), as a son (iv. 42), and as a king (iv. 39). We have already spoken of the types of character [1] that are contrasted with his. It is necessary, however, to add that, although Bhavabhūti is conscious of the original divine nature of Rāma (vii. 2), he has tried to show him (except in one or two places) as entirely human and normal. The divine does not intrude itself too prominently and so dull our sympathies, as it does in some of the successors of our poet. The play contains some splendid poetry, and, especially in acts iii and iv, some spirited dialogue.

31. Defects of the Mahāvīra-charita.—The main drawback of the play is the circumstance that its characterization, however clever in some places, is generally stiff and unconvincing; there is no such thing as character-development, unless we choose to call the *change* of mood in Paraśurāma a development. Thus, from start to finish, Rāma is always the ideal hero, the *Mahā-vīra*; what we have is a revelation of the different phases of his character, or more correctly speaking, the same phase of his character—bravery, nobility, truthfulness, and what not—revealed under different circumstances and in relation to different persons. So also with Sītā. We do not find in her that fine shading of character and blending of opposing motives, that delicate growth of passion and affection that Bhavabhūti portrays, for instance, in the heroine of the Mālatī-Mādhava. The same may be said of the minister Mālyavant (see also § 36), who in this respect

[1] We may also mention the attempt to differentiate the characters (acts iii and iv) of Janaka and Daśaratha, and of Śatānanda and Viśvāmitra and Vasishṭha.

compares very unfavourably with the sublime character of Rākshasa in Viśākhadatta's Mudrā-Rākshasa.

Another characteristic defect of the play is the poet's inability to stop when enough has been already said. Thus Mālyavant's self-revelation—the painful exposition of his motives, his hopes, and his fears—becomes positively tedious, especially in the interlude to act iv; it is not called for, and is technically a blemish. Similarly in act iii, the wordy war between Paraśurāma on the one hand, and Śatānanda and Janaka and Daśaratha and Viśvāmitra on the other, is carried to a length that may perhaps serve to display Bhavabhūti's knowledge of grammar, Yoga, Dharma-śāstra, Mīmāṅsā, and so forth, but that also betrays a radical defect in our poet, the lack of a proper sense of form and measure. As a result, awkward pauses must often have arisen on the stage, one or more characters being compelled to stop and wait till another had concluded his—perhaps poetic, but uncalled for—description or declamation. In fairness to Bhavabhūti however, it must be said that his treatment of the Bharata episode (end of act iv) and of the Vālin-Sugrīva incident can hardly be bettered. Here he gives the desired effect by a few bold strokes; and Vibhīshaṇa's remark (v. 58^{18}), 'How touching is this brevity where a prolix statement might have been looked for!' can very appropriately be applied to Bhavabhūti's own treatment of the theme, as indeed he himself probably intended.[1]

Finally we may mention that the language of the play is crude and lacks the grace and polish, and even the directness and vigour, of Bhavabhūti's later plays. The descriptions are often lengthy and involved, and the diction then becomes stilted and unnatural. The poet may also be charged with some inconsistencies of statement: cp. vii. 16^{c} with v. 38^{2}. The metrical test (see appendix 1) confirms the impression that the play is probably the earliest[2] of the three plays of Bhavabhūti.

32. The Mālatī-Mādhava.—This play was probably written not very long after the Mahāvīra-charita. It is in ten acts and is technically called a *prakaraṇa*, and its plot, taken as a whole, is the poet's own invention. Quite possibly, of course, he may have received from various sources hints for certain incidents and episodes of the story. Thus (as noted at § 4) some parts of it, such as the journey from the Berars to Padmāvatī, are perhaps autobiographical; while others, such as the marriage of a nobleman from the Berars (Mādhava) with a distinguished lady of Northern India

[1] Bhavabhūti is very fond of introducing in his plays such indirect self-praise: compare M.M. i. 35^{10}, vi. 13^{2}; U.R.C. iii. 47^{5}. But he generally takes care to introduce it so skilfully as not to destroy the stage-illusion.

[2] Compare also the prologue (i. 7^{2}), where the work is called new or *apūrva*; every play is in a sense *apūrva*, but it is usually in his *first* play that an author tries to excuse himself on this ground. Cf. Mālavikā, i. 2.

(Mālatī), may have been suggested by historic facts.[1] For the central story, Bhavabhūti seems to have been indebted to the Bṛihatkathā, which—to judge from Kshemendra's synopsis thereof[2] and from Somadeva's Kathāsaritsāgara[3]—contained three separate stories of the temple-runaways (see below, § 33, D) and the marriage in disguise (§ 33, E) and the immolation and rescue of a princess (§ 33, F).[4]

The play is of the romantic type, the central interest being a love-story, or rather a dexterous blending together of two love-stories. The plot is crowded with incident and adventure, thrilling us now with hope and now with fear, and the sequences are so far removed from the commonplace that we can never guess what is to come next until near the very end. And the action is projected upon a weird background, with tigers running wild in the streets, ghosts squeaking in the cemeteries, and mystic Kāpālikas performing gruesome rites in their blood-stained temples.

33, A. Analytic statement of the plot of the Mālatī-Mādhava.—Bhūrivasu and Devarāta, two young friends and fellow-students at the University,[5] promise each other before parting that, if they should marry and settle down, they would endeavour to pass on their friendship to the next generation by bringing about, if possible, a marriage between their own children. This promise is made in the presence of another fellow-student, Kāmandakī, and her pupil Saudāminī. The friends part. Bhūrivasu becomes minister of the king of Padmāvatī, and has a daughter named Mālatī; while Devarāta has a similar position at Kuṇḍinapura, the capital of the Berars, and has a son named Mādhava. The children grow up and Devarāta sends his son to Padmāvatī, ostensibly to complete his education, but really to remind Bhūrivasu of his early promise. Devarāta is too cautious to send his son direct to Bhūrivasu; instead, he sends him to Kāmandakī, who had now become a Buddhist nun, and was staying in a monastery (*vihāra*) at Padmāvatī, much honoured both by the king and his minister.

33, B.—Bhūrivasu comes to know of Mādhava's presence in the city, and is not averse to giving his Mālatī in marriage to Mādhava; only it so happens that the king his master has already asked Bhūrivasu to give his daughter Mālatī in marriage to an old court-favourite of his called Nandana.

[1] For two notable marriages of this kind in the Vākāṭaka dynasty of the Berars, we have epigraphic testimony: JRAS., April, 1914, p. 825.

[2] See his Bṛihatkathāmañjarī (Kāvyamālā, no. 69), xi. 6–88; 67–78; iii. 218–30.

[3] See Kathāsaritsāgara, xiii. 17–150; 158–215: iv. 146–203.

[4] It would be interesting to study the various artistic changes which Bhavabhūti made in his originals.

[5] Ancient India had famous seats of learning (Ujjain, Takshaśilā, Nālandā), each housing and feeding and teaching thousands of bachelor students. See Hiuen Tsang's description of Nālandā (book ix: S. Beal's translation, ii. 167).

It was dangerous to refuse the king's request; so Kāmandakī advises Bhūrivasu to assent to the king's wish, but to word his assent in such a way as to leave himself a loophole or chance of evasion in case of need (ii. 2^{10}), herself undertaking to contrive to bring the young people together and arrange for a private marriage. Bhūrivasu could in that case plead that he was in no wise a party to this clandestine affair, and the king—the marriage once solemnized—would have no choice but to submit. With the help of friends, Kāmandakī manages to throw the young people together in chance encounters on the road or at the spring festival of the God of Love, or in the city garden; while,—by praising to Mālatī the person and family and accomplishments of Mādhava, by painting with contrasting touches the ugliness and stupidity of Nandana, and finally by narrating to her some ancient stories of girls in like circumstances[1] who chose their husbands without regard to their parents' wishes,—Kāmandakī so works upon Mālatī's feelings that when the opportunity comes she is ready to elope with Mādhava and marry him in a place prepared by Kāmandakī.

33, C.—Such is the main plot. Interwoven with it is a by-plot, also a love-story, namely between Nandana's sister Madayantikā and Mādhava's friend Makaranda. This by-plot is clearly intended to be a foil for the main plot, an element of contrast with it. Thus the first meeting of Mālatī and Mādhava occurs at the spring festival in a most natural way. The first meeting of Madayantikā and Makaranda takes place under most exceptional circumstances: A tiger has broken loose, has killed his keepers, and is running amuck in the streets, when Madayantikā, who happens to pass by, is saved from deadly peril by Makaranda.[2] A second notable contrast appears in the characters of Mālatī and Madayantikā. Mālatī is a modest obedient girl whom Kāmandakī finds it hard to persuade to disobey her father's wishes; while Madayantikā, the sister of the court-favourite, is a flighty passionate girl who elopes with Makaranda at the very first opportunity. Further, as compared with Mādhava's love, that of Makaranda is frankly sensuous. There was nothing to prevent Makaranda from going in straightforward fashion to Nandana and asking for the hand of his sister (whom moreover he had saved from the tiger). The actual method adopted is an elopement under cover of darkness.

33, D.—The story is further complicated and diversified by the introduction of two episodic elements: 1. the marriage of Nandana to Makaranda disguised as Mālatī; 2. the two hairbreadth escapes of Mālatī, one before and one after her marriage. The purpose of the first episode is

[1] Such as Śakuntalā, Urvaśī, and Vāsavadattā.

[2] His opportune presence is adequately motivated (iv. 0^{28}). The rescuer is wounded.

to link the main plot more closely to the by-plot, since it is the event of which the union of the two pairs of lovers is the immediate sequel. The purpose of the second episode is merely to thrill the audience and to satisfy the human craving for the marvellous and even the gruesome.

The first episode comes about in this way. A clandestine marriage between Mālatī and Mādhava having been decided upon, Kāmandakī secures the opportunity as follows: It was announced that the marriage of Mālatī and Nandana would be celebrated in the evening; and, according to the custom, Mālatī was to go just before the marriage to one of the city temples and there duly worship the Goddess. It is prearranged that Mādhava and Makaranda should go beforehand into the temple and there remain hidden. Mālatī, who however is quite in ignorance of what was to follow, approaches; the attendants stand outside, only her trusty companion and confidante, Lavañgikā, going with her into the interior. Then after a scene (act vi) which is one of the best in the play, the whole plot is revealed. Makaranda was to put on the dress of Mālatī[1] and join the marriage procession and be married to the unsuspecting Nandana, Mādhava in the meantime taking the real Mālatī with him to a place prepared for them and being formally married to her.

33, E.—The same stratagem was to give Makaranda *his* wife—Madayantikā, sister of Nandana. For, after the marriage of the pseudo-Mālatī with Nandana, when the latter meets his supposed wife and makes her advances of love, he receives a cold rebuff, and finally a kick. The bridegroom walks away in high dudgeon. Now Madayantikā, the bridegroom's sister, hearing of the infamous treatment her brother received at the hands of the new bride, comes to her room to expostulate with her. What follows is easily imagined. Makaranda throws off his disguise and elopes with Madayantikā. Had he been able to reach the appointed place in safety and solemnize the marriage, the play would have ended smoothly but much too early (end of act viii). The only difficulty then would have been to pacify the king, which would not have been very difficult perhaps. What actually happens is that, as Makaranda is escaping from Nandana's house, he unexpectedly comes upon certain night-watches who challenge him. A skirmish ensues. More guards are sent, and Mādhava, hearing of the news, runs to his friend's rescue. The two friends fight so bravely that the king, who was aroused and was watching their valour, is moved to pardon them; and, coming to know of all the facts, he even acknowledges the two marriages.

[1] In judging the verisimilitude of this incident, we must consider that the part of Mālatī herself was very probably taken by a man (see appendix 11).

33, F.—Here at any rate the play might very naturally end; but no. The poet wants (see i. 6) to make as diversified an appeal as he can, and so he has introduced the second episode. It seems that at Padmāvatī, in the cremation-ground close by the river, there was a temple of the Goddess Karālā (the Terrible). This Goddess is very fond of blood, and her votaries wear garlands of skulls, and offer her animal sacrifices (sometimes even human sacrifices), and in return she grants them magic powers, such as flying through the air, rendering oneself invisible, and so forth.[1] On the very night of the day when Mālatī and Mādhava meet in the garden, and Makaranda kills the tiger—it being the uncanny night that precedes the new moon—a certain Kāpālika, Aghoraghaṇṭa by name, has arranged to offer a human sacrifice, and Mālatī is chosen as the victim. Kapālakuṇḍalā, the female disciple of Aghoraghaṇṭa, has all in readiness, and they are about to immolate Mālatī, when Mādhava, hearing Mālatī's cry, appears on the scene and rescues her. The opportune presence of Mādhava in the dead of night, and upon the cremation-ground, was, the poet frankly admits (v. 28), the merest chance. Mādhava was there trying to propitiate in some occult way the ghouls and other uncanny beings who infest such places. Mādhava kills Aghoraghaṇṭa, though he permits Kapālakuṇḍalā—as she was a woman—to escape.

33, G.—Out of this escape comes the second hairbreadth escape of Mālatī. Kapālakuṇḍalā longs to avenge the death of her master; and just when everything seems to be going well—Mādhava married to Mālatī, Makaranda securely in possession of Madayantikā, and even the king himself induced to pardon the two lovers,—she finds an opportunity to pounce upon Mālatī and lead her off with intent to kill her. There is general grief and lamentation, which fills the whole of act ix and a part of act x. This time Mālatī is saved by another fortuitous coincidence. We have already spoken (§ 33, A) of Saudāminī, the pupil of Kāmandakī. She apparently had become an adept in occult sciences, and having *by chance* come upon Kapālakuṇḍalā, she reproves her, rescues Mālatī from her hands, and restores her to her sorrowing relatives, and the play ends happily.

34. Mālatī-Mādhava: criticism of the plot.—It would be easy, of course, to criticize the plot by saying that it is no more than a loose patchwork: it lacks the consistency, the inevitableness, that should belong to every dramatic action. The poet evidently wishes to represent Kāmandakī as an expert in underhand diplomacy. She is in fact the arch-plotter

[1] Bhavabhūti, like other people of his time (see Bāṇa, Harsha-charita, iii, story of Bhairavāchārya), implicitly believed in these powers, so that we cannot reasonably charge him with an illicit introduction of the supernatural.

in the play; but her own scheming contributes far less to the ultimate result than does mere chance. In this connexion the Kapālakuṇḍalā episode is what is most frequently criticized. It gives the poet the chance to describe the cemetery-scenes, or to indulge (acts ix and x) in a pathetic outpouring of song, but it serves no other purpose.

Some go so far as to suppose that this entire episode is a later addition by the poet, prompted by a desire to emulate Kālidāsa (see § 7 above): it did not belong to the poet's original conception of the plot. It would seem that a good case could be made in favour of this theory, especially if we take into account the number of lines and stanzas and parts of stanzas that we find common[1] to this play and to the Uttara-Rāma-charita, after the completion of which latter play Bhavabhūti is believed to have reverted to the former play and enlarged it.

Now although it be true (see appendixes 6 and 8) that Bhavabhūti did revise his own plays, I am not prepared to believe in such a wholesale overhauling of the play before us as this theory would imply. For, were we to omit the Kapālakuṇḍalā episode, that would involve the falling out of not only act ix and the major part of act x, but also [2] the whole of act v and the short interlude at the opening of act vi, and even, I think, the tiger incident in acts iii and iv, seeing that one of its chief purposes is to establish a sort of a parallelism between the main plot and the by-plot: as Makaranda saves his would-be wife from the claws of the tiger, so Mādhava saves his from the clutches of the Kāpālika. We should likewise have to make a number of minor changes in the interlude to act i and the concluding part of act viii, besides omitting short sentences like iv. 7^6, where Mālatī compares her father to a Kāpālika. We have no evidence that Bhavabhūti made such extensive changes in the play.

Nor have I been able, after a careful study of the parallels adduced between this play and the Uttara-Rāma-charita,[3] to find therein anything that would make against the Uttara-Rāma-charita passages being a later modification of the corresponding Mālatī-Mādhava passages. Even Mālatī-Mādhava ix. 20 need not be an exception, as I long thought it was; see U. R. C., Note to iv. 3^5. The only case about which I do not feel quite confident is M. M. ix. 14 = U. R. C. i. 31. The stanza certainly appears to be more in place in U. R. C., and this one stanza might well have

[1] The ninth act alone—the act that has been suspected to be a later appendage—has eight such cases, namely stanzas 6, 12, 14, 20, $24^{a,b}$, 34, $51^{c,d}$, and 54^a.

[2] I do not see how we can keep Aghoraghaṇṭa without Kapālakuṇḍalā, unless Mādhava kills both. When one of the main appeals of the play consists in the story-form, it is not possible to leave the fate of a character like Kapālakuṇḍalā undecided.

[3] Complete list in appendix 3.

been inserted later into the M. M. But we must remember that much of the talk of love and grief in the M. M. is purely conventional, and it need not surprise us if the stanza after all did originally belong to it. Compare in this connexion M. M. act i, stanza 34[c], where the hero talks of the moon, when it is full day.

35. Technique of the Mālatī-Mādhava.—From the preceding analysis of the plot it is clear that in sheer inventiveness of incidents Bhavabhūti has now attained considerable power, although he does not quite realize that a mere string of incidents, however exciting or dramatic, does not necessarily lead to a climax nor give a real unity of plot. Secondly, the poet recognizes the value of suspense, but it is the sort of suspense which results from an incipient fatalism. Neither in the situation, nor in the characters, nor again in the background on which they are thrown in the early part of the play, is there a foreshadowing of the final dénouement as a thing inevitable or even antecedently probable.

In defence it may be urged that, after all, chances *do* occur in the world as it is constituted, and that the dramatist has really no right to rule chance entirely out of his creation and make the latter a rational system conformable to the demands of his own philosophy. Consider, for instance, Shakespeare's *Hamlet* or *Romeo and Juliet.* It is not antecedently necessary for the dénouement of these plays that Ophelia should die, or that Friar John be 'stay'd by accident' and not deliver the letter. Laertes might just as well have avenged the death of his father without Ophelia's drowning, and the Capulets and the Montagues might just as well have been induced to join hands and merge old feuds at the wedding of their children as at their funeral. But these irrational accidents came to Shakespeare as parts of the story proper, and the audience was willing to accept the dramatist's statement, just as we should accept that of a traveller, provided it did not overtax our credulity.

More important it is to inquire if there is any dramatic justification for these accidents: any attempt, in other words, to place us in that frame of mind in which we instinctively seem to scent dangers long before they come—scent dangers that do not come. Bhavabhūti *has* done something of the kind. Compare, for instance, passages like iv. 4[b], iv. 7; v. 27[3], v. 28; viii. 10, viii. 14; ix. 8[d], ix. 39, ix. 49; x. 13; &c. Here the poet seems to be purposely dwelling on the fickleness of Fortune, the instability of all mundane existence. This gives us the necessary mood. Stanza viii. 10 is particularly significant in this connexion.

36. Mālatī-Mādhava: its advance over the Mahāvīra-charita.—We found (see § 31) the Mahāvīra-charita weak in characterization. In the

Mālatī-Mādhava Bhavabhūti is, for the first time, truly creating character, and developing it by making it react upon its environment. This will be evident if we compare Mālyavant with Kāmandakī, Sītā with Mālatī. Mālyavant, the diplomat of the Mahāvīra-charita, is purely an academic figure. He chops logic rather too freely, and shows a preternatural insight as to the future success or failure of his schemes. There is no feeling in his strategy, and his very lamentations in act vi seem to be 'made to order'. Contrast with him Kāmandakī, who plays a similar rôle in the Mālatī-Mādhava. In her we find a genuine old lady, shrewd and resourceful, and full of learning and devotion and affection (see especially act vi, end), although one often wishes that her knowledge had not been so versatile.[1]

Compare again Sītā, as she is depicted in the Mahāvīra-charita, with the Mālatī of this play. Sītā, the moment she sees Rāma, feels a striking partiality for him, just as Sītā's sister feels for Rāma's brother. All seems to be pre-arranged: a sort of pre-natal relation, a falling in love at first sight reduced to a wooden mechanism. The same is true of the passage of love and tenderness in the second act of the Mahāvīra-charita, where Sītā seems, in a few minutes, to grow from a demure bride into a matron of phenomenal maturity of thought and sentiment. How different from her is Mālatī—tossed in the conflict between her love (intense but never obtrusive) for Mādhava and her duty of submission to her parents' wishes, a duty to which, in spite of all the artful machinations of Kāmandakī (§ 33, B) and even after the incident in the temple of Karālā (§ 33, F), she holds firmly, so that she is ready rather to commit suicide (cp. M. M. ii. 2, vi. 8^{1-5}) than do anything unworthy of a modest, well-bred girl! The same traits of her character are again brought out in that admirable love-scene[2] between Mādhava and Mālatī in the beginning of act viii.

Among other merits of the Mālatī-Mādhava we may mention that the language—particularly of the three or four best scenes in the play—is extremely good, and we also find some genuinely poetic imagery and feeling. The description of the cremation-ground at night (act v) and of the forest scenery (act ix) are some of the best that the poet ever wrote, although they may here and there seem to be overdrawn and out of place

[1] She had studied the *Kāma-śāstra*, and, what is more, she liked to make a display of her learning; or rather it is Bhavabhūti who speaks through her and Lavaṅgikā and Madayantikā. We will return to this point presently.

[2] It does not seem to have been sufficiently realized that Bhavabhūti is in this scene following very closely the instructions in Kāma-sūtra, iii. 2, even to such details as Mālatī's reply (*nāhaṁ kiṁ pi jāṇāmi*: viii. 4^{13}) and her earlier gestures.

in a play proper.[1] Taken as a whole the play may unhesitatingly be pronounced to be, both in substance and in form, a decided advance over the Mahāvīra-charita. It was written with the distinct purpose of avoiding some of the faults of his earlier work (see M. M. i. 8), and its technique is much more conscious and deliberate.

37. Defects of the Mālatī-Mādhava.—We have already commented upon the defects in the structure of the plot. In a word the play may be said to give us a particularly vivid form of story-telling, with a number of conscious critical approaches to dramatic technique. What the poet needs now is practice and, as a natural result of it, a toning down of the youthful exuberances that still mar the play. Thus we find here a constant tendency to exaggerate, to over-emphasize so as to drive a thing home, and this cannot have been wholly the result of the dullness, the tardy responsiveness, of his audience; a part of it at least must be charged to the poet's lack of restraint. He gives us dozens of long descriptions, full of lengthy compounds and mouth-filling phrases, where his delight in words as words is quite evident. It may be that his audience also shared his delight, and if only the passage as a whole conveyed an emotional mood and if that mood was adequately interpreted in suitable action, they did not care what the passage really meant. We may also note that the compounds though long are not usually involved, so that on the whole it is fairly smooth sailing.

Another characteristic defect of the play is its sentimentality. In the first act, for instance, Mādhava's love seems to be a purely intellectual affair. He loves being in love and talking about his love; and throughout the play he seems to be intent on showing how 'we that are true lovers'[2] love and run into risks and get separated and weep and even commit suicide *à la mode de* Kāma-śāstra or some other Śāstra. The long Prākrit descriptions (iii. 12^{8-49}, vii. 0^{79-91}, vii. 1^{20-47}, and elsewhere) might just as well have been, like the love-scene in act viii, taken bodily over from some ancient treatise;[3] and it is quite conceivable, seeing that the descriptions are in the vernacular, that they were expressly meant for the 'groundlings' who perhaps had a special relish for such topics; and in that case the long

[1] We must, however, remember that such descriptions have a value and a purpose, especially if the stage-properties be meagre. To me Hamlet's ''Tis now the very witching time of night' (iii. 2. 406 ff.) is more blood-curdling than all the stage-effects that electricity and modern science can produce. For a detailed statement as to the stage-conditions in Ancient India, see appendix 11.

[2] *As You Like It*, ii. 4. 55.

[3] Such as that of Aṅgiras which Bhavabhūti quotes in M. M. ii. 2^{15}. Vātsyāyana's Kāma-sūtra gives the quoted passage as an anonymous view in iii. 1 (Durgāprasāda's ed., p. 194). We have already (§ 31) commented upon the poet's fondness for displaying his learning.

compounds would rather show that Bhavabhūti did not care to make the thing too easily understood. The standards and limits of propriety as well as of prudery are different for different people, and for different epochs in the social development of the same people; and since Bhavabhūti was in this play evidently straining for effect and eager to secure from every different element of his audience all possible emotional response, any wholesale condemnation of the poet on this score would be as unfair as a similar condemnation of certain free passages in Shakespeare's poems and plays, or of the erotic verse of some of the early Christian writers.[1]

The Present Play: Uttara-Rāma-charita

38. Transition to the Uttara-Rāma-charita.—Between the two plays that we have been hitherto considering and the play before us we must assume an interval of time sufficient to account for its almost perfect development in form and technique. The poet himself calls this play a product of his mature genius.[2] Presumably therefore in the interval the poet was acquiring more practice—writing more dramas; but unfortunately none of these intervening attempts have survived. We have given above (§ 15) the external evidence that inclines us to assume such lost works; but were this evidence entirely lacking, it would yet be hard to believe that the transition from the earlier to the later work—a transition which is no ess significant than the transition from *Love's Labour's Lost* to *Romeo and Juliet*—was all made without any intermediate steps; and when we remember that there was no printing in those days and that even the manuscripts themselves (especially of works not produced for the court and not patronized by the king) did not command any extensive circulation; and when we recall further that, even with more favourable conditions, nearly half the Elizabethan dramatic literature is now almost entirely lost to us,—we need not wonder at this regrettable loss, nor grow sceptical about the existence of works other than those that have actually survived the ravages of human and non-human enemies of letters.

We turn now to a consideration of the present play, which is Bhavabhūti's masterpiece and which has earned for him, by a consensus of opinion among scholars ancient and modern, a position at least equal to

[1] I would therefore entirely dissent from Dr. Gray when, in an otherwise very kindly intentioned passage, he says (Vāsavadattā, introduction, p. 28): 'There are personal descriptions more detailed than would be desirable in the Occidental literature, together with *evident approval of relations and ideals which the less sensual Western mind rightly condemns.*' The italics are mine.

[2] Compare U. R. C. vii. 20^{d}. The allusion is purposely veiled.

that of Kālidāsa, the current view being[1] that in the Uttara-Rāma-charita Bhavabhūti has even surpassed the so-called 'Shakespeare of India'. We have given for this play in the sequel (pp. 4–14) a synoptic analysis of its plot act by act, and have tried to show the bearing of every act (and scene) upon the dénouement of the play. We will here limit ourselves to a few general criticisms.

39. Special features of the Uttara-Rāma-charita.—The play, as its title shows, treats of the later history of Rāma, from his coronation and the abandonment of Sītā to the final reunion. As we have seen (pp. liv–lxviii), the main incidents of the story—the circumstances leading to the abandonment of Sītā, her rescue, the birth of the twins and their education, the horse-sacrifice and the heroism displayed by the boys in capturing the horse, their recognition by Rāma, the final ordeal of Sītā, and presumably also the final reunion,—these were all given to the poet, not excepting even the Śambūka episode (act ii) and the Lavaṇa affair (end of act i and of act vii). The poet's task therefore was not to create a plot, nor even to make any considerable change in the sequence of given events and connect them causally, as was the case in the two earlier plays.

The problem to be answered was briefly this: How could Rāma ever think of abandoning such a wife as Sītā? and, having abandoned her—for whatever cause—how could they be again united in any real sense until all clouds, all vestiges of doubt and distrust, had been entirely banished from their minds? The Dushyanta of Kālidāsa not only repudiates Śakuntalā, but actually insults her to her face (Śākuntala, act v, *Vyapadeśam āvilayitum*, &c.); and yet, when the reunion comes in act vii, Śakuntalā has no other proof as to the penitence of the king than the indirect report coming from her mother's friend, and presumably the sad and wasted form of her husband when she first beholds him after a separation of years. True, the king begs her to forgive him (act vii: *Sutanu hṛidayāt pratyādeśa-vyalīkam*, &c.), but Śakuntalā has already acknowledged and accepted him quietly before that, although her early experience of 'that jar of poison with honey on top' might have taught her a lesson.[2] Similarly

[1] *Uttare Rāma-charite Bhavabhūtir viśishyate.*

[2] Of course, Kālidāsa, with the instinct of an artist, has tried to lessen the suddenness of the transition in various ways. One in particular must here be noted, since its artistic significance has not been sufficiently recognized; namely the difference in the background of act vii of the play as contrasted with that of the first and the following two acts. That of act vii is a hermitage in the sky far removed from the world, its passions, its hopes (*Yat kāṅkshanti tapobhir anya-munayas tasmiṅs tapasyanty amī*); that of acts i–iii is a forest on earth, a penance-grove if you will, but it is in the full bloom of spring. The wild infuriated elephant which breaks in at the end of act i, and the mild forgiving lioness in act vii which Sarvadamana robs of her cub, express

in *The Winter's Tale* it is a much grosser insult and far too unkind a treatment which Hermione receives, and yet she is reconciled to her husband on the evidence of hearsay reports of Paulina, and possibly his expressions of remorse in the statue-scene. Apparently, Bhavabhūti was not satisfied with such inadequate motivation: he was not content to bring somehow the estranged pair together and then leave them to settle their causes of dispute later—amicably or otherwise. He felt that a reunion, to be perfect, must first be a reunion of hearts; and this was the psychological problem which he deliberately proposed to himself in this play, especially in the first three acts. The complicated chain of events leading to the actual reunion and the recognition of the princes forms the burden of the last four acts.

40. Technical perfection of the opening act of the Uttara-Rāma-charita.—Nothing can show more clearly the advance which Bhavabhūti had made in his technique than a careful study of the first act of the Uttara-Rāma-charita in relation to its significance for the final dénouement. This is the act in which Rāma abandons Sītā. The prologue has already informed us (i. 6) of the circulation of a rumour which, when it reaches Rāma, makes him decide upon the abandonment of his wife. Before the rumour actually reaches him, however, it was necessary for the poet to make clear to the audience several essential points. (1) That Rāma himself would put no faith in the rumour; this is effected by U. R. C. i. 12^8–i. 14. Lakshmaṇa might just as well have said that the pictures ended with 'our return from Laṅkā', or 'our meeting with Bharata in Nandigrāma'; but he (unintentionally) happens to mention Sītā's fire-ordeal, and that gives the poet his chance. (2) That in nevertheless abandoning his wife on the basis of this false rumour, Rāma was obeying the higher call of what he owed as a king to his subjects. A king and his affairs must be above even the faintest possibility of suspicion. This stern conception of duty, and the readiness to sacrifice everything for it, is illustrated not only by i. 12 or i. 41, 42, 44, but even in the very first speech that Rāma makes (i. 7^4–i. 8). We here get the first distant echoes, as it were, of a storm that is brewing. (3) That Sītā would understand Rāma's higher motive, and would have gone herself voluntarily into exile if necessary (i. 12^1). What Sītā did resent was not that she was abandoned, but that she was abandoned in so heartless a fashion (i. 49) without her having the faintest inkling of whither she was being led and why.

symbolically this difference in atmosphere.

It is for a similar purpose that Bhavabhūti has placed the great reconciliation scene of U. R. C. act iii in the Pañchavaṭī, 'every spot in which, unto those manifold expressions of our unreserved endearments, can bear testimony.'

Wherefore did Rāma follow this unstraightforward course? In order to motivate this act adequately the poet (4) places Rāma in a peculiar situation: He is newly crowned (i. 8[6]) and has just taken upon himself the heavy responsibilities of the state; and every man who knows what it is to take charge of a new and important office will fully understand Rāma's conscientiousness, his anxious care not to seem to be wanting in the due discharge of his duties. Further Rāma is alone (i. 3); the elders and advisers, who presumably might have restrained him from such impetuous acts, are away (ii. 6[10]); and his forlornness has been brought home to him (i. 11) and has thrown him into a sort of nervous excitement just a little before the crisis comes which calls for immediate action. If the matter to be decided upon had been some non-personal affair of state, Rāma might have settled it in the way best for all; but where it was a personal affair of state, it was to be expected that he would be more rigorously self-exacting than was either right or just to himself. Finally, it was necessary to make clear (5) that, having abandoned his wife, Rāma would nevertheless suffer, and so would Sītā. The picture-gallery episode serves to show how dearly they loved each other, how they could not bear even the thought of living away from each other (i. 27[2-6], i. 30, i. 33[14]).

To bring out vividly these five points would have been achievement enough for one act, but Bhavabhūti is not content with that. In act i he is thinking of act vii, and so, besides giving us the *dohada* affair (i. 10[1], i. 33[3]) which serves as the immediate pretext for Sītā's banishment, the act gives us also the *jṛimbhaka* incident (i. 15[2]), which plays such a signal part in the recognition of the princes, as well as the allusions to Bhāgīrathī (i. 23[1]) and Pṛithivī (i. 51), who later take charge of the abandoned Sītā[1] and bring her into the action at the proper time. Two more points, which perhaps are not so very obvious at first sight: When we learn that Rāma has caused to be painted, on the walls of his palace, scenes from his past career—that career wherein Sītā was so prominent a figure,—and when we see the intense feeling and devoutness with which he looks at the pictures and recalls the memory of his past life with his beloved,—we can then readily understand his passionate clinging to these dear memories (iii. 14[4], iii. 43[13], vi. 38), and the source of mournful comfort that he will find therein even after the loss of his wife, so that we do not have to be actually told that Rāma did not marry a second time. Of course, he did not and would

[1] Herein Bhavabhūti departs from his sources. It was Vālmīki who, both according to the Rāmāyaṇa and the Padma-Purāṇa, took charge of Sītā and gave her a shelter in his hermitage. Bhavabhūti wanted to keep the twins ignorant of their parentage; hence the change.

not and could not. Secondly, there is, to my mind, a peculiarly dramatic appropriateness in the fact that the play—I mean the play proper—should open with a speech of Rāma (i. 8[4]) that was meant to console his wife for a thing which had happened and which could not but happen: the separation from her dear relatives and elders. Here we have the very keynote of the play struck once and for all. When to all this we add that the language of the entire act is exceptionally rich and poetic, that there is hardly a sentence or even a phrase which we would wish were not there,[1] hardly a word which is not just the right word, that the poet affords us a deep insight into the workings of the human heart so that the emotional tone is genuine and not mawkish or sentimental (as it was in some parts of his earlier plays), and that the whole is arranged in a sequence which is entirely natural and clearly shows that Bhavabhūti has at last mastered the art of condensing and enlarging, of choosing and omitting, and above all has learned the value of restraint,—with that we have said our last word in praise of this act and of the dramatic technique that is involved in the writing of it.

41. The Uttara-Rāma-charita as a psychological study.—In acts ii and iii we have Bhavabhūti in yet another light. Vālmīki's Rāmāyaṇa gives the story of Śambūka in vii. 74–82, and the Padma-Purāṇa gives it in v. 32, 33 and elsewhere. Both these works tell us that Rāma, after killing the Śūdra ascetic, visited the hermitage of Agastya in the Pañchavaṭī, but neither is alive to the great poetic opportunity afforded by Rāma's reappearance in the old familiar scenes after the great event of Sītā's abandonment. The Padma-Purāṇa does perhaps vaguely realize the poetic possibilities of the theme (cp. v. 35[26 ff.]), but the treatment is not to be compared with the splendid descriptive and reflective passages that we find in the Uttara-Rāma-charita, acts ii and iii. For all practical purposes then these acts might be said to be an original work of Bhavabhūti, and we have seen (§ 39) that he had a strong psychological reason for the invention. Let us now see what the poet makes of his opportunities.

[1] For the stage-omission of i. 30[9] to i. 31[d] see appendix 8. With this single exception the themes of the pictures are all well chosen. Each has a distinct purpose. The poet's treatment, of course, is necessarily allusive and the audience could easily fill in the details. His dramatic sense is shown as much by what he keeps as by what he omits; e. g. the Ahalyā incident and the fight with Vālin. Note also that Rāma does not in the play, as he does in the epic (vii. 43 f.), expressly seek information about the *kiṁvadantī* (rumour); and he abandons Sītā immediately after his interview with the spy, not the next morning, as in the epic. That the cry for help (i. 49[3]) should come just at the right moment to remind him of his kingly duty, while at the same time the allusion to *Rākshasa-trāsa* (fear of demons) should make his heart soften, is also highly artistic. So far as we know, the episode of the picture-gallery is original with Bhavabhūti.

To begin with, in Rāma there is no change of mood, no development of character. His grief is of the steady abiding kind, only made more intense and alive by the sight of Pañchavaṭī. It is Sītā who passes through a progressive emotional experience, wherein from a feeling of apathy and even resentment towards her husband she, after many a swing of the pendulum, reaches finally a state of confidence and perfect reconciliation. The various psychological moments in this process will be duly set forth in our Notes to the several passages. We will here review them briefly. In iii. 7^6 Sītā is so thoroughly estranged from Rāma that she finds it impossible to speak of him as 'My noble Lord (*ajjaütta*)', but simply as 'The King (*rāā*)'. In iii. 46^{13} she admits that 'the dart of disgraceful abandonment'[1] has been removed from her heart. What has happened in the interval is that she has seen Rāma, has heard him, has received ample apology for her wrongs. The important point to note, however, is that Sītā did not expect to get this apology, and yet she has it offered to her, and that too in a manner precluding all possibility of Rāma's being insincere, for he does not know that he is overheard by his wife, or even that his wife is alive. It is also creditable to the poet that all through this mental evolution Sītā does not appear as the stern jurist who refuses to be convinced until the last shred of evidence is in, but always as the true woman and the loving wife that she had never ceased to be.

There are three main stages in this process of *rapprochement*: 1. Seeing Rāma faint and following the impulse of the moment, Sītā runs to his rescue (iii. 10^1), but upon brief reflection she turns to withdraw (iii. 12^5), and settles down slowly into a mood of despondency and resignation to fate (iii. $22^{2\text{ ff.}}$). Sītā has, however, made sure of one thing: Rāma has not forgotten her, although why he abandoned her is yet a mystery. 2. In the second stage she goes one step further, and, when Vāsantī begins to reprove Rāma for his cruelty to his wife, it is Sītā herself who, with a truly feminine instinct, takes her husband's part against all attacks from without (iii. 26^6, iii. 27^1). This self-effacement (iii. 36^1) almost reaches a total surrender of self-respect in iii. 40^8, but Tamasā's words (iii. 43) recall her to a truer estimate of her present position. 3. Then follows a second reaction (iii. $43^{9,\,15}$, iii. 45^1), not so violent as the first; and this is immediately followed by a counter-reaction, especially when she has the assurance that her husband not only loves her as passionately as ever, but will never love or marry another. The inward reconciliation is now complete (iii. 46^{13}).

[1] Observe that it is no longer a 'causeless' abandonment as it was in iii. 14^2 and elsewhere.

It is clear that a poet who could fathom so deeply the inmost recesses of the human heart and produce a result which, from beginning to end, is so perfectly artistic because it is so perfectly natural, was a dramatist of no mean order. Similar genuinely human touches are found on almost every page of the drama.

42. Recognition-scene in the sixth act of the Uttara-Rāma-charita.—So far the poet has given us a brilliant opening and a real psychological climax, but the climax of situations is yet to come. In the latter part of the play the great act of course is the sixth, and the poet has been preparing us for it ever since the interlude to act ii. There we hear of the horse-sacrifice for the first time; Rāma confirms the news in iii. 46^{12}, and towards the end of act iv we actually see the horse. Similarly at the end of act iii Rāma is just starting in his *pushpaka* car to return to Ayodhyā, and we naturally expect him to see what was happening in Vālmīki's penance-grove on the banks of the Ganges, seeing that it lay just on the way from the south. Thus Rāma's appearance on the scene exactly when he does appear (vi. 6^4) is adequately explained. Finally, that Lava should see and capture the horse and that a battle should ensue was also quite inevitable.

The recognition itself is very artistically conceived and carried out except that here and there a point is rather over-laboured[1]—at least so it seems to us, however it may have seemed to Bhavabhūti's audience. The various steps in the process are summarized in our Notes to vi. 27^1, and here we may call attention particularly to the very natural way in which Lava is led to talk of his twin-brother (iv. 22^{15-41} and again vi. $15^{4ff.}$). Notice also how, in regard to the similarity of looks between the father and the sons, which is one of the links in the argument, the poet has tried to gain dramatic probability for the fact by letting at least three other persons besides Rāma himself be impressed by it. The whole recognition scene is worthy to be put on a par with the analogous scene in Kālidāsa's Śākuntala (act vii); in some respects it would seem that Bhavabhūti has made a distinct advance over the latter. A sort of suspense is also created by making the recognition not complete until the very end of the last act.

43. Other merits of the Uttara-Rāma-charita.—If we compare the interludes in the Uttara-Rāma-charita with those in the Mahāvīra-charita or in the Mālatī-Mādhava, we notice another great advance which the poet has made: he has now recognized the full dramatic value of the interlude. We have no longer some person or persons brought on the stage expressly to give us information (cp. interludes to M. M. ii and vii), nor

[1] I have in mind Rāma's long soliloquy in act vi, particularly vi. 27^1-vi. 28^d. The movement against soliloquies is, however, distinctly modern.

a tedious soliloquizer like Mālyavant (cp. interludes to M. V. C. ii and vi) who reveals to us the exact situation of things; neither do the characters begin, as is sometimes done, by expressly telling us who they are and what they are doing (cp. interludes to M. M. v and ix; also M. V. C. iv. 40⁴); but rather we find a group of persons with an individuality of their own who conduct the dialogue and give us the necessary information without seeming to do so. We have some approaches to this in the Mahāvīra-charita (cp. interludes to acts v and vii); but the best interludes are those to acts iv and ii of the Uttara-Rāma-charita. In these interludes there is hardly a word wasted, and they are entirely natural and adequate. The least successful is the one to U. R. C. act vi.

Secondly, the poet has developed in this play some remarkable instances of dramatic irony. Thus in that picture-gallery scene of act i, while Rāma and Sītā are enjoying the 'bliss of sorrows remembered',[1] looking upon them more or less as things of the past the memory of which is to be revived only to season the cup of present joy, the audience has already heard (i. 6) of the rumour and partly divines the fate that is hanging over the two, so that it fully understands why it is that almost in spite of himself Rāma strikes a sorrowful note[2] and seems to have a foreboding of he knows not what. And just at the moment when Rāma bursts into that sublime apostrophe to his sleeping wife (i. 38)—'What of hers is not dear, save only that unendurable separation?'—the Female-warder's 'Is come' does indeed startle Rāma,[3] but on the audience it is calculated to produce an impression not unlike that made by Iago's *aside* after a similar outburst of Othello (ii. 1. 185).[4] There is also some clever irony in acts iv and v, and throughout the recognition scene of act vi.

Finally, consider how skilfully the author has tried to bridge over the twelve-year interval that separates the first act from the rest of the play.[5] He brings the fact home to us in various ways. The nature-descriptions in act ii (especially stanza 27) and the account of the young peacock (iii. 19, 20, 21) and the elephant-cub now grown to full maturity (iii. 16, 17) make us realize that during this period growth and change were in constant

[1] Cp. Raghuvaṁśa, xiv. 25.

[2] Cp. i. 27² to i. 33ᵈ. It is worthy of remark that stanza i. 23, where Rāma invokes the blessings of the Bhāgīrathī, is in the sad dirge-like *hariṇī* metre. See appendix 1.

[3] Cp. note to the English Translation of the passage.

[4] *Othello.* O my soul's joy!
If after every tempest come such calms,
May the winds blow till they have waken'd *death*!
. . . .
Iago (*aside*). O, you are well tun'd now!
But I'll set down the pegs that make this music.

[5] Under similar conditions Shakespeare has introduced Time as the Chorus who turns his glass, and leaves 'the growth untri'd' (*The Winter's Tale*, iv. 1).

progress. Men also had grown and witnessed changes of station. Thus king Janaka has for some years given up the offices of state and sought solace in retirement (iv. 1^{27}); the demon Lavaṇa, who broke upon us at the close of act i, has been killed and his kingdom is now in the hands of Śatrughna (vii. 19^{29}; cp. Rāmāyaṇa, vii. 70–71); and the twelve-year session of the sacrifice (i. 4^{1}, ii. 6^{12}) has come to an end. But amid this fluctuation there were also elements of constancy. The mountains remain unchanged (ii. 27^{d}); the deer still remember her who used to feed them in the *kadalī* grove in the Pañchavaṭī (iii. 22^{5}, 26; cp. also Kādambarī, p. 21, ll. 19–20); Rāma is constant and devoted to the memory of his wife;[1] and above all, the holy pair, Vasishṭha and Arundhatī, still continue to guard the interests of the Raghu family, and, out of the calamities that have happened and that they in part had foreseen (iv. 17^{6}), they succeed in working a prosperous issue.

44. Defects of the Uttara-Rāma-charita.—The play, in spite of its great excellence, is not entirely free from faults. Thus the poet still retains—though in a far less degree—his old fondness for long descriptions and alliterative compounds. These are particularly obtrusive in acts v and vi. Elsewhere also the poet would have done better to condense and omit so as to secure a general quickening of the action; and if the results of appendixes 6 and 8 are correct, it would seem that the author himself sanctioned such curtailment for stage-purposes. Secondly, Bhavabhūti has not yet quite got over his fondness for display, and his points are sometimes laboured. The sentiment of the play is on the whole very real, but in its expression we sometimes catch a jarring note. Thus Rāma brings his 'heart's vitals' rather too frequently into his speeches, and not all the faintings in the play are as inevitable and as artistically necessary as that of Rāma at iii. 39^{1}. Particularly infelicitous are the Vidyādhara-Vidyādharī sentiments at vi. 4 ff. and especially vi. 5. Finally, we may mention that in none of Bhavabhūti's extant plays do we (except in U. R. C., act iv) find any pronounced humour. Bhavabhūti's humour, what little there is of it, is of the purely intellectual character and springs more from situation and irony (e. g. U. R. C. vi. $19^{12f.}$, iv. 22^{20}, iii. 46^{16}). Only once does Sītā herself indulge in a joke (i. 18^{2}) and even then it is of the sober matronly kind quite in accord with her character. This absence in Bhavabhūti's plays of anything like a pervading lighter vein[2] may be due to the fact that the poet took his subject too seriously, felt in other

[1] Cp. p. lxxix, above, and also U. R. C. iii. 14^{6}; iii. 43^{14}; vi. 38^{6}; &c.

[2] This by itself would rule out the theory that Bhavabhūti was a conscious imitator of Śūdraka in the 'Clay Cart'.

words that he had a lesson to teach; or finally that he was temperamentally incapable of dwelling long on the sunny side of life. A few more defects of a minor nature could also be pointed out; but in this connexion the more important thing is to see how many of his earlier shortcomings he has in this play successfully overcome, and so to realize, as Bhavabhūti did, that the key to consummate success lies in a constant practice in the light of earlier failures.

45. Some common characteristics [1] of Bhavabhūti's plays.—The three plays were all given as open-air performances on the occasion of a religious fair, and they end happily. The hero in all cases is devoted to one wife, and there is no illicit love of any kind. Pathos is the prevailing sentiment in the U. R. C., and it is not wholly absent in the other two plays. In all of them there appears at least one aged mourner. They show only one kind of Prākrit, Śaurasenī, and it is all prose and no verse.[2] All the three plays have characters flying through the air (two of them have aerial cars), and this circumstance, as well as the effect of light and shade given by the stanza *vyatikara iva*,[3] is of importance in connexion with the stage-properties.[4] We have already spoken (§ 37) of the long Prākrit passages in the Mālatī-Mādhava as an indication of the nature of Bhavabhūti's audience; we may further note that all the three plays contain a number of learned allusions to different Śāstras, and this must be meant as an appeal to another element of the audience. Finally, what are called unities of time and place are entirely absent in the plays. The action moves in a rapid succession from the interior of a house or a palace to the garden surrounding it, the street, the cemetery, the river, or the forest, sometimes indeed the high regions of the atmosphere. Then as to time, the first play covers a period of some fifteen years, the last about twelve years. The action of the Mālatī-Mādhava occupies nearly three months. The only unity recognized is the unity of plot. About that we have spoken elsewhere. All these circumstances make it likely that the plays were given by one and the same company of actors; and this is an important factor in determining the authorship of the stage-emendations discussed in appendix 8.

[1] Mere parallelisms in words, images, and sentiments will be found collected in appendix 3.

[2] M. M. vi. 10 and 11 are so worded as to have one form both in Sanskrit and in Prākrit.

[3] M. M. ix. 54; x. 8; U. R. C. v. 13; M. V. C. has the thing (i. 43) but not the words. This last circumstance might be additional proof that the M. V. C. was the earliest of the three plays.

[4] See appendix 11.

Bhavabhūti as a Poet

46. Bhavabhūti's shortcomings.—So far as it is possible to separate the functions of a dramatist from those of a poet, we will now try to bring out some of the special qualities of Bhavabhūti's poetry; and first we will speak of his shortcomings because they are so very few. Most of them are on the surface, and are the more often felt because critics attempt to apply to the poet standards which belong neither to his country nor to his time; but some are radical defects, and belong as much to the man as to his works. Thus, especially in his early works, the poet does not seem to have risen above the standards imposed upon him from without. He came after Bāṇa, or at least at a time when long mouth-filling words were regarded as the very essence of poetic composition. Words had to be arranged in a particular way so as to give a particular *rīti*, a particular kind of alliterative effect, which was supposed to represent a particular kind of emotional mood. Softer emotions were expressed in simpler words, the more fiery or warlike emotions in harsh, guttural sounds, uttered in rapid succession.[1] The result has been those long descriptive passages in the Mālatī-Mādhava and elsewhere, which do not even contain ideas sufficiently poetic to offer a sort of a justification for the poet. It may be that his own audience was trained to such language, and grasped it more readily than we can do now, but the very fact that, as he advanced in his work, he gave up his earlier and more cumbrous style in favour of the simpler style of the Uttara-Rāma-charita, is an argument against such a supposition. Where there is such a deliberate straining after effect we need not be surprised if here and there we meet some infelicities of expression.[2] Secondly, Bhavabhūti now and then exhibits a tendency to exaggerate, and so to transcend the bounds of what is poetically probable. We must not, however, in this case judge the poet too harshly. Almost all romantic writers, Oriental or non-Oriental, modern or ancient, not infrequently indulge in exaggeration for the sake of deeper colour and stronger effect. A third fault in Bhavabhūti is pithily expressed by the formula that he has more passion than poetry. As Dr. Bhandarkar puts it, where Kālidāsa *suggests*, Bhavabhūti *expresses*. 'The characters of the latter, overcome by the force of passion, often weep bitterly, while those of the former simply shed a few tears, if they do so at all.'[3] Now with an external manifestation of emotions as such, we need

[1] This is best illustrated in U. R. C. v. 26, where the first half has a different *rīti* from the last half. Most of the illustrations which follow are purposely chosen from this play only.

[2] Thus *guñjat* used of an elephant's roar (U. R. C. v. 6a); *ghaṭā* used of a flock of owls (U. R. C. ii. 29a); &c.

[3] Mālatī-Mādhava, 2nd ed., preface, p. xii.

have no quarrel; it is a characteristic as much of a people as of a man, or of a particular period in the life of a man. Thus the ancient Greeks had it to a great extent, and even Kālidāsa's Dushyanta shows enough of it in the sixth act of the Śākuntala. Is the emotion genuine? is the expression natural? that is the main question. And we saw (§ 37) that such is not always the case in the Mālatī-Mādhava. In the Uttara-Rāma-charita the emotion is genuine, but the expression (especially fainting) is, to say the least, peculiar. A few other defects, such as the poet's use of the miraculous and his fondness for display, have already been mentioned.

47. Bhavabhūti's merits.—The real merits of the poet far outweigh his defects. We have spoken of his cumbrous style; this, however, is true only of his descriptive prose, and of less than a fourth part of his verse. Elsewhere, and whenever something stirring or momentous is happening on the stage, his language becomes notably simpler and simpler, until in some of the most intense situations he seems to have abjured compounds altogether.[1] No writer in fact has succeeded in keeping his prose and his poetry on two so entirely distinct footings. Then as to the ability to *suggest* the picture by a few, bold strokes, Bhavabhūti is not entirely devoid of such power;[2] more usually, however, instead of seeking for artistic similes and figures of speech, which were Kālidāsa's *forte*,[3] Bhavabhūti likes to select a few typical aspects of a situation or an emotion, and state them barely in succession; and this is equally effective in spite of, or rather because of, the absence of any poetic embellishments.[4] We have already commented sufficiently upon the poet's skill in portraying the deeper emotions of the human heart. This he does quite as much by a cumulation of epithets, as by a solitary word or sentence put into the mouth of some character. Instances of the former kind are not far to seek;[5] of the latter we may mention the exquisitely self-revealing speech of Sītā as she awakes to find herself alone (i. $51^{2\text{ ff.}}$), or, in the words of Wilson, the truly Shakespearian device (U.R.C. i. 8^{6}) of the chamberlain's addressing the newly crowned king first as 'Rāma dear' and then as 'Your Majesty'. Similarly the other chamberlain of the play (act iv), true to his calling, merely repeats or paraphrases the words of his betters.

[1] Cp. U. R. C. ii. 27; iii. 31 ff.; iii. 46; iv. 13; vi. 11; vii. 6; &c.

[2] Compare for instance U. R. C. i. 29, or that beautiful description of the peacock in iii. 19 and 20.

[3] '*Upamā Kālidāsasya.*' Some of Bhavabhūti's particularly happy similes in our play are: i. 45; ii. 4; iii. 5; iii. 30; iii. 43; v. 11; vi. 4; vi. 17; &c.

[4] Compare i. 27; i. 43; ii. 27; iii. 16; iii. 38; iv. 1; iv. 4; vi. 19; &c.

[5] As typical ones we may mention U. R. C. i. 35 f.; ii. 26; iii. 11 f.; iii. 32; iii. 36; iii. 39; vi. 9; &c.

It is touches like these[1] that tell us as much about the character of the chamberlain as the two descriptions of it given by Kālidāsa (Śākuntala, v. i; Vikramorvaśīya, iii. 1). In this connexion we may observe that the poet is at pains to put in the mouth of each character words the most appropriate. Thus Lava, pupil of the saint Vālmīki, speaks a language that is tinged with religious learning (v. 31[1]), just as the language of Janaka is tinged with the philosophy for which he is so famous in the Upanishads. Tamasā, the River-goddess, is full of similes drawn from her experience in the water.[2] The two ascetic youths in the interlude to act iv, Uttara-Rāma-charita, take a keen pleasure in logical discussions, attempting to detect fallacies and draw subtle distinctions, just as students might have done in the great mediaeval universities of India. Bhavabhūti has also given us some very beautiful pictures of animals, investing them of course with human feelings.[3]

48. Conclusion.—But it is hardly necessary to enumerate all such merits one by one. Appreciative criticisms of this sort are more or less subjective, and it is no longer the fashion for a translator or an editor of an ancient text to take his reader by the button, stop him in front of every picture, and ask him to admire it, and even to tell him *how* he should admire it. If a modern reader, and especially a foreigner, is given just the help necessary to understand the exact situation, and to get from it the exact implication that was got by a Hindu of Bhavabhūti's time who saw the play acted, that is all that can be expected in an edition like this.

Once the preliminary ground has been cleared, and the needful information given, the play can confidently be left to win its own conquests. It will not lack readers. In India it has never lacked enthusiastic admirers.

> Never, O never mayest Thou condemn me to sing my song unto
> hearts that answer not!

Such was the prayer of an old Sanskrit poet. A deeper note was struck by Bhavabhūti:

> It may be that a spirit kindred to mine will some day be born;
> for time is endless, and the world is wide!

[1] Cp. also our Note to U. R. C. iii. 26[2].

[2] Cp. U. R. C. iii. 13[d]; iii. 24; iii. 30; iii. 35[b]; iii. 43[c]; and iii. 48.

[3] Cp. iii. 15 f.; iii. 20 ff.; iv. 1[ab]; iv. 26; &c.

TRANSLATION

DRAMATIS PERSONAE[1]

A. Main Characters.

Rāma, King of Kosala (capital Ayodhyā), son of Daśaratha and Kausalyā.
Ashṭāvakra, a Brahman messenger.
Durmukha,† a state spy.
An aged chamberlain (*kañchukin*).
A female warder† (*pratīhārī*).
Śambūka, a Śūdra ascetic killed by Rāma.[2]
Kausalyā,† Rāma's mother, widow of King Daśaratha.[3]
Gṛishṭi, a chamberlain in attendance upon her.
Sītā,† Rāma's wife, daughter of King Janaka and Earth-goddess.
Janaka, Sītā's father, King of Videha (capital Mithilā).
Arundhatī, wife of sage Vasishṭha, Rāma's family-preceptor.
Kuśa and Lava, twin sons of Rāma and Sītā.
Vālmīki, foster-father and teacher of the twins, author of the Rāmāyaṇa.
Lakshmaṇa, Rāma's half-brother, son of Daśaratha and Sumitrā.
Chandraketu, son of Lakshmaṇa and Ūrmilā.
Sumantra, Chandraketu's charioteer.
A man (*purusha*) from Chandraketu's army.

[1] Speakers behind the curtain and persons addressed *ākāśe* are not separately mentioned here.

[2] He is immediately reborn as a celestial being.

[3] Often spoken of in the plural: *Daśarathasya dārāḥ* or *mahishyaḥ*, *Rāmasya mātaraḥ*, *ambāḥ*, &c. This may be a plural of respect, although there is also the implication of the mere presence of the step-mothers of Rāma.

† These four characters speak Prākrit; the rest, Sanskrit.

B. Interlocutors.[1]

For the Prologue at the beginning of Act i.

Reciter of the customary Invocation (*Nāndī*).

Stage-manager (*Sūtradhāra*).

An actor.

For the Interlude at the beginning of Act ii.

Vāsantī, a sylvan deity of the forest of Daṇḍakā.[2]

Ātreyī, a former student of Vālmīki's.

For the Interlude at the beginning of Act iii.

Tamasā, Goddess of the river Tamasā.[2]

Muralā, Goddess of the river Muralā.

For the Interlude at the beginning of Act iv.

Bhāṇḍāyana, Saudhātaki,† } ascetic boys, fellow-students of the twins at Vālmīki's.

For the arrival of the horse, near the end of Act iv.

Boys (*baṭavaḥ*) much excited upon seeing the unfamiliar animal.

For the Interlude at the beginning of Act vi.

An air-sprite (*Vidyādhara*), His mate (*Vidyādharī*),† } witnesses, in an aerial car, of Lava's combat with Chandraketu.

For the play within the play in Act vii.

Stage-manager, for the Prologue in Vālmīki's little play.

Sītā,† a heavenly nymph (*apsaras*) representing Sītā.

Earth-goddess (*Pṛithivī*), mother of Sītā, Goddess of the river Bhāgīrathī (Ganges) } nymphs enacting these parts.[3]

Twin boys, just born.

[1] These figure mainly in the Prologue and the Interludes, and give information of events not enacted on the stage.

[2] Takes also an active share in the main plot of Act iii.

[3] The real Pṛithivī and Bhāgīrathī have only a stanza in common (vii. 17), and each has separately a short speech from behind the curtain.

† These three characters speak Prākrit; the rest, Sanskrit.

SYNOPTIC ANALYSIS OF THE PLAY

PROLOGUE: i. 1—i. 7^2

TRANSLATION, PAGES 15–17.

Scene* **1** (i. 1—i. 2). Ujjain (?): a booth at the fair of Kālapriyanātha. The Director recites the customary Invocation (i. 1); he withdraws upon the entrance of the Stage-manager (i. 1^1), who announces the title of the play, with a few words about its author (i. 1^3—i. 2).

Scene 2 (i. 2^1—i. 7^2). Ayodhyā: a large square near Rāma's palace. The Stage-manager, now representing one of the many bards assembled for the coronation of Rāma after his victory at Laṅkā, inquires (i. 2^3) why the festal music in the squares has ceased. Enters an actor and replies that it is because the coronation is over and the guests are gone. He adds that the Queen-mothers and other persons of age and authority have left Ayodhyā [1] to attend the twelve-year [2] sacrifice (i. 3) at the hermitage of Ṛishyaśṛiṅga, the husband of Rāma's sister Śāntā, and that they did so reluctantly, as it involved their leaving behind them Sītā, now far gone with child. The actor also alludes incidentally to a false rumour about Sītā (i. 6), and expresses assurance (i. 6^2) that sages and deities will intervene [3] in order that no evil may come out of it. Upon inquiry they learn that Rāma is just returning home to comfort the disconsolate Sītā (i. 7), and so the Stage-manager and his companion go about their duties (i. 7^1, i. 4^3).

* In this synopsis the play has been divided into scenes, irrespective of the canons of Hindu dramaturgy, which do not recognize such a division. The entrances and exits and the place of action have served as the guiding principle.

1 This statement makes it clear that, in the absence of persons to whose authority Rāma owed deference (his *gurus*), he is acting of his own accord when he abandons his wife. Compare ii. 6^{10}, iv. 10^5.

2 This period represents the interval between the first Act and the rest of the action of the play. It is alluded to more than once later; compare ii. 6^{12}, iii. 34, vii. 15, &c.

3 And this in fact they do, thus bringing about a non-tragic ending to the play. Cp. iii. 3, vii. 17, vii. $18^{6ff.}$

ACT I. THE PICTURE-GALLERY

TRANSLATION, PAGES 17–30.

Scene 1 (i. 7^{3}—i. 14^{3}). Ayodhyā: A chamber in Rāma's palace. Enter Rāma and Sītā. He tries to console her. Enters the chamberlain (i. 8^{6}) to announce the arrival of Ashṭāvakra, a messenger from Ṛishyaśṛiñga's hermitage, and exit. Enters Ashṭāvakra with his message: A. that all is well with the Queen-mothers and the rest, and that they confidently expect (i. 9^{1}) for Sītā heroic[1] progeny; B. that all the women enjoin upon Rāma to satisfy promptly any longings of pregnancy (i. 10^{2}) that Sītā may have; and C. that his family-preceptor, Vasishṭha, exhorts Rāma to do his utmost to keep his subjects pleased.[2] Exit Ashṭāvakra, announcing the entrance of Lakshmaṇa. Enters Lakshmaṇa and proposes (i. 12^{5}), as a diversion, a visit to the picture-gallery.

Scene 2 (i. 14^{4}—i. 33^{16}). Ayodhyā: the palace-corridor with paintings on the walls depicting Rāma's earlier history. Rāma and Sītā inspect the paintings,[3] Lakshmaṇa serving as cicerone or guide and explaining them (i. 14^{4}—i. 33^{2}). The pictures of these familiar scenes arouse in Sītā a longing (i. $33^{6\,f.}$) for an excursion to the Ganges. Rāma orders Lakshmaṇa to bring forthwith an easy carriage for her (i. $33^{11\,f.}$). Exit Lakshmaṇa (i. 33^{16}).

Scene 3 (i. 33^{17}—i. 51^{15}). Ayodhyā: a balcony near the palace-corridor. After the pictures Sītā feels fatigue. Rāma begs her to rest; she does so, her head pillowed on Rāma's arm, and falls asleep (i. 37^{3}). Enters a female warder (i. 38^{1}) to announce Durmukha, an old and trusty spy, and exit. Enters Durmukha (i. 38^{3}), who, with grief, whispers to Rāma (i. 39^{7}) the scandalous rumour about Sītā. Rāma knows her innocence and yet, to please the people, resolves to abandon her (i. 40^{1}).

[1] The Sanskrit word for 'heroic' means both 'valorous' and 'male'.

[2] This message has an important bearing on the action of the play. A. The confident expectation as to the sex of Sītā's offspring, and Rāma's further knowledge (cp. vi. 28) that it was to be twins, serve as important links in the recognition and final identification of the two sons when Rāma encounters them in Act vi. B. gives Rāma the pretext under cover of which Sītā is led away (cp. i. $33^{7\,f.}$, i. 43^{1}, i. $51^{9\,f.}$). C. Vasishṭha's reminder fortifies Rāma in his resolve (i. 41^{1}, i. 42).

[3] This episode gives occasion for the tender love between Rāma and Sītā to show itself, and thus heightens by contrast the grief of their ensuing separation. Incidentally the sight of the picture of the magic missiles (*jṛimbhakāstra*) leads Rāma to assure Sītā that the actual missiles shall be at the service of her offspring (i. 15^{2}). The picture of the Ganges calls forth from Rāma a prayer to the river for Sītā's welfare (i. 23^{1}). Both these incidents are important in the dénouement of the play.

He bids Durmukha tell his change of plan to Lakshmaṇa (i. 43^1). Exit Durmukha (i. 44^2). Rāma tears himself gently from his sleeping wife (i. 46). His lamentations (i. 46^1—i. 49^2). A voice behind the curtain tells him of a danger threatening some of his Brahman subjects from the demon Lavaṇa (i. 50). The voice recalls him to his kingly duty. He resolves to send his brother Śatrughna against the demon (i. $50^{1\,f.}$). With the prayer[1] (i. $50^{3\,f.}$), 'O holy Earth, watch over thy daughter Sītā', Rāma leaves her and exit. Sītā wakes and finds herself alone (i. 51^3). Enters Durmukha (i. 51^9) and tells her that Lakshmaṇa has the carriage in readiness for her. She rises (i. 51^{11}) to go—as she supposes—with Rāma to the Ganges. Exeunt all.

ACT II. DAṆḌAKĀ REVISITED

TRANSLATION, PAGES 31–40.

Between Act i and Act ii is an interval of twelve years.

Scene 1, Interlude (ii. 0^1—ii. 9^2). The forest of Daṇḍakā. Vāsantī, the sylvan deity of Daṇḍakā, welcomes, from behind the curtain, Ātreyī, who enters in the habit of a traveller. Vāsantī herself follows (ii. 0^4). They exchange compliments and fall into a conversation, in the course of which Ātreyī explains why, although studying at Vālmīki's, she is compelled to travel southwards in search of instruction (ii. 3): because 1. she could not keep pace (ii. 4) with Kuśa and Lava, twins of unknown lineage, of whom Vālmīki is both teacher and foster-father (ii. $3^{13\,ff.}$); and because 2. Vālmīki himself was recently much occupied with the composition of a new poem, the Rāmāyaṇa (ii. $5^{5\,f.}$). Having rested (ii. 5^{10}), Ātreyī rises to go, but the incidental mention (ii. 5^{11}) of some places associated with the life of Sītā in the Daṇḍakā arouses painful memories. Vāsantī, ignorant of the happenings in the distant Ayodhyā, makes anxious inquiries. Ātreyī tells her all, including the most recent act of Rāma—his starting out (ii. $8^{1\,f.}$) in search of a Śūdra ascetic, Śambūka, whose austerities[2] have caused the premature death of a Brahman's son. As Śambūka is in the Daṇḍakā, Vāsantī

[1] A prayer which did not remain unheard: cp. iii. 2^6, vii. $18^{9\,f.}$

[2] The law permitted only Brahmans to practise austerities. Śambūka's doing so was therefore an offence which, if unpunished, might cause trouble in the kingdom.

expresses hopes (ii. $8^{3\,f.}$) of soon meeting Rāma there. It is midday (ii. 9); so they both retire.

Scene 2 (ii. 9^3—ii. 30^1). The forest of Daṇḍakā, particularly that portion of it called Janasthāna. Enters Rāma, in his aerial car[1] named *Pushpaka*, sword in hand, and makes a pass as if to kill some one behind the curtain (ii. 10^1). Enters a celestial being who explains that he is no other than Śambūka, the Śūdra ascetic of the Daṇḍakā, just killed by Rāma (ii. 11 and ff.). The mention and the actual sight of Daṇḍakā and Janasthāna arouse very painful memories in Rāma (ii. 17—ii. 18). Śambūka's eloquent description (ii. 19^1–21) of the forest scenery affects Rāma all the more, and Rāma consequently dismisses him (ii. 21^1). Śambūka, however, goes away to pay his respects to the sage Agastya, who lived near by, before mounting the car to heaven (ii. 21^3). A pathetic soliloquy (ii. 22–28) by Rāma follows. It is interrupted by Śambūka who reappears with the word that Agastya's wife, Lopāmudrā, desires that Rāma will stop a while at her hermitage before returning to Ayodhyā (ii. $28^{1\,ff.}$). Rāma accepts the invitation and goes away followed by Śambūka, expressing, however, the intention of visiting the old familiar scenes once more (ii. 28^6) before leaving for his kingdom.

ACT III. THE SHADOW

Translation, pages 41–59.

The interest of this Act is mainly psychological. Act i saw the separation of Rāma and Sītā, and the motif of Acts ii–vii is their union, which, to be complete, must be both mental and physical.[2] Act iii achieves the former, and Acts iv–vii the latter. Accordingly, what seems here to be lacking in dramatic movement is more than made up by the richness and faithfulness of its psychology.

Scene 1, Interlude (iii. 0^1—iii. 5^2). That part of the Daṇḍakā called the Pañchavaṭī. Time: afternoon of the same day as Act ii. Enter two River-goddesses, meeting. The first, Muralā, is the bearer of a message from Lopāmudrā, who has asked (iii. 0^4—iii. 2) the river Godāvarī to try, by means of cool scented breezes, to soothe and revive Rāma in

[1] It is not clear whether Rāma gets down from the *Pushpaka* before striking the blow. Probably he does.

[2] The same motif underlies Acts vi–vii of Kālidāsa's Śākuntala, but his treatment is somewhat different from that of our poet. Compare Introduction, sections 39 and 41.

case the sight of Pañchavaṭī proved too much for his sorrowing heart. The second, Tamasā, relates (iii. 2^{4-8}) that Queen Sītā, abandoned by Rāma in the forest, there gave birth to twin sons, whom her mother, the Earth, and the divine Ganges have placed in charge of Vālmīki; and that the holy Ganges, anticipating Rāma's present visit to Pañchavaṭī, has contrived to bring Sītā herself there (iii. 3^{1-4}); and that being, by the favour of the Ganges, rendered invisible (iii. 3^{13}) to men (like Rāma) and sylvan deities (like Vāsantī), Sītā can now, in a case of need, revive Rāma by her touch.[1] Thereat Muralā goes to carry the news (iii. 3^{16}) to Lopāmudrā, and Tamasā to bear company with Sītā.

Scene 2 (iii. 5^{3}—iii. 10^{2}). Place and time, the same as before. Enters Sītā, gathering flowers and listening to the speech of Vāsantī behind the curtain. This speech refers to an attack by another elephant upon a young elephant once the pet of Sītā (iii. 6). Sītā, in great excitement, calls upon Rāma to protect her pet, but realizing her situation faints away (iii. 6^{4}). Enters Tamasā to comfort her. Sītā is in fact comforted by the sound of Rāma's voice behind the curtain (iii. $6^{9\,ff.}$). Tamasā explains that Rāma was then in Pañchavaṭī on state business (iii. 7^{4}). 'How fortunate', observes Sītā (iii. 7^{6}), 'that the King is so very assiduous in the discharge of his *kingly* duties!' Greatly overcome by grief, Rāma, still behind the curtain, calls out Sītā's name and faints (iii. 9^{5}). This affects Sītā deeply, and on Tamasā's asking her (iii. 10) to do so, she hurries to where Rāma was (iii. 10^{1}).

Scene 3 (iii. 10^{3}—iii. 15^{19}). Place and time as before. Enters[2] Rāma, at Sītā's touch reviving from his swoon. Sītā, afraid lest Rāma might blame her for presenting herself unbidden before him, suggests to Tamasā that they withdraw. The latter reminds her that she is invisible to Rāma[3] (iii. 12^{11}). Enters Vāsantī (iii. 15^{4}) to announce the fight of the elephants, whereupon the whole party—including Sītā and Tamasā—proceed to where the fight was going on (iii. 15^{19}).

[1] The mysterious power of the beloved one's touch is the constant theme of our poet. Cp. i. 18, 34, 35, 38; iii. 10-12, 14, 39^{9}, 40, 41, 42; iv. 21^{11}; vi. $4^{4\,ff.}$, 8, 13, 22; vii. 18.

[2] In the absence of curtains which could be raised up or pulled sideways, it would seem that Rāma had to enter the stage walking, and then assume the necessary position. Sītā comes in shortly after, while Tamasā, whose exit is not indicated at the end of the last scene, watches, along with the spectators, the whole course of events.

[3] This may appear dramatically improbable, but so is the statue-scene in The Winter's Tale (Act v, sc. iii). Each, however, has the same purpose to serve, and it is unfair to question a poet's premises. Invisibility was regarded in India as one of the incidental attainments due to the practice of Yoga (cp. Yoga-sūtra, iii. 21), and is constantly employed as a dramatic device: cp. Śākuntala vi, Vikramorvaśīya iii, Bhāsa's Avimāraka iii, &c.

Scene 4 (iii. 15[20]—iii. 49[1]). Another part of Pañchavaṭī: At a distance, the river Godāvarī, with elephants fighting in the waters. Characters same as before. The elephant-fight has resulted in a victory for Sītā's pet (iii. 15[21]); all rejoice in consequence (iii. 16 ff.). Vāsantī now avails herself of the occasion to point out a number of other objects (iii. 19, 22, 37[5], 38, 44) connected with their earlier life in Pañchavaṭī, as if casually, but really with a view to reprobate Rāma's conduct towards his wife. Rāma in reply lays his whole heart open to Vāsantī (iii. 27[6 ff.], 29, 32, 33, 34, 36, 37, 39), who is much moved by his sorrows and his sufferings and the sublime grandeur of his soul. All this takes place, of course, within the hearing of Sītā, though neither Rāma nor Vāsantī was aware of her presence. The result is that Sītā, who in Scene 2 (iii. 7[6]) was full of just resentment against her husband, gradually finds herself softening towards him,[1] until finally she absolves him from all wrong whatsoever (iii. 46[13 f.]). As it was getting late, Rāma rises to go to Ayodhyā and take part in the holy horse-sacrifice (iii. 48[1]).[2] Exeunt all.

ACT IV. KAUSALYĀ AND JANAKA

TRANSLATION, PAGES 60–72.

This Act is practically synchronous with the last two, and is partly meant as a humorous relief after the intense emotional excitement of Act iii.

Scene 1, Interlude (iv. 0[1]—iv. 2[2]). Vālmīki's hermitage on the Ganges: An open space near by. Enter two pupils. One of them admires the beauty of the hermitage, which is now putting on its best appearance (iv. 1) to welcome some venerable guests. The other—evidently a youngster[3]—is delighted at the thought that the guests bring with them also a holiday for the schools (iv. 1[1]). In the course of their conversation it transpires that the guests are no other than Arundhatī, Vasishṭha, and the Queen-mothers, who, on the conclusion of Ṛishyaśṛiṅga's twelve-year sacrifice (cp. i. 3), not caring to return to Ayodhyā where Sītā was not, have repaired to Vālmīki's hermitage. Among the day's guests there is also Janaka (iv. 1[23]), Sītā's father, come on a friendly visit to Vālmīki (iv. 1[33]). The boys go off to play.

[1] The psychological moments in this process are described at length in the note to iii. 7[6]. They show the poet's thorough understanding of human passions, and a deft handling of them.

[2] For the nature of this sacrifice compare Introduction, § 18, P.

[3] Who cannot yet speak his Sanskrit properly.

Scene 2 (iv. 2^3—iv. 26^{11}). A yard adjoining Vālmīki's hermitage. Enters Janaka, seated sorrowing at the foot of a tree. His lamentations for his daughter (iv. 3–5) are interrupted by the appearance of Arundhatī and Kausalyā, who, led by a chamberlain and under instructions from Vasishṭha, are coming to meet Janaka. Janaka is not at first well-disposed towards Kausalyā, the mother of 'that shepherd of the people', meaning Rāma (iv. 10^3); but he soon relents at the sight of the grief-stricken old widow of his late friend Daśaratha (iv. 13, 14). A noise of the boys making merry over their holiday-games is heard from behind the curtain (iv. 18^1). Among the boys all watch with interest one—evidently a Kshaṭriya youth (iv. 20)—who resembled in his looks not only Rāma but Sītā also (iv. 19, 22). Arundhatī, who has had the secret (iv. 18^7) from Bhāgīrathī (the Ganges), knows that he must be one of the twin sons of Rāma. They send the chamberlain (iv. 20^3) after the boy, who comes and announces himself (iv. 21^3) as Lava. They inquire after his parentage (iv. 22^1), but he naïvely answers (iv. 22^5) that he belongs to Vālmīki (who of course never married). A voice behind the curtain conveys to the soldiers of the army Prince Chandraketu's order (iv. 22^9) to the effect that they must not molest the hermitage in any way. Janaka and Kausalyā rejoice at the prospect of meeting Chandraketu (iv. $22^{10\text{ ff.}}$), and in reply to Lava's inquiry they tell him that Chandraketu is no other than Lakshmaṇa's son (iv. 22^{20}). Lava, who knew Vālmīki's Rāmāyaṇa by heart, was instantly able to identify Chandraketu. Janaka now asks Lava (iv. 22^{23}) if from the Rāmāyaṇa he could tell them some of the Later History of Rāma. Lava replies that Vālmīki has composed that portion, but, wishing to give a dramatic representation of it, he has sent it, in charge of Lava's brother Kuśa, to the sage Bharata.[1] The published portion of the Rāmāyaṇa, he adds, ends with the abandonment of Sītā (iv. 22^{43}). The memory of that event calls forth a passionate expression of grief from Janaka (iv. 23), and Lava now learns who all the elders were (iv. 23^2). At this point a number of disorderly boys break in upon the stage and inform (iv. 26) Lava of a wonderful sight—a horse—that they have seen. They drag Lava off the stage (iv. 26^2). The rest of the party also go away anxious to meet Vālmīki and learn from him, if possible, the secret of Lava's parentage (iv. 26^{11}).

Scene 3 (iv. 26^{12}—iv. 29^1). Another open space near Vālmīki's hermitage: the sacrificial horse in sight. Re-enter[2] the boys with Lava. Lava at

[1] Author of the Nāṭyaśāstra, the earliest extant book on Hindu dramaturgy. This whole account sounds like a bit of autobiography: cp. Introduction, § 4.

[2] Not strictly 're-enter'. The boys merely withdraw to a remote part of the stage

once perceives that it is a sacrificial horse, and the boys, from inquiry, learn (iv. 27) that it is let loose by Rāma, 'the foremost hero of the seven worlds'. The youthful Lava, incensed at this supposed insult to his own heroism asks his companions to capture the horse (iv. $28^{1\text{ f.}}$). Enters an enraged soldier to prevent the capture. Lava makes ready to fight (iv. 29). Exeunt all.

ACT V. PRINCES IN COMBAT

TRANSLATION, PAGES 73–81.

In the short interval—an hour or so—between this Act and the last, Lava has utterly routed the army.

Scene 1 (v. 0^1—v. 36^2). An open space near Vālmīki's hermitage. Enter Chandraketu in a chariot, and Sumantra his charioteer. Chandraketu has heard of the fight and is hastening to the rescue (v. 1). He cannot help admiring Lava's appearance and courage (v. 2, 3, 5) and feels abashed to find that Lava singly has defeated the whole army (v. 6^3). Chandraketu now invites Lava for a personal combat (v. 7). Enters Lava, bow in hand, leaving the army, who, however, continue to harass him (v. 8^4, v. 10^4) the moment his back is turned upon them. Finding no other way to stop them, Lava makes use of the magic missiles[1] (v. $12^{2\text{ f.}}$). The hubbub in the army is now at an end (v. 13) and the two youths meet face to face (v. 15^3). Chandraketu courteously offers Lava a chariot (v. 28^2), which Lava as courteously, but not without a mixture of pride, declines (v. 28^6). Lava adds that the fight was partly forced upon him (v. 29) by the insolent vaunting (iv. 27) of the attendants of the horse. Chandraketu wonders if Lava really believed himself superior to the great Rāma (v. 29^1, 34). Lava, who knew the Rāma story well, replies that no great man need be absolutely perfect, and mentions a few weak points (v. 35) in Rāma's earlier career. This provokes Chandraketu and both repair to a place where they can fight undisturbed (v. 36^1).[2]

at the end of Scene 2, and now come to the centre.

[1] Called *jṛimbhaka* or stupefying. Their use, so naturally brought in, plays an important part in the final recognition in Acts vi and vii.

[2] According to the canons of Hindu dramaturgy, combats could not be represented on the stage.

ACT VI. THE PRINCES RECOGNIZED

TRANSLATION, PAGES 82–93.

In respect of time, this Act is an immediate sequel to the last.

Scene 1, Interlude (vi. 0^1—vi. 7^3). Place: aerial regions above Vālmīki's hermitage. Enter an air-sprite (*Vidyādhara*) and his mate, viewing the combat between Lava and Chandraketu from an aerial car. They describe the fight: how one missile supersedes another only to be itself superseded by a third. Victory trembles in the balance. At last they see Rāma returning from Daṇḍakā in his *Pushpaka* car (vi. 6^5) and stopping the battle. The air-sprites go away.

Scene 2 (vi. 7^4—vi. 42^3). The fighting-ground at a considerable distance from Vālmīki's hermitage. Enter Rāma, Chandraketu, and Lava. Chandraketu tells Rāma of the fight and particularly of Lava's valour (vi. 8^2). Rāma feels an unaccountable attraction towards Lava (vi. 9, 12). Lava, in his turn, is deeply impressed (vi. 10, 11) by the sight of the great man, who, Chandraketu tells him (vi. 12^5), is no other than the hero of the Rāmāyaṇa. Rāma embraces Lava (vi. 13). Lava begs to be pardoned for his insolent conduct (vi. 13^3) but Rāma praises him for it (vi. 14). Chandraketu then points out how by his *jṛimbhaka* missiles Lava has thrown the whole army into a stupor (vi. 14^2). Rāma asks Lava to withdraw the missiles and sends Chandraketu away to comfort his army. Exit Chandraketu. Rāma inquires of Lava how he came to have this power over the missiles (vi. 15^3). Lava explains that they two were born to the knowledge of them. 'Who is the other?' asks Rāma. The answer is partly given by a voice behind the curtain, inquiring in great agitation, after Lava (vi. 16). This is Lava's elder brother, Kuśa, returning from his errand to sage Bharata (vi. 17^1, cp. iv. $22^{33\text{ ff.}}$). Enters Kuśa, bow in hand. Rāma admires his bearing (vi. 19). Lava introduces him to Rāma, who embraces him (vi. 21). As the day was growing hot, Lava suggests reposing under the shade of a tree (vi. 22^1), which they all do. The appearance and the deportment of the two boys (vi. 23 f.), their resemblance to Rāma and Sītā (vi. 25–27), their presence near the place where Sītā was abandoned, their inborn power over the missiles, which Rāma remembers now to have transferred in anticipation (i. 15^2) to the offspring of Sītā, and particularly the fact of the boys being twins, as he knew would be the case with Sītā's issue (vi. 28),—all this seems to him to be mournfully tantalizing. Rāma weeps. Lava expresses concern for him (vi. 29). Kuśa wonders why Lava, knowing the Rāmāyaṇa, should be surprised at Rāma's grief (vi. 30). If Rāma had hoped to ask the boys about their parentage and learn something definite, all his hopes were now at an end. The boys spoke of the hero of the Rāmāyaṇa in the most unconcerned way imaginable. Rāma now asks the boys to recite some stanzas from the Rāmāyaṇa (vi. 30^{3}). Kuśa (vi. 31, 32) and after him Lava (vi. 36) hit upon passages which awaken the most painful memories in Rāma's mind (vi. 34, 37). At this point a voice behind the curtain states that Vasishṭha, Vālmīki, the Queen-mothers, Janaka, and Arundhatī, having heard of the fight between the boys and anxious for their safety, are coming that way (vi. 39). Rāma and the boys go away hurriedly to meet them (vi. 42^{3}).

ACT VII. THE REUNION

TRANSLATION, PAGES 94–102.

In the interval between Acts vi and vii Rāma has met all the elders. When their first grief had abated a little, all plied Vālmīki with questions regarding Kuśa and Lava. Vālmīki, anticipating all this, has arranged to have the Later History of Rāma enacted (play within play), in the sight of gods and men, by the celestial nymphs trained by Bharata (cp. iv. 22^{31}).

Scene 1 (vii. 0^{1}—vii. 20^{1}). An extensive open-air stage on the banks of the Ganges, near Vālmīki's hermitage. Time: afternoon of the same day. Enters Lakshmaṇa, who announces that the stage is ready and the audience seated. Enters Rāma (vii. 1^{1}) who orders the players to commence (vii. 1^{7}).[1]

Play within play, Prologue (vii. 1^{8}—vii. 2^{1}). Enters Stage-manager, who requests the audience to be graciously attentive to the play of Vālmīki, 'the speaker of the Truth'. The lament of a woman is heard from behind the curtain (vii. $1^{13\,ff.}$). The Stage-manager explains that it is Sītā, who, unable to bear the pangs, is throwing herself into the Ganges (vii. 2). Exit Stage-manager.

Play within play, Scene 1 (vii. 2^{7}—vii. 15^{10}). Enters Sītā fainting, supported by two Goddesses—Earth and the Ganges—each with an infant in her lap. The Goddesses congratulate Sītā on the birth of twin sons (vii. 3). Sītā inquires who they were, and on learning

[1] The play within the play which follows is of the one-act kind known as *prekshaṇaka*. The characters of the original play interrupt the course of this secondary play by occasional remarks. For convenience the inner play is here given all by itself.

that one of them was her mother, the Earth, she embraces her and swoons away (vii. 3[13]). On recovering, the Earth-goddess reproaches Rāma bitterly for his conduct (vii. 4[a, b], 5), while Bhāgīrathī (the Ganges) tries to defend him (vii. 6). Sītā requests her mother to receive her into her womb (vii. 7[2]), but the Earth-goddess reminds Sītā of her duty by her two sons. A noise behind the curtain (vii. 8[3]). This is caused by the appearance of the *jṛimbhaka* missiles, who [1] have come, in accordance with Rāma's wishes (cp. i. 15[2]), to wait upon Sītā's offspring (vii. 10). The missiles are asked to depart, with an injunction that they should attend the twins whenever called upon (vii. 11). Sītā is at a loss to know (vii. 12[2]) how her sons were to be reared and educated. Bhāgīrathī proposes to give them over into the charge of Vālmīki (vii. 13[1 f.]). Sītā once more prays the Earth-goddess to receive her into her womb (vii. 15[3]), but is asked to wait till the boys are weaned (vii. 15[7]). Exeunt all the characters of the **play within the play.**

Rāma,[2] who all along was watching the play and experiencing alternating impulses of grief and joy, is quite overcome at its conclusion and goes into a swoon (vii. 15[12]). Lakshmaṇa calls upon Vālmīki for succour. A voice behind the curtain orders (vii. 15[14]) the removal of the stage-apparatus. It is not a drama but a reality that is happening now; for, from the heaving waters of the Ganges arise the forms of Bhāgīrathī, the Earth-goddess, and Sītā (vii. 16). The two Goddesses hand over the virtuous Sītā into the charge of Arundhatī, who now enters leading Sītā (vii. 18). Sītā touches Rāma, who revives, and is overjoyed to meet his lost Queen. The Goddess Bhāgīrathī reminds Rāma (vii. 18[6]) of his prayer to her (i. 23[1]), which she heard and has granted. The Earth-goddess also reminds Rāma (vii. 18[9]) of his parting adjuration (i. 50[3]) to her, which she has faithfully followed. Arundhatī now admonishes the assembled people for their past conduct (vii. 18[12 ff.]), and they salute Sītā in token of acceptance. Rāma also readily accepts his wife (vii. 19[3]). Exit Arundhatī (vii. 19[9]). Enters Vālmīki who now presents Kuśa and Lava as the sons of Rāma and Sītā (vii. 19[13]). To fill the cup of joy, Śatrughna, who had been sent (cp. i. 50[1]) against the demon Lavaṇa, returns victorious (vii. 19[29]). Vālmīki now asks Rāma if he desires anything else (vii. 19[32]). The customary benediction (vii. 20) brings the drama to a happy close.

[1] Conceived as persons with human speech. They, however, speak from behind the curtain.

[2] At this point the first scene of the play proper is resumed.

UTTARA-RĀMA-CHARITA

OR

LATER HISTORY OF RĀMA

ACT I

UNTO the Bards of yore this tribute of homage we tender, and bow down [next] unto [the Goddess of] Speech, that portion (*kalā*) immortal of the Supreme-spirit. **1**

After [*this*] *Invocation*—

Stage-manager—Enough: Why make it too long?—To-day, indeed on this festival (*yātrā*) of the Exalted Lord Kālapriya,[1] I have a request for this distinguished assembly. Your honours will be pleased to understand that there is a worthy scion of the Kāśyapa family, bearing the appellation of Śrīkaṇṭha and known [also] as Bhavabhūti:

On whom, [as on God] Brahmā, the Goddess [of] Speech attends like a submissive handmaid. The Later History of Rāma, composed by him, is [here] going to be represented [by us]. **2**

Here now, in deference to the matter in hand, I am transformed into an inhabitant of Ayodhyā[2] and a contemporary [of Rāma]. *Looking about him.* How now, Sirs! This the period of the coronation of His Majesty the Honoured Rāma, the fire that consumed the race of Pulastya[3]—when this [period] is, day and night, to be celebrated with incessant festive music, wherefore then, to-day, are the bards silent in these quadrangles?

An Actor, *entering*—Sir, they have been sent away to their homes by His Majesty—the high-souled Demons and Monkeys and [other] allies [of Rāma] in the war at Laṅkā,[4] as also the priestly and the royal sages—the sanctifiers of the various quarters—that had honoured the ceremony by their attendance, and as a mark of respect unto whom there was this festivity this many a day. And now—

[1] Of whom there is a famous temple in Ujjain in Central India. See on this point, however, Introduction, § 3.

[2] Capital of Kosala, the kingdom of Rāma.

[3] The grandfather of Rāma's enemy, the demon Rāvaṇa.

[4] Seat of Rāvaṇa's kingdom and identified with Ceylon.

Headed by Vasishṭha,[1] the Queen-mothers of Rāma, following the lead of Arundhatī,[2] are gone to the hermitage of [their] son-in-law for a sacrifice. **3**

Stage-manager—Ah, that explains it.

Actor—Being a stranger I ask, who can [this] son-in-law be?

Stage-manager—King Daśaratha[3] begot a daughter named Śāntā,

whom—as an adopted child—he made over to king Lomapāda.[4] **4**

Her, Ṛishyaśṛiñga, the son of Vibhāṇḍaka, married. He [Ṛishyaśṛiñga] has now commenced a [sacrificial] session of twelve years; and, in consequence of that, leaving behind their daughter-in-law Jānakī,[5] far gone with child though she is, the elders (*guru*)[6] have gone thither. But what is [all] this to us? Come, let us rather repair to the royal portal, there to discharge the duties befitting our caste.[7]

Actor—If so, please your honour to think of some form of benediction—absolutely flawless—wherewith to approach [the King].

Stage-manager—Mārisha,[8]

It behoves us ever to be doing [whatever lies next]; for there is no escaping censure [any way]. As of women, so of compositions, people are malicious as to their purity (*sādhutva*[9]). **5**

Actor—Ultra-malicious, say rather:

For, even in the case of Queen Vaidehī,[10] the people are not without their wicked talk. Her staying in the house of the Rākshasa[11] is at the bottom of it, and, as to the fire-ordeal,[12] they are not convinced. **6**

Stage-manager—Should this scandal now come to [the ears of] His Majesty, it would be very unfortunate!

Actor—In every wise will the sages and the deities work out a happy issue. *Walking about.* Ho, friends! Where now is His Majesty? *Listening.* So say the people:

Coming hither to greet [Rāma] out of affection and having passed these days in festivity, Janaka has to-day gone to the Videhas.

[1] The family-priest of Rāma.

[2] Vasishṭha's wife.

[3] Father of Rāma.

[4] Of the kingdom of the Añgas.

[5] I. e. Sītā, wife of Rāma, daughter of Janaka.

[6] A word almost impossible to render by one English word. It is applied to any one to whose authority deference is due: parents, elderly relatives, teachers, and persons of piety and learning.

[7] The actors were supposed to be Śūdras.

[8] The regular form by which the stage-manager addresses an actor, who in turn calls him Bhāva.

[9] The word means both chastity and excellence.

[10] I. e. Sītā, daughter of Janaka, king of the Videhas.

[11] I. e. the demon Rāvaṇa who had abducted her.

[12] Which Sītā underwent after Rāma had secured her release.

To solace the Queen, disconsolate on that account, from his judgement-seat the Lord of men [Rāma] is now entering the residential palace. 7

They both go out.

END OF PROLOGUE.

Enters Rāma seated, and Sītā.

Rāma—Cheer up, cheer up, my Queen, Vaidehī! The elders (*guru*) certainly would not have been able to leave us,

Except that the urgency of the [stated religious] observances restricts their liberty [to stay here]; for verily the life of householders who have set up their Sacred Fires is hampered with [such] restraints. 8

Sītā—I know it, my noble Lord, I know it; and yet separations from [dear] relatives do cause pain.

Rāma—Yes, just so. These things of the world do indeed gnaw at the very vitals of the heart; and it is from disgust with these that men of wisdom give up all interests and find peace in a forest.

Chamberlain, *entering*—Rāma dear—*breaking off apprehensively*—I mean, Your Majesty!

Rāma, *with a smile*—Nay, Sir! In the mouth of an [old] attendant of my father's, 'Rāma dear' is just the fitting mode of address for me. Address me then as you have been used to do.

Chamberlain—From Ṛishyaśṛiñga's hermitage Ashṭāvakra has arrived.

Sītā—Then, Sir, why delay?

Rāma—At once let him in.

Exit Chamberlain.

Ashṭāvakra, *entering*—Blessings on you both!

Rāma—Exalted Sir, my obeisance. Be seated here.

Sītā—Salutations unto you. Are all my elders (*guru*) and the noble Śāntā doing well?

Rāma—In performing Soma-sacrifice I hope my brother-in-law, the exalted Ṛishyaśṛiñga, is meeting with no hindrances?—And the noble Śāntā too?

Sītā—And does she [ever] think of us?

Ashṭāvakra, *seating himself*—Yes, certainly. Queen, the revered Vasishṭha [your family-preceptor], sends you this word:

The All-sustaining [Earth], the exalted one, gave birth unto thee.[1]
A king, the equal of [God] Prajāpati,[2] Janaka is thy sire.

[1] Janaka came upon Sītā while he was ploughing and preparing the ground for a holy sacrifice. Sītā means 'furrow'.

[2] I. e. Creator.

A daughter-in-law art thou, O gladdening one, of those kings of whose house the Sun[1] is the head (*guru*) and we are the preceptor (*guru*). **9**

What else then can we wish thee, save this?—Be thou the mother of heroes!

Rāma—We are [in this mightily] favoured;

For, the speech of the worldly-wise saints follows the course of the event (*artha*), whereas, of the ancient sages, it is the event which speeds after [their] utterance. **10**

Ashṭāvakra—This is what the exalted Arundhatī and the Queen-mothers and Śāntā have told again and again: Whatever longing[2] Sītā may conceive, that should without fail be forthwith gratified.

Rāma—We *are* doing whatever she says.

Ashṭāvakra—And her sister-in-law's husband, Ṛishyaśṛiṅga, says this unto the Queen: Far gone with child as thou art, thou, my child, hast not been brought here. Dear Rāma also, for thy solace, has been left behind. So now we shall see thee, the long-lived one, with sons gracing thy lap.

Rāma, *with a smile of joy and bashfulness*—So be it! Has not the exalted Vasishṭha, however, any mandate for *me*?

Ashṭāvakra—Listen:

This sacrifice at the son-in-law's has kept us engaged; thou art but a boy and new to thy kingdom: In the propitiation of thy subjects be thou [therefore] diligent. What glory comes out of that is your supreme treasure. **11**

Rāma—As [Vasishṭha] the exalted son of Mitra and Varuṇa says.

Affection and compassion and felicity—yea, even this daughter of Janaka [Sītā]—for the propitiation of the people I can abandon and feel no pangs. **12**

Sītā—And hence it is that my noble Lord is the foremost of the [race of] Raghus.

Rāma—Ho, some one without, let Ashṭāvakra be attended to.

Ashṭāvakra, *rising* [*and*] *walking about*—Lo, it is prince Lakshmaṇa coming. *Exit.*

Lakshmaṇa, *entering*—Victory attend my noble brother! Noble Sir, that painter has, as ordered by us, drawn, in this corridor here, [scenes from] your career: Will the noble Lady have a look?

Rāma—Thou knowest, dear brother, [how] to divert [the mind of] the sorrowing Queen. How far do these pictures go?

1 Rāma belonged to the Solar race of kings.

2 Pregnant women are supposed to have longings, the prompt satisfaction of which promotes perfect development of the unborn child.

Lakshmaṇa—As far as the fire-ordeal of the noble Lady [Sītā].

Rāma—Peace!

Pure even in her [very] birth, what need has she of other [external] purifications? Holy Water and Fire surely do not need to be made pure by *other* things. **13**

O my Queen, sprung from the [very] sacrificial ground of the Gods, pardon! Here is unto thee my life-long homage.

Hard [to please] is the people, and those whose wealth is [the fame of] their family *have* to follow [the people's] humours! So, whatever unkindly I spoke[1] unto thee was unmerited by thee. By its very nature unto a sweet-smelling flower is ordained a place on the head, and never tramplings under the feet. **14**

Sītā—Never mind, noble my Lord, never mind. Come, let us rather, if you please (*dāva*), see [those pictures of] your career.

They rise and walk about.

Lakshmaṇa—Here is the painting.

Sītā, *inspecting it*—Who now are these up above, standing close together and seeming as if praising my noble Lord?

Lakshmaṇa—These are those *jṛimbhaka*[2] missiles and their spells (*rahasya*), which from the exalted Kṛiśāśva were passed on to the son of Kuśika, [I mean] to sage Viśvāmitra[3]—that friend (*mitra*) of the universe (*viśva*), who in his turn, at the killing of Tāṭakā[4], presented the same as a favour to my noble brother.

Rāma—Salute, my Queen, these divine missiles:

Brahmā[5] (*Brahmán*) and others, in the interest of the Sacred Truth (*bráhman*), practised penances for over a thousand autumns. And then those Sires (*guru*) of old obtained a vision of these [missiles] as if these were the very fires of their own penances. **15**

Sītā—My homage unto these.

Rāma—Assuredly now these will attend upon thy offspring.

Sītā—This is a [great] favour.

Lakshmaṇa—This here is the scene at Mithilā.[6]

Sītā—Lo! Like a newly-expanding blue lotus dark and soft and tender and fully developed in the charms of his person—[my] father gazing in rapt amazement on his mild and lovely form—the bow of [God] Śaṅkara

[1] At the time of the fire-ordeal at Laṅkā.

[2] I. e. missiles producing stupor. They are conceived of in a human shape.

[3] Rāma's instructor in archery and warfare.

[4] A frightful she-demon and molester of pious sacrifices. She was killed by Rāma.

[5] Creator of the universe.

[6] Capital of Janaka and the place where, after successfully passing through the test of wielding the heavy bow of God Śiva (or Śaṅkara), Rāma and his brothers married Sītā and her sisters.

broken [in twain] with a careless ease—the [waving] tufts of hair gracefully adorning [his face]—thus is my noble Lord painted here!

Lakshmaṇa—Look, noble Lady, look at this:

To these relatives headed by Vasishṭha here is thy father [Janaka] offering worship—as also Śatānanda, the son of Gotama and priest of the Janaka-family. 16

Rāma—This is a sight to see!

Of the family of Janaka with that of Raghu[1] to whom is the union not pleasing?—wherein both the giver and the receiver is the son-of-Kuśika [Viśvāmitra] in person. 17

Sītā—Here in sooth are all ye four brothers—your *godāna*[2] ceremony just performed—ready (*dīkshita*) for the wedding. Ah! I feel as if in that very same place, on that very same occasion I were [again] present.

Rāma—To me [also] it seems to be again that self-same hour when, like unto a great festival incarnate, it thrilled me with joy, O fair-faced one,—this thy hand offered [me] by the son of Gotama and begirt with lovely [nuptial] bangles. 18

Lakshmaṇa—This [here] is my noble Lady; this again, the noble Māṇḍavī[3]: This here, likewise, [our] daughter-in-law, dear (*vadhū*) Śrutakīrti.[4]

Sītā—And who, dear brother (*vatsa*), is this other one here?

Lakshmaṇa, *with a bashful smile*,[5] *aside*—I see, it is [my] Ūrmilā that the noble Lady is asking for. Well, I'll change the subject. *Aloud.* Here, my noble Lady, here is something worth seeing; for here is the exalted son of Bhṛigu.[6]

Sītā—Oh, how I tremble!

Rāma—My homage to thee, O sage!

Lakshmaṇa—Behold, behold, noble Lady! Here is this [sage], by my noble brother—

Rāma, *impatiently interrupting him*—Don't you see there is much more to be seen: show us what follows.

Sītā, *gazing* [*at Rāma*] *with affection and deep respect*—How well dost thou, my noble Lord, shine in this thy excess of modesty!

Lakshmaṇa—Here is our arrival at Ayodhyā.

Rāma, *with tears*—I remember, alas! I remember:

1 A famous ancestor of Rāma.

2 Literally, 'hair-clipping' ceremony. For its nature see Notes.

3 Wife of Lakshmaṇa's elder brother, Bharata.

4 Wife of Lakshmaṇa's younger brother, Śatrughna. Notice the difference in the mode of address. Since a younger brother is in the status of a son, his wife is the elder brother's daughter-in-law.

5 For one may not utter his wife's name, especially before elders.

6 Paraśu-Rāma or Rāma with the axe, a Brahman warrior and sage whom Rāma, the hero of this play, vanquished.

Our most honoured sire [1] still alive—we only just wedded to our brides—the Queen-mothers looking to all our needs: gone indeed are those [happy] days of ours! **19**

And then too this daughter of Janaka [Sītā]—

With her fine, slender, and charming locks-of-hair glistening at the ends [as they were wafted by the wind]; with her bud-like teeth enhancing the beauty of her face—child as she yet was; with her delightfully lovely—as if made out of moon-beams—and guilelessly sportive and sweet and tender limbs: she was the joy of our Queen-mothers! **20**

Lakshmaṇa—This is Mantharā.[2]

Rāma, *passing on silently to another place*—Queen Vaidehī,

This is that *iṅgudī* tree in the city of Śṛiṅgavera, where, formerly,[3] we came in contact with that friendly king of the Nishādas [hill-tribes]. **21**

Lakshmaṇa, *with a smile, aside*—So, I see, my noble brother has skipped over the story of our second (*madhyama*) mother!

Sītā—Ha! This is the scene at the tying [4] of the matted-hair (*jaṭā*).

Lakshmaṇa—With their sovereignty transferred to their sons what the old sires of [the race of] Ikshvāku [5] undertook, that, in his [very] youth, my noble brother undertook—the holy vow of an anchorite. **22**

Sītā—This is the exalted Bhāgīrathī [Ganges] with her serene and holy waters.

Rāma—Goddess! Presiding-divinity of the race of Raghu! Salutations unto thee.

Busily engaged in search of the [lost] horse, when—at the time of Sagara's [6] [horse-]sacrifice—[his sons] cleft the earth open and were through [sage] Kapila's wrathful radiance burnt to ashes, it was Bhagīratha, practising penances heedless of the sufferings of his body, who was able, after a very long time, to save [those sixty

1 His father Daśaratha.

2 An old nurse and attendant of Kaikeyī, the second wife of Daśaratha, and the moving spirit of the intrigue which brought about Rāma's banishment, instead of his installation as heir-apparent.

3 After crossing the Ganges on their way to banishment.

4 In preparation for assuming a forester's life.

5 Another famous ancestor of Rāma.

6 King Sagara of the Solar race commenced a horse-sacrifice. But the horse was stolen away. In search, the sixty thousand sons of Sagara ripped the earth open. There they came upon sage Kapila, who burnt them to ashes for their insolence. Their great-grandson, Bhagīratha, brought the Ganges down from the skies; and as the holy waters touched the ashes, the sixty thousand sons attained heaven. The Ganges is called Bhāgīrathī after Bhagīratha.

thousand sons,] those grand-sires of his own sire, when, O exalted one, they [their ashes] were touched by thy [holy] waters. **23**

Be thou, therefore, O [divine] mother, towards [this] thy daughter-in-law, Sītā, ever cherishing kindly thoughts—even like Arundhatī [herself]!

Lakshmaṇa—Here, on this way leading to the [mountain] Chitrakūṭa, which was shown us by [the sage] Bharadvāja—[here] upon this bank of the [river] Kālindī [Jumna]—is the banian-tree named Śyāma.

Sītā—Does my noble Lord remember this region here?

Rāma—How can I, darling, forget it!

For it was here that these tender limbs of thine, lovely and languid and drooping like a crushed lotus-stalk—exhausted with the journey's fatigues, [and so] close [mutual] embraces [alone] doing the work of their shampooings—[these limbs of thine] thou didst on my bosom repose and so sink into sleep! **24**

Lakshmaṇa—Here is [the demon] Virādha obstructing [our] entrance into the Vindhya-forest.

Sītā—Have done with this. I would rather see how—my noble Lord's hand holding a tāla-branch as an umbrella over me and [thus] shielding me from the sun—how we journeyed through the Southern Forest.

Rāma—These here, along the banks of the mountain-rillets, these are the penance-groves of the hermits who find shelter under the trees. In these [groves], ever intent on hospitality, the peaceful dwellers, cook their handful of wild-rice (*nīvāra*) and have their dwellings. **25**

Lakshmaṇa—[This mountain,] with its dense clusters of trees imparting a deep glossy blueness to the forests on its slopes, [forests] which hem in [the current of the river] Godāvarī and [thus] cause the ravines to resound —[this here,] with its blueness still further enhanced by the incessantly pouring clouds [on its top]—here, situated in the heart of Janasthāna,[1] is this mountain Prasravaṇa.[2]

Rāma—Dost thou, O fair-limbed one, remember, on this mountain— while Lakshmaṇa attended upon us and chased away all our cares—those days [that we once passed]? Dost thou likewise remember [the river] Godāvarī with its refreshing banks? And dost thou also remember our strolls in its neighbourhood? **26**

Here likewise—

While those delicious nothings (*kimapi*) softly, gently—cheek meeting cheek in [close] contact—we kept talking at random; while a fast embrace kept of us both a hand each engaged—

[1] The habitable section of the forest of Daṇḍakā.

[2] Literally, 'streaming' or 'full of streams'.

its watches speeding unnoticed [in succession]—thus did the night come to an end! **27**

Lakshmaṇa—Here is Śūrpaṇakhā [1] in the Pañchavaṭī.[2]

Sītā—Alas! my noble Lord! No sight of thee hereafter!

Rāma—O thou, frightened at [the mere thought of] separation, this is only a picture!

Sītā—Be that as it may, a wicked person is [ever] the source of unhappiness.

Rāma [3]—Why, in sooth, this Janasthāna incident *does* seem as if [happening in the] present.

Lakshmaṇa—Hereafter the demons, through the trick of the disguise [in the form] of the golden deer [4]—the wicked ones—did in this wise [as represented in the picture] that which [even now] smarts us, though it has been washed off [in the enemy's blood]. In the void of Janasthāna these doings of my noble brother, in his piteous helplessness, they cause even the stone to weep and the heart of adamant to burst! **28**

Sītā, *with tears, to herself*—Alas! Thus, O thou Joy of Raghu's race, [thus] wast thou on my account afflicted!

Lakshmaṇa, *looking at Rāma, significantly*—What is this now, my noble brother?

These thy welling (*ogha*) tears—like some broken threads of a pearl-necklace—trickle down and roll on the ground in streams of shattered drops. Restrained though it is, this emotion, which in its excess swells and fills thy heart, doth [nevertheless], through thy quivering lips and nostrils, become inferable by others. **29**

Rāma—Dear brother,

Born of that [former] separation from my beloved [that fire of grief]—tormenting as it was—it was, in the hope of vengeance, then endured by me. Now once again that [same] fire of grief, as it flares out in my mind, like a [festering] wound in the vitals of the heart doth it smart me with pain. **30**

Sītā—Alas! Alas! I too, in the intensity of my anguish, feel myself as if sundered from my noble Lord!

[1] Sister of the demon Rāvaṇa. Foiled in her attempt to seduce Rāma and Lakshmaṇa, and being punished by them, it was she who incited Rāvaṇa to abduct Sītā.

[2] That part of Janasthāna where Rāma lived with his wife and brother.

[3] A slight interval during which they pass in review a few more pictures (such as Rāma's fight with the fourteen thousand, cp. ii. 15) must here be presupposed. This renders intelligible Rāma's change of feeling between this speech and his speech immediately preceding.

[4] This was the trick used to draw Rāma and Lakshmaṇa away from Sītā, whom Rāvaṇa forthwith seized and carried off.

Lakshmaṇa, *to himself*—Well then, I will create a diversion. *Looking at the picture, aloud.* Here now, aged by [the full length of] an eon,[1] is this king of vultures, father Jaṭāyus[2] of honoured name, and [here] the illustration of his valorous conduct.

Sītā—Alas, father! To its most bitter end (*nir-*) hast thou carried [this] thy filial love!

Rāma—Alas, father! Thou descendant of Kaśyapa [and] monarch of the winged tribes! Where can there be found, once again, another like thee—a store of holiness, a saint?

Lakshmaṇa—This here, west of Janasthāna, is what they call Chitrakuñja[3] —a portion of the Daṇḍakā forest inhabited [once] by the headless Danu. This on the mountain Ṛishyamūka is the hermitage of [sage] Matañga, and the grounds (*padam*) adjoining it. Here is the most saintly Śabara lady, Śramaṇā by name. That again is the lily-pool called Pampā.[4]

Sītā—Here, as I learn (*kila*), my noble Lord—[all] his passion [for revenge] (*amarsha*) and courage forsaking him—wept aloud and in the very fullness of his heart (*kaṇṭha*).

Rāma—My Queen, lovely is this [lily-]pool [to me]:

> [For,] in this [pool]—when in their youthful merriment the [blue-beaked] *mallikāksha* birds shook with their wings the broad and tremulous stalks of the [white] lotuses—in the intervals between the risings and fallings of tear-drops, I perceived the regions to be full of [blue] lotuses.[5] **31**

Lakshmaṇa—This is the noble Hanūmant (Māruti).[6]

Sītā—This is he who has conferred a mighty blessing on this [entire] living world by uplifting it from the despair wherein it was long plunged—he of resistless prowess, Māruti!

Rāma—Happily this is he of mighty arms—the source of Añjanā's[7]
> joy—by whose valour blessed [in the attainment of their end] are we ourselves and [all] the worlds! **32**

Sītā—Dear brother, this here, with the full-plumed peacocks (*barhin*) dancing upon its flowering *kadamba* trees, by what name is this mountain called?—where, his majestic grace being all that is left of his pale beauty—

[1] A *manvantara* or eon = 306,720,000 human years.

[2] The vulture Jaṭāyus was a friend of Rāma's father, and met death in the attempt to prevent Sītā's abduction.

[3] Lit. 'having many bowers'; the monster Danu infested it.

[4] For all these persons and places see the Notes to the passage.

[5] By a transference of the birds' colour to the lotuses on which they were perching.

[6] A monkey-chieftain, ally of Rāma. He met Sītā in her captivity at Lañkā, and carried news of her back to Rāma.

[7] The mother of Māruti.

about to swoon and supported by thy sorrowing [hands]—in the shade of this tree, my noble Lord is depicted?

Lakshmaṇa—This is that mountain perfumed with the [fragrant] *kakubha*-[trees], Mālyavant by name, on whose peak is perching an early rain-cloud, glossy and blue.

Rāma—Desist, my dear brother, desist from this: no farther can I endure. Come back to me once again, meseems, is that separation from [this] daughter of Janaka. **33**

Lakshmaṇa—Hereafter [come], both of my noble brother and of the valorous Monkeys and Demons, these countless and waxingly marvellous deeds. Fatigued, however (*cha*), is my noble Lady here. Pray, therefore, rest a while.

Sītā—Noble my Lord, the sight of these pictures has created [in me] a longing, which prompts me to beg that—

Rāma—Why, you are free to *command.*

Sītā—I feel once again like amusing myself in the serene and lovely woodlands, and having a plunge in the holy, cool, and translucent waters of the exalted Bhāgīrathī.

Rāma—Dear Lakshmaṇa!

Lakshmaṇa—Here, at your service.

Rāma—That such longings should be forthwith gratified has even just now been enjoined upon us by [our] elders (*guru*). Have ready therefore a chariot that runs smoothly and without jolting.

Sītā—And *you*, my noble Lord, you are coming thither—aren't you?

Rāma—Why, you hard-hearted one! This—needs it to be *said*?

Sītā—Then, indeed, I am content.

Lakshmaṇa—So, as my noble brother commands. *Exit.*

Rāma—Dearest! Here, in this sheltered-balcony (*apavartaka*), let us repose a while.

Sītā—So be it. Through fatigue I am really overpowered by sleep.

Rāma—If so, cling to me close and we will go [thither] together:

As if infusing life into me, let this thy arm—moist with drops of perspiration due to excitement and fatigue—let it be thrown around my neck: [thy arm] in all the loveliness of a necklace of *chandrakānta*[1] beads, dripping [as when gently] kissed by the moon-beams. **34**

While helping her to do so, in joy. Dearest! What can this be?

Impossible to decide if this be joy or if this be grief, if a swoon or a slumber; whether this be a slowly-creeping poison or an

[1] The 'moon-stone' is believed to have this property.

infatuation [of some sort]: for, at every touch of thine, a [certain] feeling, benumbing all my senses, [possesses me, and] now bewilders my soul (*chaitanya*) and now paralyses it quite! **35**

Sītā, *with a smile*—'Tis all your unchanging affection: how *else* then could it be?

Rāma—Causing the drooping flower of my life to bloom—filling me with transport—ravishing all my senses—these endearing words of my lotus-eyed one: they are as ambrosia to the ear and as elixirs to the mind! **36**

Sītā—Come, thou of honeyed words! Let us rest. *Looks about for something to sleep on.*

Rāma—And what, pray, wouldst thou look for?

Ever since the time of our wedding, at home or in the forest, in girlhood and then again in young-womanhood, what has [ever] lulled thee to sleep and what no other woman can claim—Rāma's arm, thy pillow, is here. **37**

Sītā, *going into sleep*—It is even so, my noble Lord! It is even so. *Sleeps.*

Rāma—Why, with sweet words on her lips she has already fallen asleep on my bosom! *gazing, in fondness*—

She to the house a very Lakshmī[1]—to the eyes an ambrosial pencil—this touch of hers like a thick sandal-juice to the body—this [her] arm round [my] neck, cool and tender as a pearl-necklace: what of hers is not dear, save only that unendurable separation? **38**

Pratīhārī,[2] *entering*—Has come, my liege!

Rāma—And who?

Pratīhārī—The personal attendant of Your Majesty—Durmukha.[3]

Rāma, *to himself*—Oh, Durmukha, who is on duty about the harem? Him I had employed as a spy upon my subjects in the city and in the country. *Aloud.* Let him come in.

Exit Pratīhārī.

Durmukha, *entering, to himself*—Alas! how now, concerning the Queen Sītā, such an unthinkable public slander may I report unto the King? But (*adhavā*) such indeed is the lot of [men like] me, ill-starred.

Sītā, *talking in her sleep*—Alas! Gentle my Lord! Where art thou?

Rāma—How now! Of that torment-giving separation this must be the [latent] impression[4] (*bhāvanā*) which my Queen received while looking at

[1] The Goddess of wealth and plenty.

[2] A female warder. Her words 'has come' Rāma construes with the last word of his speech, 'separation'; hence his surprised question. 'Separation' in Sanskrit is masculine.

[3] 'Foul-mouthed' or 'with face of evil omen'.

[4] The poet is here purposely technical.

the pictures, and which is [now] causing her these perturbed dreams. *Affectionately stroking her.*

Uniform (*advaita*) in happiness and in sorrow—conformable (*anuguṇa*) to all the conditions [of life]—in which the heart finds solace—the flavour of which age cannot stint—which with time, as the veil-of-reserve (*āvaraṇa*) drops away, abides as a perfect and ripened affection—that one supreme-blessing (*bhadra*) [only] the fortunate among mankind, and after a sore trial (*katham api*), attain. **39**

Durmukha, *approaching*—Victory unto Your Majesty!

Rāma—Speak what you have found out.

Durmukha—They praise Your Majesty—the people both in the city and in the country—saying, 'King Rāma has made us forget King Daśaratha'.

Rāma—A mere compliment this: tell me of some fault or other so that it may be set right.

Durmukha, *with tears*—Let the King listen [then]. *In his ear* [*whispers*] *so and so.*

Rāma—Alas! How sudden in its blow is this thunderbolt of a speech! *Faints.*

Durmukha—Take heart, my King!

Rāma, *coming to himself*—

Alas, oh alas! That scandal, due to the residence in a stranger's house of this daughter of the Videha-King, [that scandal] which [formerly] through means miraculous we had put down—that, like a mad hound's venom, is once again, by an adverse turn of fortune, spreading fast (*pra*) everywhere! **40**

What then—ill-starred that I am—may I do in this case? *After reflecting, mournfully.* Or, what else is there [to it]?

For good men, by some means or other, propitiation of the people [must be] a sacred duty (*vrata*)—[a duty] which, moreover (*hi*), my father fulfilled,[1] though [thereby] losing me and his [own] life. **41**

Just a short while ago did the exalted Vasishṭa send [me] his mandate.[2] Furthermore,

[That long career] which hath been made glorious by the Children of the Sun—the rulers of the Earth, the foremost of men—if that pure and unblemished career [of this Solar race] should, on my account, by some foul calumny be disgraced—then, alas! fie on me, the unblessed! **42**

[1] For the palace-intrigue which caused Rāma's banishment and his father Daśaratha's death, see Introduction, § 18, E. Compare stanza 11, above.

Alas, my Queen, who hast uprisen from the [very] sacrificial ground of the Gods! Who by thy birth hast graciously purified [the womb of] the Earth! Who hast been a joy to Janaka and [the whole race of] Nimi![1] O thou whose character [even] Fire and Vasishṭha and Arundhatī have commended! Thou to whom Rāma is life and all! Thou the dear companion of my residence in the great wilderness [of Daṇḍakā]! Dear unto my [honoured] father! Sweet and measured in thy words! How is it that of one like thee such here should be the fate?—

> Through thee [are] the worlds holy—unholy [are] the world's rumours about thee! Thou art the world's protection—without protector thou wilt [now] perish! **43**

Go, Durmukha, say unto Lakshmaṇa: This is what thy *new* King, Rāma, commands thee. *In his ear [whispers] so and so.*

Durmukha—And wherefore [unto the Queen] whose purity has been attested by the fire-ordeal and who bears in her womb the [hopes of the] continuance of this holy race of Raghu—[wherefore] unto a queen, on base wretches' words, has Your Majesty resolved to mete out such treatment?

Rāma—Peace! The people of my city and my country—base wretches?

> Ikshvāku's race hath [ever] been beloved of the people: and [yet in it] hath arisen, as Fate will have it, an occasion of scandal. And as for that miraculous event at the time when the Queen was cleared [by the ordeal]—who will believe it, since it took place [in Lañkā] so far away? **44**

Go therefore.

Durmukha—Alas, Queen! *Exit.*

Rāma—Woe and alas! Detestable in my actions—a savage—have I been!

> From childhood on, with kind cares (*priyaiḥ*), to her wants have I ministered—my dearest, who in her love hath naught but me on whom to rest: her I am treacherously handing over to Death, as does a butcher his pet house-bird! **45**

Wherefore then should I—the untouchable criminal—[yet continue to] pollute the Queen [by my touch]? *Gently uplifts Sītā's head, withdrawing his arm.*

> [Me,] an outcaste whose deeds it were hard to match, let me go, thou artlessly-innocent one! Thou hast clung, mistaking it for a sandal-tree, to what is only a poison-tree with fruit of bane. **46**

Rising. Alas! [to me] topsy-turvy now is this world of life. Ended is the life-purpose of Rāma. A void, now, a wasted wilderness, is the universe. Robbed-of-its-charms is my existence [hereafter]. My body a mere abode

[1] Ancestor of Sītā's father, Janaka.

of woes. No help remains to me and no choice: what can be done? Surely (*athavā*)—

It is only to make me feel [the pangs of] sorrow that into [me,] Rāma, consciousness has been put; and my life is stubborn like a dart of adamant: it pierces the vitals [and *will* not be pulled out]! **47**

O Arundhatī that hast been a mother to me; ye venerable Vasishṭha and Viśvāmitra; O holy Fire and thou O all-sustaining Goddess [Earth]!—Alas, father! Alas, Janaka! Alas, ye my [dear] mothers!—Thou O loving friend, King Sugrīva;[1] gentle Hanūmant; Vibhīshaṇa,[2] ruler of Lañkā [and] my great benefactor; [and not the least] thou O friendly Trijaṭā[3]—ye do all stand robbed, stand insulted, by this wretch of a Rāma! Or rather, what right have I now to call on them?

For, I think, that they of noble mind, when their names are taken on the lips of me of base and ungrateful mind, [that they] perhaps are polluted by my deed of wrong, **48**

in that I—

Am casting away her who in confidence on my bosom reposing has gone to sleep—my dearest consort, the glory of my house;—her whose womb is heavy with its painfully throbbing and full-grown burden—[her] like a victim unto the Flesh-eaters[4] I am ruthlessly throwing away! **49**

Placing his head on Sītā's feet. Queen, Queen! Here now—but [alas!] for the last time—Rāma's head toucheth thy lotus-feet. *Weeps.*

[**Voice,**] *behind the curtain*—An outrage against a Brahman, an outrage!

Rāma—Find out, some one, what it is.

[**Voice,**] *again behind the curtain*—

Of sages fierce in their austerities and dwellers on the banks of the Yamunā, a throng, harassed by [the demon] Lavaṇa, is approaching unto thee their defender. **50**

Rāma—How,—even *yet* are the demons harassing? Then I must forthwith send [my brother] Śatrughna to destroy this wicked son of Kumbhīnasī.[5] *Pacing a few steps and again coming back.* Alas, my Queen, how—situated as thou art—[how] wilt thou fare? O holy [Earth, thou] Giver of all blessings! This thy virtuous daughter do thou look upon with kindness—this daughter of Janaka:

[1] An ally of Rāma.

[2] Brother of Rāvaṇa; he assisted Rāma in his fight with Rāvaṇa, and was by Rāma installed king of Lañkā.

[3] She solaced Sītā in her captivity.

[4] Demons or beasts of prey.

[5] Mother of the demon Lavaṇa. He infested the region around Mathurā (modern Muttra in the N.W. Provinces).

Of Janaka's and of Raghu's families the all-in-all of auspiciousness, and to whom—of holy character—in the holy sacrificial ground of the Gods thou didst give birth. **51**

Exit.

Sītā, *talks in sleep*—Alas, gentle my Lord! *Rising abruptly.* Why now, what a fool I am! Deceived by the malignant dream, I am crying after my noble Lord! *Looking [around].* How now! Could it be that leaving me here alone and sleeping, my dear Lord has verily gone away? What *can* this mean? Well, well! I must be angry with him—provided [of course] that when I look upon his face I am master of my [actions]! Who is in attendance here?

Durmukha, *entering*—Queen! Prince Lakshmaṇa requests: The car is ready; will the Queen [be pleased to] get in?

Sītā—Here I am, ready. *Rising.* I feel something like a throbbing in my womb: let us go slowly.

Durmukha—This way, this way, Queen!

Sītā—My salutations[1] unto the Presiding-deities of the race of Raghu!

Both go out.

[1] It is usual, when leaving the house, to make this homage.

END OF ACT I

CALLED

PICTURE-GALLERY.

ACT II

[**Voice,**] *behind the curtain*—Welcome unto [you] the store of holiness!

Enters a female ascetic in a traveller's habit.

Female Ascetic—O, I see: This is a sylvan deity approaching me respectfully with an offering [1] of leaves and fruits and flowers.

Sylvan Deity, *entering, and making the offering*—

Open unto your unhindered enjoyment is this forest here; this is for me a day of bliss. For, the meeting of the good with the good happens but rarely [and then, only] by [reason of some special] merit. Sheltering arbours, water, and whatsoever of food for [your] penance be suited—fruit or root—all alike is entirely at your command here. 1

Female Ascetic—Needs this to be said?

A habitual complaisance of manners; a temperance in speech agreeable by its modesty; a disposition naturally benevolent: a friendship [absolutely] irreproachable—thus first and last [and ever] invariable in its sweetness, may this secret of a sage's [life] —free from stains and hindrances—[may it ever] prosper! 2

Both sit down.

Sylvan Deity—By what name, now, may I know your ladyship?

Female Ascetic—I am Ātreyī.

Sylvan Deity—Honoured Ātreyī, and from where is it that you have come, and what may be your purpose in coming to this Daṇḍakā forest?

Ātreyī—Here in this region are dwelling—with Agastya [2] at their head—many [scholars] learned in the Sāma-Veda. To acquire from them the Upanishad (*nigamānta*) lore, hither have I come journeying from Vālmīki's place. 3

Sylvan Deity—If now even other [distant] students (*muni*), to realize Brahma, sit at the feet of that same venerable discourser of Brahma [Vālmīki], that son of [God] Varuṇa, what means then this your ladyship's journey?

[1] It is usual to honour a guest with such an offering.

[2] Believed to be the earliest explorer of Southern India. His hermitage was in Pañchavaṭī, near Rāma's own.

Ātreyī—There [occurred] a great hindrance to the course-of-studies (*adhyayana*); and so was this long journey undertaken.

Sylvan Deity—Of what sort [may this hindrance be]?

Ātreyī—To him, the exalted one [Vālmīki], some unknown (*viśesha*) divinity has made over two boys in every respect marvellous and being of an age when they were just weaned. These boys have indeed captivated the inmost hearts not only of [Vālmīki] himself but also of all movable and immovable beings[1] whatsoever.

Sylvan Deity—And are their names known?

Ātreyī—That same divinity, 'tis said, announced Kuśa and Lava as their names, and [declared also] their prowess.

Sylvan Deity—Prowess, of what nature?

Ātreyī—They have—so runs the report (*kila*)—a mastery from their very birth over the *jṛimbhaka* missiles with their secret spells.

Sylvan Deity—This, to be sure, is passing strange!

Ātreyī—Now these [boys] the exalted Vālmīki, having taken upon himself the duties of a nurse, has brought up under his care. As soon as they had gone through the *chaula*[2]-ceremony he [Vālmīki] assiduously grounded them—with the exception of the three Vedas—in the three[3] other branches of knowledge. And then when the [boys] had reached the eleventh year from their conception, they were, according to the rites proper to a Kshatriya, invested with the Sacred Thread and instructed in the knowledge of the Three [Vedas] also.[4] Now with these two [boys], possessed of exceedingly brilliant power of comprehension and retentiveness as they are, [students] like us cannot keep pace in the studies. For,

> The preceptor imparts unto the clever, instructions just the same as unto the dull, and in no wise doth he their power of comprehension either make or thwart; and yet there *does* result a vast difference as to the outcome: for we know (*tad-yathā*) that [only] a pure crystal is able to take in images, and not a [mere] lump of clay. 4

Sylvan Deity—And this then is the hindrance to your course-of-studies?

Ātreyī—[There is] yet another.

Sylvan Deity—And what can this other be?

Ātreyī—Then, once upon a time, this Brahman-sage [Vālmīki], for his

[1] Not only animals and plants, but even mountains and rivers and the whole mineral kingdom, in fact, possess souls.

[2] Lit. 'forelock'-ceremony: clipping a boy's hair with the exception of five little tufts or locks. At the time of marriage these 'forelocks' give place to a single central tuft or *śikhā*.

[3] Logic, Economics, Politics: the Vedas form the fourth branch. See Kauṭilīya, p. 6.

[4] The Vedas may not be taught before the Sacred-thread ceremony.

[customary] midday oblations, went unto the river Tamasā; and there, of a pair of curlews sporting together (*chārin*), he sighted one as it was being pierced by a fowler. Then did [the sage] burst forth in words divine, spontaneous-and-intuitive, blameless [in their form] and adapted to the metre of an *anushṭubh* stanza:

> 'Never, O Nishāda,[1] through all the years eternal, [never] shalt thou attain stability, because thou hast killed one of these two curlews maddened with love [for its mate].' **5**

Sylvan Deity—Wonderful is this introduction of new metres outside the Vedas![2]

Ātreyī—And then, about the same time, unto that exalted one—unto the sage [Vālmīki] in whom shone forth the light of Brahma in the form of the Word—approached the exalted Author of all beings, the Lotus-born [Brahmadeva], and spake,—Sage! Awakened art thou to that Brahma whose essence is Word: Speak out, therefore, the History of Rāma. Unimpeded in its illumination [be] thy inspired and prophetic vision! Thou art the first of poets. So saying He [forthwith] became invisible. Then [Vālmīki,] that exalted son of Varuṇa, composed what is the first [of its kind] among mortals: that transformation (*vivarta*) of Brahma-in-the-form-of-Word—the History called Rāmāyaṇa.

Sylvan Deity—This, to be sure (*hanta*), is an adornment to the world.

Ātreyī—And hence, as I said, there occurred a great hindrance to our course of studies.

Sylvan Deity—I see now (*yujyate*).

Ātreyī—I have had my rest, kind lady! Now unto [sage] Agastya's hermitage point me the way.

Sylvan Deity—Enter Pañchavaṭī on this side here, and then proceed onwards along this bank of the Godāvarī.

Ātreyī, *with tears*—Can it then be that this penance-grove is Pañchavaṭī—that this river is Godāvarī—that this mountain is Prasravaṇa—and [finally] that you are the Deity of the Janasthāna, Vāsantī?

Vāsantī—Even so: all [as you say].

Ātreyī—[Alas] Jānakī, my child![3]

> Here are those loving companions of thine, on [all] occasions the theme of thy conversation, who, as I see them [here] now, bring thee visibly before our eyes, though [alas!] only the name of thee now remains behind! **6**

[1] Forester.

[2] Vālmīki is regarded as the father of poetry and the Rāmāyaṇa as the first poem. Before this the Vedas were the only metrical works.

[3] Ātreyī apparently is an elderly lady.

Vāsantī, *with apprehension, to herself*—How! 'only the name of thee now remains behind,' she says! *Aloud.* What calamity then, noble lady, has befallen the Queen Sītā?

Ātreyī—Not a mere calamity but a calumny to boot! *In her ear* [*whispers*] *so and so.*

Vāsantī—Alas! A cruel stroke of destiny! *Faints.*

Ātreyī—Compose yourself, gentle lady, compose yourself.

Vāsantī—Alas, my loving friend [Sītā]! Thou Fortune's favourite! That such should be the lot of thy life!! Rāma, dear! Dear Rāma!—Or rather I have had quite too much of thee. But, I say, honoured Ātreyī, after Lakshmaṇa's departure from that forest where he had left her, what became of Queen Sītā? Is there any tidings as to that?

Ātreyī—No, not the least.

Vāsantī—Woe and alas! And when Arundhatī and Vasishṭha were guardians to the scions of the Raghu-race—[even] in the [very] life-time of the aged Queen-mothers—how was this suffered to happen?

Ātreyī—In Ṛishyaśṛiṅga's hermitage the elders were then living. Now [however] that twelve-year [long] session [of the sacrifice] has come to an end; and Ṛishyaśṛiṅga, after paying them the [customary] honours, has bidden the elders (*guru*) farewell. Then spake the exalted Arundhatī,—'I will not return to Ayodhyā if our daughter-in-law [Sītā] is not there'; to this too Rāma's Queen-mothers assented; and in compliance with that the exalted Vasishṭha uttered his holy word to the effect that they should [all] repair unto Vālmīki's penance-grove and there abide.

Vāsantī—And the King[1]—what is *he* doing now?

Ātreyī—The King has now undertaken a horse-sacrifice.

Vāsantī—Oh, fie! Has he even married [again]?

Ātreyī—No, Heaven forfend, no!

Vāsantī—Who then is there to participate in the religious offices[2] connected with the sacrifice?

Ātreyī—A golden image of Sītā.

Vāsantī—Ha!—Really?

> Than even an adamant, harder; softer than even a flower: the minds of those that tower above the common sort—who is there that can [ever] fathom [them]? 7

Ātreyī—And the sacrificial horse has been let loose consecrated by [sage] Vāmadeva;[3] and for [the horse] have been assigned, agreeably to the Shastras (Scriptures) the [proper number of] guards, and at the head of

[1] She would not call him 'Rāma dear' now.

[2] The wife took part in all religious ceremonies.

[3] Who officiated in the absence of Vasishṭha.

these is commissioned the son of Lakshmaṇa, Chandraketu by name, who has been initiated into the [traditional] knowledge of celestial missiles and who is leading an army [fully] equipped in all its four divisions (*aṅga*).[1]

Vāsantī, *in curiosity and with tears of affection*—Even Prince Lakshmaṇa has a son, and I, O mother, am [still] living [to see it]!

Ātreyī—Meantime a Brahman lays down his dead son at the royal gate and beating his breast proclaims that an outrage has been committed against a Brahman. Then, since in the absence of some failing of the king himself no untimely death can overtake any one of his people, our dear Rāma mournfully began to examine [his past conduct to discover] some fault of his own: when all of a sudden an incorporeal voice broke forth—

> 'Tis Śambūka by name—a Śūdra—who on [this] earth is practising penance. His head it behoves thee, O Rāma, to cut off: by killing him bring thou the Brahman [boy] to life. **8**

Hearing this, sword in hand and mounting his aerial car, *Pushpaka*,[2] the Lord of the World [Rāma] has [now], in search of that Śūdra ascetic, begun to traverse all the cardinal and intermediate points.

Vāsantī—A Śūdra, Śambūka by name, who inhales the smoke,[3]—in this very Janasthāna does he practise penance. Can it then be that Rāma dear[4] will once again grace this forest [by his presence]?

Ātreyī—Kind lady, let me go now.

Vāsantī—So be it, honoured Ātreyī; for, the day has grown oppressive—

> As the itching elephants[5] rub their rounded temples against them, [the trees] shaken violently shower down their flowers, [already] through heat loosened from the stalks, and [with this shower] pay [their midday] offering [as it were] to the [river] Godāvarī. In their shade [are] these birds that, as they scrape [for food], peck with their beak and drag forth insects [hidden] under the bark; [perched] on their [tops are] these troops of fine pigeons and [wild] fowl cooing [in languor]: such [now], along this bank, are [all] these nesting-trees. **9**

They move about and exeunt [severally].

END OF INTERLUDE.

[1] Elephants, horses, chariots, and foot-soldiers.

[2] Lit. '[light as] a flower'. It came into Rāma's possession after the victory of Laṅkā. The car was as swift as the mind, and obeyed automatically all the wishes of the rider.

[3] By hanging from a tree head downwards.

[4] He has become 'Rāma dear' again!

[5] Their temples itch when they are in rut.

Then enters Rāma in his Pushpaka, raised sword in hand, and full of compassion.

Rāma—O my right hand, for the revival of the Brahman's dead son do thou hurl at [this] Śūdra ascetic thy sword! Thou art a member of Rāma's [body]—[of that Rāma] who found it easy (*paṭu*) to send away Sītā, [although she was] languishing with [the weight of] the burden she bore:[1] Compassion—how can it be thine? **10**

Reluctantly striking. Done is a deed worthy [only] of a Rāma! May it be that the Brahman boy will now come to life?

A Celestial Person, *entering*—Victory, victory unto Your Majesty!

With you, rod in hand [to mete out punishment and] to grant immunity even from the Lord of Death, revived is that boy and mine hath been this glory: This is Śambūka with his head bowing at your feet. Coming from contact with the good even death brings salvation! **11**

Rāma—Both [the events] please us [equally]. May you now enjoy the reward of your fierce penances!—

Where there is all bliss and delight—wherein through merit [alone] is [a person] born: may those realms of light—Vairāja as they are called—be yours for ever! **12**

Śambūka—It is your gracious feet that have brought me this greatness. What has my penance to do in the matter? Or rather [I should say] a mighty boon has my penance conferred upon me:

You are the One to be sought after in this world—the Lord of men, their [supreme] refuge; [and you] in search of me—this mere Śūdra—have over hundreds of leagues traversed, and come [hither]: This great favour it is my penance that hath conferred upon me; were it otherwise, from the [distant] Ayodhyā what possibility was there of your coming once more to this forest of Daṇḍakā? **13**

Rāma—What! Is this indeed Daṇḍakā? *Looking in all directions.* Yes, indeed!

Mild and shady in some places, in others harsh in [the immensity of] their frightful expanse; here and there filling the quarters with the roar of their gushing streams: these, interspersed with forests,

[1] This indicates that even after the lapse of twelve years Rāma is still haunted by the memory of his wife, whose loss he mourns as bitterly as ever. Compare also iii. 3^{6}.

abounding in [holy] bathing-places and hermitages and mountains and rivers—[they] appear to be, familiar as they have been to me, the [same old] regions belonging to the wilderness of Daṇḍakā. **14**

Śambūka—Surely this *is* Daṇḍakā; and—as I have learnt—by Your Majesty when formerly living here—

Fourteen thousand Demons, frightful in their deeds, and the three:
Dūshaṇa,[1] Khara, and Trimūrdhan, in battle were slain. **15**

And hence it was that in such a saintly resort—in this Janasthāna—even timid persons like me could roam at will, apprehending danger from nowhere.

Rāma—So, not merely Daṇḍakā, but this is even Janasthāna?

Śambūka—Assuredly: For, smiting all creatures with horror—hosts of furious and savage beasts infesting [all] its inaccessible mountain-recesses—there in sooth are those extensive forests outlying the skirts of Janasthāna and stretching [from there] towards the south. For—

Noiseless and [profoundly] silent in places; in places resounding to the roarings of ferocious beasts; huge and horrible serpents, stretched out in repose, making with their [fiery] breath [the whole forest] ablaze: these [indeed] are those bordering regions having [very] little water flashing in their clefts, so that the thirsty lizards [must] drink the sweat exuded by [mighty] pythons! **16**

Rāma—I do [indeed] behold Janasthāna, once the abode of [the demon] Khara; and as if [happening] just before my eyes those former events I do now experience! **17**

Looking carefully all around. Yes (*hi*): And the daughter of the King of Videha [my Sītā] always loved these woodlands (*ārāma*). Here, to be sure, are those [very] forests: Than this can anything be more terrible? *With tears.*

'With thee will I dwell in those dales where the scents are sweet' —[this was her thought, and] with that alone here was she happy—such was her love [for me]! **18**

Though doing nothing, by the very joy [of being together] we chase away all sorrow: Indeed it is a treasure indescribable when some one has some one to love. **19**

Śambūka—Let us, if you please (*tad*), turn away from these impenetrable [forests]. But here are these others,—studded with hills that wear the soft tinge of a lusty and tuneful peacock's throat—decked with clusters of

[1] For the names see Introduction, § 18, H and I.

young trees thickly planted and yielding an ample and bluish shade—with the numerous herds of deer fearlessly [roaming about]: let the noble one [now] look at these, these serene and awe-inspiring central forests:

Here, as the [youth-]intoxicated birds invade the *vānīra* creepers, the flowers [dropping down into the rillets] suffuse with fragrance their cool and limpid waters;—as the *jambū* clusters, darkling with the load of ripening fruit, impede [the rillets in] their path, their [broken] currents incessantly murmur: thus do these [mountain-]rillets glide along. **20**

Furthermore—

Here, of the young bears that have their lairs in [these] caverns, the spluttered growls (*ambūkṛita*) become augmented by the echoes that they send forth; [and] cool and bitter and pungent as it is, the exuding fragrance of the *śallakī*[1] branches, torn from their joints and scattered about by [rutting] elephants, is [also] augmented. **21**

Rāma, *stemming [the flow] of his tears*—Friend, happy be your path! May you attain the Course celestial,[2] leading you on to the Realms of the holy!

Śambūka—Meantime I shall do my homage to the ancient Brahman sage, [the venerable] Agastya, before I enter the Abode eternal. *Goes out.*

Rāma—This, once more, is that same, same forest that to-day I behold, [the forest] wherein formerly for many many days we lived [together], as foresters and as householders, duly discharged our [several] duties, [and] knew the taste of [all] the charms of life. **22**

Here are those selfsame mountains alive with the cries of peacocks—these the same wooded ridges full of the lustily sportive deer. Here again, vocal with [the rustlings of] the lovely *vañjula* creepers, are those same river-banks densely fringed with the sable *nichula* [trees]. **23**

And this here that, like a range of clouds, one can well make out even from a distance—this is the mountain Prasravaṇa, where is the river Godāvarī. **24**

It was on the mighty crest of this very [mountain] that the king of vultures [Jaṭāyus] had his abode; and at its foot we likewise found our comfort in those leafy cottages. The waters of the

[1] A tree the twigs of which form the favourite food of wild elephants. The idea is, as the caverns deepen the growls of bears, so the exudations of *śallakī* intensify the pungent smell of the elephants' rut.

[2] See Note to the passage.

Godāvarī reflecting the glory of its sombre trees and the birds filling the skies with their incessant warblings—such is this charming woodland [scenery]. **25**

And even here is that Pañchavaṭī every spot in which can bear witness, in the course of our long residence, to those manifold expressions of unreserved endearments, and where my dear wife's dear friend, Vāsantī, [has her abode]. What then is this that has to-day befallen this Rāma? For now—

Like the virulent essence of some poison [dormant hitherto but now] after such a long time diffusing itself all over and causing spasms [of acute pain]—like the splinter of an arrow [imbedded in flesh and smarting now] as when, from some cause or other, it is violently shaken—like a [festering] ulcer overgrown with flesh [on the outside but] bursting open in the very vitals of the heart—even so my [long and so to say] solidified grief [now] unmans me as would a recent [grief]. **26**

Still, these friends of old—these landscapes here—I will see. *Looking* [*more*] *closely.* Ha! How changed [now] is the aspect of this region!—

Where once was the stream [itself], there now are the sands of the rivers; of the sprouting trees (*kshiti-ruh*) the denseness and the sparseness have exchanged places:[1] This forest, seen after [such] a long time, seems to me like another [forest]—only the unaltered position of the mountains confirms the idea that it is the same! **27**

Alas! Though trying to avoid it, my attachment to Pañchavaṭī forcibly draws me, as it were, towards it. *With pathos*—

[That Pañchavaṭī] wherein, in that [blissful] manner, those days with her I passed, and later, in our home, with long talks about which [Pañchavaṭī] we constantly whiled away our time: alone, now, after being the cause of the loss of his dear [wife], how should Rāma, sinful as he is, visit that very same Pañchavaṭī, or how pass on regardless of it? **28**

Śambūka, *entering*—Victory unto Your Majesty! The exalted Agastya hearing from me of your presence [here], sends this word unto you:—'Having in readiness all the auspicious preparations for your welcome, the kindly Lopāmudrā awaits you, as do also all the sages [in our neighbourhood]. Come then: honour us [with your visit]. With your swift *Pushpaka* you can thereafter return to your country in time for the horse-sacrifice.'

[1] I. e. where the trees were dense, now they are sparse, and vice versa.

Rāma—As the exalted [Agastya] commands.

Śambūka—Let Your Majesty then turn the *Pushpaka* this way.[1]

Rāma—O Pañchavaṭī [of] revered [memory]! Being constrained by [this call from] those to whom deference is due (*guru*), for a while let this transgression of Rāma be forgiven [him].

Śambūka—Behold, Sire, behold!—

> [These clumps here—] when in the tiny-nests (*kuṭīra*) within their bushes the flocks (*ghaṭā*) of owls do hoot—they constrain the troops of rooks[2] to silence: these vast stretches (*āḍambara*) of the melodious (*guñjat*) bamboo-clumps (*stambha*) [growing on] this mountain called Krauñchāvata; [this mountain] wherein [also] are to be seen—frightened by the cries of the hovering (*prachalat*) peacocks—these snakes[2] climbing in fear around the trunks of ancient sandal trees. **29**

Furthermore,—

> These here, with their caverns rumbling and roaring with the torrents (*vāri*) of the Godāvarī[3]—the clouds overhanging their blue and towering peaks—[these] are the lofty Southern ranges. [Here likewise—] with mutual clashings overwhelmed and surging with the tumult of their noisily dashing billows—here are the confluences of these holy and fathomless streams. **30**

Exeunt both.

END OF ACT II

CALLED

DANḌAKA REVISITED.

[1] It would seem that throughout the act Rāma was in his aerial car, though it is not a necessary supposition. See Notes for further discussion of the point.

[2] Rooks fear the owls as snakes fear the peacocks. Snakes are inordinately fond of sweet-smelling sandal trees.

[3] It is not possible to reproduce in translation the alliteration of the original. It suggests Southey's 'Lodore'.

ACT III

Then enter two River[-goddesses].

First [River-goddess]—Friend Muralā, why do you seem to be in a [great] flurry?

Muralā—Honoured Tamasā! I am sent by the exalted Agastya's wife—Lopāmudrā—to say unto the great river Godāvarī as follows: "You already know that ever since [Rāma] abandoned our daughter-in-law [Sītā]—

Through the imperturbable gravity [of his nature] carrying concealed within [himself] commotions of intense agony, like an iron-vessel-closed-and-boiling (*puṭapāka*) is the impassioned grief that Rāma is enduring. **1**

So that, born out of that misfortune which befell one that was so dear to him, his long-continued sorrow, now [wellnigh] coming to a climax, has made dear Rāma sadly pine away. As I look upon him my heart seems as if trembling to its [very] root! Now, furthermore, as dear Rāma has once again come here, he would certainly not fail to see these spots in the woodlands of the Pañchavaṭī that could speak to him (*sākshin*) of those unreserved endearments that he had had in the company of his wife. And in those [spots], firm by nature though he be, still—under such conditions—through the overwhelming emotions of a sorrow settled-and-profound, at every step, it is to be feared, would arise occasions for great mishaps. Do you, therefore, O exalted Godāvarī, be watchful about it:

With breezes borne over [your] waves and surcharged with cooling sprays and wafting along the perfumes of [your] lotus-filaments—every time dear Rāma sinks-under-his-grief (*mohe*)—do you [O Godāvarī] his senses revive, gently, gently fanning him." **2**

Tamasā—This assiduous-care is worthy indeed of the affection [Lopāmudrā bears for Rāma]; but for dear Rāma's revival, the only-natural-remedy-that-there-is (*maulika*), is here at hand to-day.

Muralā—How so?

Tamasā—Listen. You-may-not-perhaps-know (*kila*) that, after abandoning her in the outskirts of Vālmīki's penance-grove, when Lakshmaṇa went back, Queen Sītā—as travail came upon her—in the very vehemence of her pangs, threw herself into the stream of the Ganges; and then, even there, she was delivered of a pair of sons. She was then comforted by [her mother] Earth and the river Jāhnavī[1] [Ganges] and by them taken to the Nether regions. Then as the twins [grew of an age to be] weaned, them the Goddess [of the] Ganges handed over in person to the son of Varuṇa, to the great sage [Vālmīki].

Muralā, *with amazement*—

> Of such [as Rāma and Sītā] even an [adverse] turn [of fate] proves to be full of miracles, in that even persons [as exalted] as these [the Earth and the Bhāgīrathī] serve as instruments [to their ends]. **3**

Tamasā—And now, in consequence of this affair of Śambūka, [Bhāgīrathī] being led to anticipate, through the [river] Sarayū's[2] report, that Rāma would come hither to Janasthāna, and, what the exalted Lopāmudrā out of affection [for Rāma] apprehended, apprehensive of the same, the exalted Bhāgīrathī, in the company of Sītā and under pretext of some household rite or other, has come here on a visit to the Godāvarī.[3]

Muralā—This is a happy thought of the exalted [Bhāgīrathī]. For when indeed [he is] stationed in his capital and engrossed in all those activities conducive to the world's progress, it is possible to keep dear Rāma's mind away [from his grief[4]]; whereas [now] with nothing [else] to occupy [his thoughts] and face-to-face-with naught but his sorrow, this his revisiting of the Pañchavaṭī [will be] an unfailing source of mischief. But how—as-things-stand (*idānīm*)—is Queen Sītā going to comfort Rāma?

Tamasā—Thus spake [unto Sītā] the exalted Goddess Bhāgīrathī: "My child, thou that hast sprung from the [very] sacrificial ground of the Gods, Sītā! To-day, as-you-know (*khalu*), it being the twelfth birthday of the long-lived ones—of [our] Kuśa and Lava—for their ensuing prosperity (*abhivardhate*) we must tie the auspicious twelfth (*sañkhyā*) knot.[5] Therefore, unto thy ancient Father-in-law, the Progenitor of all this race of Royal sages beginning with Manu,[6] [I mean] unto the God Sun, the dispeller

[1] When Bhagīratha brought down the Ganges (cp. p. 21, note 6, above), the river in its course washed the sacrificial sheds of Jahnu, who in anger drank it all up. At Bhagīratha's intercession he let the river out again through his ears. Hence the name Jāhnavī.

[2] A tributary of the Ganges: Ayodhyā, Rāma's capital, is situated on it, and so the river knew what happened in that city.

[3] A physical fact, believed even now to occur at stated intervals: see Notes.

[4] Or, it is quite possible to keep dear Rāma's mind from running off [to the one subject that harrows him].

[5] A thread tied around the wrist or the arm, one knot being added each succeeding birthday.

[6] The seventh of his name, Son of the Sun, and founder of the Solar race of kings.

of all that is evil, do thou, with flowers collected by thy own hands, pay thy homage. And as thou wilt tread the surface of the earth—through my sure contrivance (*prabhāva*)—not even deities shall [be able to] see thee, still less mortals." [Likewise] thus was I commanded: "Tamasā, for you this daughter of Janaka, this [our] dear daughter-in-law, has already conceived a great affection; do you, therefore, yourself keep her company." Accordingly I am now going to do what I am bidden.

Muralā—And I for my part will [now] unto the exalted Lopāmudrā convey this news. Dear Rāma, I think, is just coming here.

Tamasā—And here is she, issuing from the deep basin of the Godāvarī—

With her face lovely even in the [very] paleness of its emaciated cheeks and with the braid of hair all dishevelled[1]—the very image of Pathos[2] or like Grief-of-separation incarnate: so unto the woodland goes this daughter of Janaka. **4**

Muralā—And this to-be-sure (*hi*) is she!

Her long and remorseless sorrow, parching up the flower of her heart, withers away her body [which is] like a tender sprout torn from its stalk, and all pale and emaciated—as does the autumnal heat the inmost petal of a *ketakī* flower. **5**

Both walk about and go out.

END OF INTERLUDE.

[**Voice,**] *behind the curtain*—O how unfortunate, how unfortunate!

Then enters Sītā busied in collecting flowers and listening with pathetic eagerness.

Sītā—Ha! I know it is my dear friend Vāsantī that is speaking.

[**Voice,**] *behind the curtain*—

That youngling of an elephant who was [fed] formerly by Queen Sītā with tender *śallakī* leaves gathered by her own hands, fed as he stood before her fond and expectant— **6 a, b**

Sītā—[And] what of him?

[**Same Voice,**] *behind the curtain once more*—

he, sporting in the water in the company of his mate, is busily engaged in combat by a mighty leader of another herd of tuskers, who has in wanton-pride (*darpa*) assailed him. **6 c, d**

[1] A woman in separation does not plait her hair.

[2] Here, as in several other places, the word Pathos is used in a technical sense. Pathos is one of the eight or nine or ten sentiments that, according to Hindu writers on Rhetoric, should pervade a poetic composition.

Sītā, *in flurry advancing a few steps*—To his succour, Noble my Lord, to the succour of my fondling! *Recollecting, and with dejection.* Alas, alas! Those same long-familiar words, at the sight of [this] Pañchavaṭī, come up to my lips—unhappy that I am! Alas, my noble Lord! *Swoons.*

Tamasā, *entering*—Look up! Courage, my child!

[**Voice,**] *behind the curtain*—[Stay,] thou best of aerial cars, stay right here!

Sītā, *recovering, with trepidations of joy*—Ha! Like a swollen rain-cloud's tremulous roar, deep and massive, whence now is this thrilling voice which, as it fills the hollows of my ears, quickly brings even me, the luckless one, back to life?

Tamasā, *with a tearful smile*—What now, my darling?

> At this sound, indistinct and coming thou knowest not whence, here art thou standing thus startled and eager—as might a pea-hen at a thundering cloud! 7

Sītā—'Indistinct'—does your ladyship say? [No.] By the tone of voice I do recognize that it is my noble Lord himself who is saying this.

Tamasā—It has [indeed] come to our ears that, for laying chastisement upon a Śūdra practising penance, the Royal descendant of Ikshvāku has come to Janasthāna.

Sītā—It is happy that [he] fails not in [the discharge of] his *kingly* duties—the King!

[**Voice,**] *behind the curtain*—

> Where trees no less than the deer were my comrades; where long in the company of my beloved I have stayed: here, along the margin of the Godāvarī, are those very same mountain-slopes with many a cave and waterfall. 8

Sītā, *observing*—Alas! How now? [Is this then,] like the orb of the moon at daybreak, wan and weak and wasted in his look, and only through his own proper mild and serene grandeur recognizable—is this then none other than my noble Lord? [Honoured Tamasā] lend me now your support. *Falls in Tamasā's arms, overwhelmed with emotion.*

Tamasā, *supporting [her]*—Take heart, my child, take heart!

[**Voice,**] *behind the curtain*—Through this sight of Pañchavaṭī—

> Of the fire of my grief [long] dormant within and now about to blaze forth wildly, this gloom is as it were the column of smoke that, as a precursor [of the coming fire], is now enveloping me. 9

Alas, my dearest! Thou daughter of Janaka!

Tamasā, *to herself*—This it was that the [kind] elders had also dreaded.

Sītā, *recovering herself*—Ha! How comes this?

[**Voice,**] *behind the curtain*—O Queen, dear companion of [my] residence in the Daṇḍakā forest! Thou daughter of the King of Videha!

Sītā—Alas, alas! Calling upon me—ill-starred that I am—and closing his blue eye-lotuses [my Lord] has really swooned! Look, how on the [bare] surface of the earth—all languid and helpless—he is lying outstretched! Quick, honoured Tamasā, run, run to the rescue: restore my noble Lord to life. *Falls at her feet.*

Tamasā—Do thou, rather, O blessed one, thyself restore the Lord of the world to life. The touch of thy hand carries bliss: on it rests all the burden. **10**

Sītā—Be it [then] as it will: As your ladyship commands.

Exit in great flurry.

Then enters[1] *Rāma stretched on the ground and touched by the sorrowing Sītā and reviving and full of joy.*

Sītā, *rather joyfully*—I think life seems to have again returned unto the [Lord of the] three worlds!

Rāma—Ha! What, in sooth, can this be?

Is it, perchance, an anointment of the juice [pressed out] of the [tender] *harichandana* leaves; or is it rather a sprinkling of [the essence] kneaded out of a sprout of moon-beams? Of the scorching fire of my life the all-allaying [balm], is it an extract from some life-giving herb poured upon my heart? **11**

A touch from of old familiar—certainly it is that same, giving life to my soul and [anon] overwhelming it with languor: It hath at once dispelled the gloom which came from my grief, but hath [also] thrown me once more into a lassitude of joy! **12**

Sītā, *withdrawing in excitement and sorrow*—Even this much now for me should more than suffice!

Rāma, *sitting up*—Surely it could not have been my Queen come, out of affection, to favour me?

Sītā—Alas, alas! Wherefore [now] should my noble Lord worry himself (*maggissadi*)[2] about me?

Rāma—Well: I [must] find out.

Sītā—Honoured Tamasā, let us depart. Should he see me, for thus approaching him without leave, the King will be ever so much more displeased with me.

[1] 'Is discovered' we should say in modern theatrical terms.

[2] Or, what opinion will he have (*mantissadi*) of me [if he should find me here, as he probably will]?

Tamasā—But don't-you-recollect (*ayi*), child, that, by virtue of Bhāgīrathī's sure-contrivance (*vara*), even unto deities thou hast become invisible?

Sītā—Ah, yes: so it is.

Rāma—Dear Jānakī! Why, I say, my dearest Jānakī!

Sītā, [*as if*] *choked with passion*—Noble my Lord! Inconsistent this really is with all that has happened! *With tears.* Or rather, wherefore, when I have [here] obtained, as if in another life, this sight of him that I should never have aspired to attain; [wherefore] at a time when towards one so ill-starred as I am, he is so brimful of affection and kind words: [wherefore,] hard as adamant though I be, should I against my noble Lord be so relentless? For, I know his heart, and he knows mine.

Rāma, *looking in all directions, with dejection*—Why! nobody here!

Sītā—Honoured Tamasā! Although the author of my causeless banishment, still, as I see him in this his plight, I know not what sort of emotions surge foremost (*anubandha*) in my heart.

Tamasā—I know it, child, I know it:

> Apathetic through despair and yet stirred with a sense for thy wrongs; in this long long separation as if forthwith ardent for reunion: gracious in thy [innate] goodness and filled to its depths with pity for thy dear Lord's piteous plight, and melting in affection—thus now, meseems (*iva*), all in a moment thy heart has become. **13**

Rāma—Queen!

> Like a favour incarnate, thy touch, cool and full of affection,—even now it bedews me with joy: but where art thou, thou my Joy? **14**

Sītā—These, in sooth, revealing the treasure (*sambhāra*) of an affection inward and unfathomed, [and] overflowing [me] with joy—these words of my noble Lord I have [once again] heard: [words] which, as I drink them in (*jāṇaṁ pachchaeṇa*) now—though the barb of my unmerited abandonment still rankles within [my heart]—they make me prize this my life [so] highly.

Rāma—No (*athavā*), it could not by any chance be my dearest. Verily, springing out of the perfection of his practised meditation [on her], this must be Rāma's illusion.[1]

[**Voice,**] *behind the curtain*—Oh, how unfortunate, how unfortunate!

> That youngling of an elephant who was [fed] formerly by Queen Sītā with tender *śallakī* leaves gathered by her own hands, fed as he stood before her fond and expectant— **15 a, b**

[1] I. e. thinking too intently upon an object you get a hallucination of the same.

Rāma, *with sympathetic eagerness*—Well, what of him?

[**Same Voice,**] *behind the curtain, once more*—

he, sporting in the water in the company of his mate, is busily engaged in combat by a mighty leader of another herd of tuskers, who has in wanton-pride (*darpa*) assailed him. **15 c, d**

Sītā—Who now will succour him?

Rāma—Where, where is that wicked [beast] that is assailing one who was as a son unto my dear wife—and that too while he is enjoying his mate's company? *Rises.*

Vāsantī, *entering, greatly agitated*—How! Is it the King, the joy of Raghu's race?

Sītā—Why! It *is* my dear friend, Vāsantī!

Vāsantī—Victory attend Your Majesty!

Rāma, *observing* [*her*]—Who! My Queen's dear friend, Vāsantī?

Vāsantī—Haste, Sire, haste: along this way, south of Jaṭāyu's peak, past [what they call] Sītā's Ford, do you descend down to Godāvarī's bank and honour [by your visit] the Queen's [foster-]son, [the elephant].

Sītā—Alas, father Jaṭāyu! Void without thee[1] [now must be] this Janasthāna!

Rāma—Alas! They really tear the [very] vitals of my heart—these familiar allusions!

Vāsantī—This, this way, Sire!

Sītā—Honoured [Tamasā]! And is it indeed true that even sylvan deities can't see me?[2]

Tamasā—Knowest thou not (*ayi*), darling, that superior by far to [that of] all other divinities is the power of the divine Mandākinī [Ganges]? Why dost thou fear then?

Sītā—In that case—let us go after [them].

[*Sītā and Tamasā*] *walk about.*

Rāma—My homage to thee, exalted Godāvarī!

Vāsantī, *observing*—Sire! Rejoice at the victory [gained] by the Queen's [foster-]son [that is there] in the company of his mate.

Rāma—May victory and long life attend him!

Sītā—Oh! And has he grown thus [big]!

Rāma—Queen! Here is something to be glad of—

With his tapering tusks, just sprouting and soft like fibres of lotus, [he] who used to pull, O fair-bodied one, the *lavalī* leaves

[1] See note 2, page 24, above.

[2] It is necessary to bear in mind that throughout this Act Sītā and Tamasā remain invisible to Rāma and Vāsantī. The poet himself draws our attention to this fact whenever we seem most near forgetting it.

that decked thy ears[1]—this [is he] that [foster-]son of thine, [now] a vanquisher of sturdy and rutting elephants, by whom, what in growing youth is a bliss, that[2] has already been achieved. **16**

Sītā—Only, unseparated from this his gentle-looking mate[3] may he for ever live!

Rāma—Look, friend Vāsantī, look! The youngster has even learnt—though only by half—the art of courting his mate's favour!—

When the bunches of lotus stalks, in frolic uprooted, had been [by her] bitten off, he transferred [unto his mate] trunkfuls of water perfumed with the blooming lotuses; then indeed a bath from the sprays of his trunk he gave her, but, when through with that, he has not, in his affection, [pulled out] a straight stalk of lotus, [leaf and all, and] held [it] as a sunshade over her. **17**

Sītā—Honoured Tamasā, thus now has this one grown up: but the other two—through all this [long] time—my Kuśa and Lava, I know not how [big] they have grown.

Tamasā—As this one here, so likewise those two [sons].

Sītā—Thus ill-starred am I that [I am condemned] not merely [to] an eternal separation from my noble Lord but even [to] a separation from my sons!

Tamasā—Thus Fate hath decreed.

Sītā—And why have I given birth unto sons [at all], if, of both of them, so [lovable] as they are, those unspotted lotus-like faces—with cheeks blooming by reason of their teeth, tender, white, and rather sparse—rippling with a laugh charming and musical—and [decked] with little locks plaited over their ears and forehead—if [their faces] my noble Lord has not kissed?

Tamasā—May it so happen by the favour of the Gods!

Sītā—Honoured Tamasā! Now, as I am fondly (*saṁ*) thinking of my sons, my bosom heaves and longs to suckle them; and, with their father[4] here by me, I feel as if—just for a moment—I were restored to my domestic felicity!

Tamasā—Needs this to be said? A child is the utmost perfection of the love [between man and wife]. It is the closest link that can hold them together:

As being the meeting-ground (*saṁśraya*) for the mother's and

[1] The young elephant was then only of a man's height.

[2] I. e. love and triumphant valour.

[3] A characteristic benediction!

[4] This mode of referring to the husband, says one of the commentators, indicates that the author was a Dravidian. The inference does not, however, hold.

the father's affection, in a child we [so to say] tie in a [common] knot of joy [the several strands of] their inmost hearts. **18**

Vāsantī—And this way, likewise, let Your Majesty turn his eye:

He, in the full intoxication [of his youth], has ended [with a flourish] his mirthful dance, this peacock, whose smooth and wavy feathers have [only] recently sprouted forth—here [he is now] with his expansive plumage [sitting,] like a jewelled coronet, on the top of this *kadamba* tree, [and] rejoicing in the company of his mate. **19**

Sītā, *in curiosity and with tears*—This is he!

Rāma—Rejoice, darling! [Ever] rejoice!

Sītā—So be it!

Rāma—At each of thy whirlings, [O peacock,] her eyes, rolling around[1] within the lids, had their charm enhanced by the skilful dancings of her tremulous eyebrows, as she, [my wife,] in the fondness of her heart (*mugdhayā*) taught thee to dance, keeping time by the clapping of her hands, delicate like a sprout—thus it is [O peacock] that I think on thee, as on a son, with a mind brimful of affection. **20**

Why! Even animals[2] remember (*anurudhyante*) old friendships!—

That *kadamba* tree, displaying just a sprinkling (*katipaya*) of flowers, which my dearest had once reared up;— **21 a, b**

Sītā, *observing, with tears*—Rightly [indeed] has my noble Lord recognized [the tree].

Rāma—[that *kadamba*,] this mountain-peacock remembers as having been [once] favourite to the Queen: hence it is that on it he is feeling merry. **21 c, d**

Vāsantī—Here, in the meantime, let Your Majesty take a seat:

This here, situated in the middle of the *kadalī* grove, [this] is that same slab of stone which did duty as a bed for you and your wife; and because, sitting here, Sītā would give frequent [morsels of] grass to the deer, therefore [those fondlings] refused [ever] to leave her [alone]! **22**

Rāma—This, I cannot [even] endure its sight [now].

Sits elsewhere, weeping.

Sītā—Friend Vāsantī! What hast thou achieved by showing this [place] to my noble Lord and to myself? Alas, alas! Here [now] is my noble Lord [ever] the same; here the same Pañchavaṭī grove; and here the

[1] To follow the circular movements of the dance.

[2] Cp. Jātaka, No. 156, story of the grateful elephant. [C. R. L.]

selfsame dear companion of mine—Vāsantī. Here [likewise] are these [mute] witnesses to our varied and confidential intercourse—these woodland spots on [the banks of] the Godāvarī: and these [again] are the very same deer and birds and trees—all esteemed by us like our own children. To me, however, though present before my [very] eyes, they are all—such is my fate—no better than non-existing! Such then are [some of] the vicissitudes of this world of mortals!

Vāsantī—Sītā, my friend! Dost thou not notice [thy] Rāma's condition?[1]

With his limbs lovely like the petals of a blue lotus, he [formerly] used to cause supreme delight to [thy] eyes; and, although thou couldst see him always and at will, he did [then] look new and ever newer to thee: But [now] here he is with his limbs all lifeless, overspread with pallor, and extremely (*pari*) enfeebled by grief; not without difficulty can he be recognized as the same, though he [to be sure] still continues to delight [our] sight. **23**

Sītā—I see it, my friend, I do see it.

Tamasā—Mayest thou, [my dear] daughter, see what is dear[2] to thee!

Sītā—Alas, [cruel] Fate! He without me and I without him—would any one [ever] have thought this possible? Let me therefore—just for a moment and through my tears—take a look at my noble and loving Lord, whom I, as if in a second birth,[3] am able [here] to behold.

Remains looking [*at him*].

Tamasā, *embracing* [*Sītā*], *with tears of affection*—

Floating in an overwhelming flood of tears both of joy and of sorrow and wide open in thy eagerness [to see him], thy eyes (*dṛishṭi*) seem as it were to bathe the Lord of thy heart in an overflow of affection—as [if by] a stream of milk, white and copious and charming. **24**

Vāsantī—Let trees, with flowers and fruits that drip with their [sweetest] juices, yield an offering [unto Rāma]—surcharged with the fragrance of full-blown lotuses, let breezes blow over the dales—let the [youthful and] full-throated birds pour forth their incessant melodies—for here, once more, unto this forest, has our Lord Rāma himself returned. **25**

Rāma—Come, dear Vāsantī! Won't you take a seat here?

[1] Vāsantī purposely assumes ignorance as to Sītā's fate.

[2] Either i. her husband's face or ii. a termination of her sorrows.

[3] It was in an earlier life, as it were, that I was his wife and he my Lord: so changed are our present relations.

Vāsantī, *seating herself, with tears*—My liege Lord! Is dear Lakshmaṇa doing well?

Rāma, *pretending not to hear*—

With water and wild-rice and grass—offered with her own lotus-like hands—these trees and birds and deer[1] that the daughter of the King of Mithilā[2] [once] used to feed: as I sight them [now] an indescribable emotion wells up within me; [an emotion] that, like an oozing [in some rock], must end (*yogya*) by breaking my heart [in twain]. **26**

Vāsantī—I was asking, My liege Lord, Is it all well with dear Lakshmaṇa?

Rāma, *to himself*—Ah! 'My liege Lord' [is] a mode of address devoid of cordiality and her inquiry referred to the son of Sumitrā [Lakshmaṇa] only; her voice [too was choked] with tears [and] faltered: so I fear she already knows the news about Sītā. *Aloud.* Ah, yes: Prince Lakshmaṇa is doing well. *Sobs.*

Vāsantī—Why, O King, why art thou [so, so] cruel?

Sītā—And what art *thou*, dear Vāsantī, when thou couldst reproach [him] thus? My noble Lord certainly deserves kind consideration from all—and particularly from *my* dear friend.

Vāsantī—"Thou [art] my life; thou art my second heart; thou the moon-light of my eyes: thou the [immortal] ambrosia to my body"—with these and hundreds of other endearments her simple-and-loving (*mugdhā*) soul thou didst beguile; and her now—alas! why utter the rest? **27** *Faints.*

Tamasā—Quite natural indeed that [thus] she should break off in her speech and faint away.

Rāma—Compose thyself, friend, compose thyself.

Vāsantī, *recovering*—Wherefore, then, has Your Majesty done this unworthy deed?

Sītā—Desist, dear Vāsantī, desist.

Rāma—Because the people would not put up with it.

Vāsantī—And why?

Rāma—They themselves know—I-know-not-what (*kimapi*).

Vāsantī—O thou hard-hearted one! Is it honour that you profess (*kila*) to hold dear? What dishonour I ask (*nanu*) is more dreadful than this? And what, in that forest, may have been the fate of that fawn-eyed one [your wife]? Alas! Tell me, My Lord, what *do* you think about it? **28**

Tamasā—After a [very] long time [indeed comes] this reproof!

[1] Respectively.

[2] Mithilā was the capital of King Janaka.

Sītā—Friend Vāsantī! 'Tis thou that art terrible—that art cruel, in that thou dost thus fan [his] flames.[1]

Tamasā—It is thy love [for thy Lord] that thus speaks—[thy love] and thy grief.

Rāma—Dear friend! What [else] *could* any one think about it?

She whose eyes were tremulous like those of a fawn, just a year old, [when it is] taken with fright, [and who was] languid with the quick and throbbing burden in her womb—her dear creeper-like form, [a form that was] as if the very quintessence (*mayī*) of moon-beams and [delicate] like a soft and lovely lotus—[her form] the flesh-eating Monsters must certainly have swallowed up. **29**

Sītā—I am still alive, dear my Lord, still alive!

Rāma—Alas, dearest! Thou daughter of Janaka, where art thou?[2]

Sītā—Alas, alas, that even my noble Lord, in the fullness of his heart, should cry aloud!

Tamasā—This, my child, is nothing but proper. Those in grief must [at times] give vent to their grief: For—

When put to a strain by the flood, for a tank, an overflow is the [only] remedy; so, when agitated by grief, the heart only through laments is restrained-from-breaking (*avadhāryate*). **30**

And especially for [our] dear Rāma this world of life has been full of unusually great and manifold troubles:

This entire world he has to protect assiduously and in [strict] conformity with the law; [then there is] this sorrow for his beloved, which withers, like heat, the flower of his life; having himself brought about [his wife's] abandonment, what relief there is in lamentations, even that is not easy for him: still he continues to draw his breath [in this world]—is not weeping then a real gain? **31**

Rāma—Oh, these torments!

My heart with its intense tumults [of grief] is near to bursting, but it [*will*] not break in twain; this shattered frame succumbs [again and again] to a swoon, but it [*will*] not part with consciousness; an inward anguish burns my body, but [*will*] not consume it to ashes: Fate strikes me down and pierces my vitals, but [*will*] not cut this life away! **32**

Sītā—So it is [even with me]!

Rāma—Ye my worthy citizens and subjects!

[1] Dost increase his sorrow. [2] See page 47, note 2, above.

When I indeed knew (*kila*) that you did not wish my Queen to stay in the house, her, like mere chaff, in that void wilderness, I abandoned, and not even so much as mourned! [But] these scenes long familiar [unto me]—[they] have to-day set my heart melting, so that in sheer helplessness—forgive me [my people]—I am here—weeping! **33**

Tamasā—Deep is the roar of this ocean of grief.

Vāsantī—My Lord! As matters that have been, it behoves you to endure [them] with courage.

Rāma—What is it you say, friend!—courage?

Since when this world was deprived of its Queen, this is the twelfth year: Even her very name seems to have vanished quite: and yet Rāma has *not* ceased to be! **34**

Sītā—These words of my noble Lord—by them I am beguiled [into forgetfulness of my own grief].

Tamasā—And no wonder, my child!

These words, brimful of affection [but withal] terrible by reason of grief—it is not an unmixed pleasure (*priyatama*) that they bring thee: they are streams of honey and poison a-dripping upon thee. **35**

Rāma—And [furthermore,] Vāsantī, have I not indeed—

[This dart that] like a glowing spear-head driven deep and athwart, or like a fang of venom—this pointed dart of grief [that rankles] within my heart [and] tears my vitals to pieces: [have I not then patiently] endured it? **36**

Sītā—Such is my hard lot that I am once more[1] a cause of trouble to my noble Lord.

Rāma—Although, therefore, [by an extreme effort] I have firmly restrained my mind, still to-day the sight of these various familiar scenes has thus overpowered me. For—

To stem the swelling commotions of this wild and tumultuous heart, every single effort that I somehow bring to bear upon it—all those [efforts], one after another, some mysterious impulse within breaks forcibly through, and gains ground for itself (*prasarati*), as would a torrent of water a dam of sand—[a torrent when] unchecked in its course. **37**

Sītā—This my noble Lord's outburst of grief [that is] growing (*ārambha*) more and more alarmingly irresistible, it has revived the [smouldering] grief of my own heart and makes it tremble [in agitation].

[1] The earlier occasion was when she was abducted by Rāvaṇa, and Rāma had to fight and win her back.

Vāsantī, *to herself*—To a piteous plight has His Majesty come; let me, therefore, create a diversion. *Aloud.* Will now Your Majesty [be pleased to] have a look at these [sights] long familiar [to him]—these spots in the Janasthāna?

Rāma—So be it. *Rises and walks about.*

Sītā—The very things that would inflame the sorrow, my dear friend [Vāsantī] conceives [them] as remedies to allay it!

Vāsantī, *with pathos*—Sire, Sire!

It was under this, this very bower of creepers that once you stood, your eyes watching [expectant] for her return; while she, attracted by the sight of the [sporting] swans, tarried a little longer [than usual] on the sands of the Godāvarī. But as she returned, observing your slight displeasure, at once did she fold, in tremor, her supplicant hands—[hands that were] graceful like a bud of [red] lotus! **38**

Sītā—Oh, cruel, cruel art thou, Vāsantī, in that with these thy efforts to drive the darts deeper and more firmly into the vitals of the heart, thou art again and again making my noble Lord remember me—ill-starred that I am!

Rāma—O thou ruthless one, thou daughter of Janaka! I seem to see thee here and there [and everywhere], and yet thou wouldst have no pity on me!

Alas, alas, O Queen! My heart is bursting asunder; the frame of my body is flying to pieces; all void seems [now] this world to me; an incessant flame [of anguish] from within, inflames me; immersed in utter darkness, this lonely soul within me seems to plunge down [in deep despair]: an all-overspreading stupor paralyses me—O miserable wretch that I am, what can I do? **39**

Faints.

Sītā—Alas, alas! Once again my noble Lord has fainted!

Vāsantī—Be comforted, Sire, be comforted.

Sītā—Alas, My noble Lord! That for the sake of me, the ill-starred one, thou on whose blessed life (*jammalābha*) rests the happiness of this entire living world, [that thou] shouldst be reduced to such a terrible plight and that thy very life should be in frequent danger!—Wretch, wretch that I am.

Faints.

Tamasā—Take heart, take heart, my child! Once again it is the touch of thy hand that is the only remedy for bringing dear Rāma to life.

Vāsantī—How now, he does not yet recover! Sītā, my dear friend! Where art thou, alas! Come and rescue this Lord of thy life.

Sītā in excitement approaches [Rāma] and touches his heart and forehead.

Vāsantī—Happily dear [1] Rāma has come to life again!

Rāma—[This touch,] as if anointing with ambrosial anointments, both within and without, all the tissues of my body—this touch that has [just] brought me to life—once again, it has, all of a sudden, produced, through joy, an infatuation in me—[only] of a different kind. **40**

With eyes still closed in joy. Friend Vāsantī! Here is a matter for rejoicing.

Vāsantī—And what may it be?

Rāma—What else, my friend? She has returned—the daughter of Janaka!

Vāsantī—Why, my dear Rāma, where is she?

Rāma, *enjoying the felicitous touch*—Look! Is not she just here in front?

Vāsantī—Wherefore, my dear (*ayi*), [wherefore,] with these frightful excesses of thy ravings that pierce the very vitals, dost thou again [and again] burn me [in anguish], ill-starred that I am, and already burnt up with [the sorrow consequent upon] the sufferings of my dear friend [Sītā]?

Sītā—I do wish to withdraw: but this my noble Lord's touch, gentle and cooling by reason of his enduring affection, has all of a sudden allayed even my long and cruel grief, and has held fast, as if with adamantine cement, [this] my moist and powerless hand, [causing it] to tremble in helplessness.

Rāma—No: not 'ravings', my friend!

That [hand,] begirt with bracelet, which formerly, at the time of marriage, I had held [in mine], and which, since then, through all that long time, had been familiar to me by its cooling and ambrosial touch—[touch] that was [once, alas!] mine for the asking— **41 a, b**

Sītā—Noble my Lord! Thou art [ever] the same—[then and] now!

Rāma—that same hand of hers, resembling a tender stalk of *lavalī* but most happily compared [only] with her own other hand—that hand here I have grasped. **41 c, d** *Seizes it.*

Sītā—Oh, fie! Carried away by my noble Lord's touch I have really committed a blunder!

Rāma—Friend Vāsantī! With my eyes (*indriya*) closed in [the ecstasy of my] joy and in my [present] excited state I am [no longer] master of myself: Do you therefore hold her likewise.

Vāsantī—Why! This is sheer madness!

[1] This is the first time in this Act that Vāsantī uses this familiar mode of address.

Sītā hastily snatches away [her hand] and stands aloof.

Rāma—Oh, fie! What a folly!

That hand of hers, [tender] like foliage and tremulous and perspiring [1]—[that hand], in my listlessness, I have all of a sudden let slip from my own hand, [no less] tremulous and perspiring! **42**

Sītā—Why, alas! Even yet—with his eyes [now] inert [and now] rolling unsteadily all about—he has not yet regained his composure!

Tamasā, *observing [Sītā], with affection*—

With a thrill of joy over her moist and tremulous body, my dear child [Sītā] has, at her dear Lord's touch, become like a branch of *kadamba*, blooming with buds as when washed by early showers and shaken by [gentle] breezes. **43**

Sītā, *to herself*—Why! For this loss of self-control I have really been put to shame by the honoured Tamasā! What indeed will she think [of me but this]?—Such [*was*] thy abandonment and such [*is*] thy [persistent] attachment!

Rāma, *looking all about [him]*—Alas! Is she then really not there? [2] Why, I say, thou pitiless daughter of the King of Videha!

Sītā—Pitiless I certainly must be, in that, seeing thee in this thy plight, I yet continue to live.

Rāma—Where then art thou, Queen? Take pity on me! Do not, I beg, abandon me in this plight!

Sītā—Why, noble my Lord! Quite otherwise stand the facts! [3]

Vāsantī—Please, Sire, with your own proper all-transcendent courage, do, I beg you, restrain-and-compose yourself; your self-deception has gone beyond all bounds. How, [how] could my dear friend [Sītā] have been here?

Rāma—Clearly then she is not here; otherwise how could even Vāsantī have failed to see her? Can this then have been a dream? But I was not dreaming; for, sleep has fled [long] away from Rāma! Undoubtedly then this must be that almighty Self-deception which was induced by my repeated meditations [upon her] and which persistently clings to me.

Sītā—'Tis I then, the ruthless one, that have caused his deception!

Vāsantī—Behold, Sire!

Broken to pieces by Jaṭāyus, here is the iron-chariot of the grandson of Pulastya [Rāvaṇa]. Behold these, in front [of the chariot], the bony remains of the goblin-faced donkeys.[4] Here on this side are the wings of Jaṭāyu clipped off by [Rāvaṇa's] sword.

[1] When the hands of lovers meet, perspiration at the finger-tips is one of the signs of their love—such is the poetic convention.

[2] Cp. page 47, note 2.

[3] It is you that have abandoned me.

[4] Yoked to Rāvaṇa's chariot.

From here the enemy [Rāvaṇa], lifting up Sītā all blazing [with ire], the enemy—even like a [black] rain-cloud gleaming (*antaḥ*) with the tremulous flashes of lightning—rose up into the sky. **44**

Sītā, *in alarm*—Noble my Lord! Our father [Jaṭāyu] is being killed—And he is carrying me too away! Save me!

Rāma, *swiftly rising*—You wretch, you robber of father [Jaṭāyu's] life Where will you escape?

Vāsantī—Why, King! You [are] the fire that has consumed the race of Demons: can there still exist any object for your [avenging] wrath?

Sītā—Forsooth! I came near losing [all] my wits!

Rāma—Much to the purpose indeed are these my [useless] rantings now!

Remedies being available, through the exploits of heroes it [that earlier separation] became [for them] a source of constant and engrossing occupation, and for the world a theme for its wondering admiration: such was my [earlier] separation from my fair-eyed [Sītā]; and it did indeed come to an end with the slaying of my enemy [Rāvaṇa]: but how am I to endure, all in silence, this [my present separation,] which has no remedies and knows no end? **45**

Sītā—Knows no end?—then alas for me!

Rāma—Woe and alas!

Where even my friendship with the mighty King of the Monkeys [Sugrīva] avails not—where [equally] unavailing is the valour of the Monkeys themselves as well as the talents of even a Jāmbavant[1]—where even the son of the Wind [Māruti] is denied access, and where even Nala,[2] the son of the Architect of the universe, is unable to construct a path—where even the arrows of the son of Sumitrā [Lakshmaṇa] cannot penetrate: in what region then [so inaccessible] art thou, my dearest? **46**

Sītā—So [a time has come when] I must prize more highly my earlier separation!

Rāma—Dear Vāsantī, nothing but grief can the sight of Rāma now bring to his friends. How long then must I keep you weeping? Permit me to go, therefore.

Sītā, *leaning upon Tamasā in agony and dejection*—Honoured Tamasā! [Look!] My noble Lord is going away!

Tamasā—Compose thyself, child, compose thyself. Let us then, likewise,

[1] Did signal service to Rāma first during the expedition in search of Sītā, and later in the war at Lankā.

[2] Constructed the bridge between India and Lankā (Ceylon).

repair to the exalted Bhāgīrathī and [there] perform the auspicious birthday (*varsha-vardhana*) rites of the long-lived ones, [our] Kuśa and Lava.

Sītā—Pray, honoured [Tamasā], permit me, just for a moment [longer], to see him [a sight of whom must be] so rare [hereafter].

Rāma—Furthermore, there is, to participate in the sacred rites of the horse-sacrifice,—

Sītā, *with trepidation*—Who, my noble Lord?

Rāma—A golden image of Sītā :—

Sītā, *with a sigh* [*of relief*]—Now art thou indeed he—my noble Lord! Ha! Now has my noble Lord plucked out [from my heart] that [rankling] dart of abandonment and disgrace!

Rāma—And with the sight of it [the image] I shall now for my tear-dimmed eyes seek solace.

Sītā—Blessed is that [image] which is so highly esteemed by my noble Lord and which, affording solace to my noble Lord, has become the stay for [all] the hopes of this living world!

Tamasā, *embracing* [*Sītā*] *with a sad and affectionate smile*—Don't you see, my child, that this amounts to praising thy own self?

Sītā, *looking down abashed, to herself*—I have brought honoured Tamasā's smile upon me!

Vāsantī—This your visit has indeed been a great favour for us. As for your going, be it so that no neglect of duty may ensue.

Sītā—This time [for once] Vāsantī is acting against my interests.

Tamasā—Come, child, let us go.

Sītā, *reluctantly*—We might—might do so.

Tamasā—Or rather, how canst thou move from hence, as long as, of thy eyes—

> As if riveted upon thy dear Lord and wide open in eagerness—[of thy eyes] the withdrawal [from their object] has not yet been completed—[a withdrawal] that is sure to (*para*) tear thy vitals? **47**

Sītā—Homage unto my noble Lord's lotus-feet, this sight of which some exceptional merit [of mine] has vouchsafed me. *Goes off in a swoon.*

Tamasā—Take comfort, my child! Be of good cheer.

Sītā, *recovering*—Yes: for, how long[1] may it be that amidst enveloping clouds one can win a glimpse of the full moon?

Tamasā—How marvellous has been the course of events![2]

[1] Not very long: so I must be content with this short visit.

[2] Or, the arrangement of incidents. The author is here doing the very thing for which, a while ago, he blamed Sītā: indirectly praising himself!

[All through] it is the one sole sentiment of Pathos that, by a diversity of causes [and attending circumstances], has become diverse and assumed distinct manifestations; just as water assumes eddies and bubbles and billows and other manifestations, whereas it is all [in reality] nothing but mere water. **48**

Rāma—This way, my best of aerial cars!

All rise.

Tamasā *and* **Vāsantī,** *to Sītā and Rāma [respectively]*—

May the Earth and the River of the Immortals [Ganges], together with those like us [1]—may the revered Preceptor [Vālmīki] who is the Father of metrical compositions—may also sage Vasishṭha along with Arundhatī: may [all] these bestow blessings upon you, conducive to your eternal welfare! **49**

Exeunt all.

END OF ACT III

CALLED

THE SHADOW.

[1] I. e. Rivers and sylvan deities respectively. Regarding this joint speech, see Notes.

ACT IV

Then enter two ascetic [boys].

First [boy]—Saudhātaki, just look at the beauty! of this hermitage of the exalted Vālmīki, wherein to-day, by reason of the arrival of a great crowd of guests, some elaborate preparations are on foot. For—

The scum of boiled rice (*nīvāra*) that was left over after his mate, [the doe]—that has just brought forth young—had partaken of it, [that scum,] warm and savoury, this deer from [our] penance-grove is [now] sipping to his heart's content. Slightly blended with the diffusing odour of boiled rice mixed with ghee, the fragrance of vegetables cooking, as well as of *karkandhū* fruit, is spreading everywhere. 1

Saudhātaki—Welcome, special welcome unto these harbingers of holiday—unto these [reverend] grey-beards!

First [boy], *with a laugh*—Extraordinary indeed, O Saudhātaki, is the motive that inspires this your reverence for the *gurus*!

Saudhātaki—I say, Bhāṇḍāyana, what now is the name of the chief leader of this huge train of females—of this guest that has come?

Bhāṇḍāyana—Fie! No joking here! For, don't you see it is the exalted Vasishṭha come from Ṛishyaśriñga's hermitage, escorting the [late] King Daśaratha's wives who have come hither following the lead of Arundhatī? Why do you then talk this foolish way?

Saudhātaki—Indeed! Vasishṭha?

Bhāṇḍāyana—Why, yes.

Saudhātaki—I for my part thought that he was a tiger, maybe a wolf!

Bhāṇḍāyana—What! what is it that you say?

Saudhātaki—Why, hardly had he come when that poor dear heifer of ours he gobbled up with a swoop!

Bhāṇḍāyana—Out of deference to the Scriptures that prescribe meat as a part of the welcome-offering (*madhuparka*), upon the arrival of a learned Brahman [pious] householders offer him either a heifer or a bull or a goat. And this same practice the authors of the Dharma-sūtras also enjoin.

Saudhātaki—There now, I have caught you!

Bhāṇḍāyana—How, pray?

Saudhātaki—For, when the holy Vasishṭha comes the heifer is slain; whereas on the arrival, later this very day, of the royal sage Janaka, even the exalted Vālmīki makes his welcome-offering merely with curds and honey: the heifer is let off.

Bhāṇḍāyana—The former (*evaṁ*) ritual is laid down by the sages for those who have not abjured meat; whereas venerable Janaka *has* abjured meat.

Saudhātaki—And why?

Bhāṇḍāyana—Because as soon as he heard of that adverse turn which Queen Sītā's fate had taken, he took up the life of an anchorite. And so it is now some years since he has been practising penance in the penance-grove [called] Chandra-dvīpa.[1]

Saudhātaki—If so, why has he come here?

Bhāṇḍāyana—Merely to see the [exalted] son of Varuṇa, [Vālmīki,] his old and intimate friend.

Saudhātaki—Has he then to-day met his relatives, or has he not?

Bhāṇḍāyana—It is only just now that the exalted Vasishṭha sent the exalted Arundhatī unto the Queen[-mother] Kausalyā, bidding her to go in person and meet the King of Videha [Janaka].

Saudhātaki—As these old folks have congregated together, so likewise let us band our comrades together and—as is meet (*sambhāvemha*)—play in celebration of this [great] holiday.

They walk about.

Bhāṇḍāyana—And this here is that discourser in Brahma, that ancient royal sage, King Janaka, who, having paid his honours to Vālmīki and Vasishṭha, is now reposing under the shade (*mūla*) of this tree outside the hermitage: he who—

> With Sītā's sorrow ever preying upon his heart, is burning [within himself]; like unto an ancient tree invaded by some inwardly-consuming fire. 2

Both go out.

END OF INTERLUDE.

Then enters Janaka.

Janaka—Kept alive (*vishakta*) by that great and intense and agonizing,

> by that heart-rending calamity that fell upon my child [Sītā], this my acute and incessantly flowing grief that grides my vitals like a saw, even with this lapse of time it ceases not, as if it were a recent [grief]! 3

Oh, woful luck, that while age and this overwhelming sorrow, and

[1] Lit. Moon-island.

furthermore, the [severe] penances of *parāka*,[1] *sāntapana*,[2] and so forth—while all these are using up its substance and humours, this accursed body of mine, bereft of its staying [tissues], even now it refuses to fall! Those are the so-called Sunless regions enveloped in blind darkness; [and they,] say the sages, are assigned [after death] unto the men who slay themselves.[3] Even after the lapse of so many years, these transports of a grief that is as poignant as though it were fresh, and that, through my continual broodings over it, is steadily gaining in vividness—[these transports] know no abating. Alas, alas! O thou that didst spring from the [very] altar of the [holy] sacrifice, my Sītā, such has come to be the lot of thy life that, for very shame, I cannot even cry aloud at will. Alas, alas, [my] daughter!—

> I remember—when thou wast yet a child—that little lotus-like mouth with its capricious cryings and laughings, [that mouth] blooming with the tips of a few tender and bud-like teeth, and stammering over thy sweet and thoughtless prattle. **4**

Exalted Earth! Thou certainly art excessively hard:

> Thou and Fire and the Sages—[sage] Vasishṭha's wife [Arundhatī] and the [holy] Ganges—when ye all and when even the great *guru* of Raghu's family, the divine Sun himself, knew her greatness; when, as the [sacred] Word unto Learning, thou unto her didst thyself give birth, and who was no less divine than [Learning herself]: Of such a daughter wherefore then didst thou, O ruthless one, permit that outrageous death[4] (*viśasana*)? **5**

[**Voice**,] *behind the curtain*—This way, your exalted Ladyship—This way, my great Queen!

Janaka, *looking*—Oh, it is Gṛishṭi, showing the way to the exalted Arundhatī. *Rising.* But whom now does he style great Queen? *Observing.* Alas! Is she then no other than the wedded wife of the great King Daśaratha—Kausalyā, my dear friend? Who indeed can believe that she is the same?

> In Daśaratha's house she was like the Goddess of Wealth: or rather, why say *like*? She was the Goddess of Wealth *herself*. But woe and alas! Now, following the decree of Fate, she has become like some strange and unfamiliar being, all made up of grief: Alas for the outcome! **6**

[1] A twelve-days' fast.

[2] A modified form of fast in which only one variety of food—milk, curds, ghee, and so forth—is eaten every day.

[3] Or, in Shakespeare's words—'O . . . that the Everlasting had not fix'd His canon 'gainst self-slaughter!'

[4] Nearly every one thinks that Sītā is dead. So Janaka here, and so Rāma at iii. 34.

Here is another unhappy reversal of circumstances:

> That very same person [Kausalyā] that, formerly, was unto me like an embodiment of festal joy, the sight of her has now become unendurable, like brine upon an [open] wound! 7

Then enter Arundhatī and Kausalyā and a chamberlain [*Gṛishṭi*].

Arundhatī—Why, I say, aren't you directed by your family preceptor [Vasishṭha] to go in person and see the King of Videha? It was for this too that I am sent. What means then, at each step, this your extreme lack of determination?

Chamberlain—Queen, compose yourself, I beg you, and follow the direction of the exalted Vasishṭha.

Kausalyā—That in times like these I should have to see the Lord of Mithilā [Janaka]—this makes my griefs well up all at once within me: I am powerless to hold together my heart the roots of which are as if loosening from their bonds.

Arundhatī—This, no doubt, is quite natural:

> Although never [quite] ceasing to flow entirely, the sorrows of men, caused by separations from dearest relatives, become, at the sight of some very dear friend, altogether unendurable and as if in thousands of floods they seem to gush forth. 8

Kausalyā—And how may we—when my dear daughter-in-law [Sītā] has fared thus—[how may we] look upon the face of her father, the royal sage?

Arundhatī—And here he is, your noble connexion and the sustainer of the family of the Janakas—he whom sage Yājñavalkya has initiated into[1] the knowledge of Brahma. 9

Kausalyā—And this is he who was a delight to the heart of my great King [Daśaratha]—the father of my dear daughter-in-law [Sītā]—the royal sage. Ha! I am put in mind of those times when every day brought forth many an unbidden festivity. Alas, O Fate, that it should be no more!

Janaka, *approaching*—Exalted Arundhatī! This is Vaideha, the Sīradhvaja,[2] making homage unto you.

> In your company [your husband] regards himself as [more] holy, although he is himself the store of holy light—your husband who, of all the *gurus* of yore, is indeed the supreme *guru*; with my head bowing low down to the earth I salute you, the exalted one, who for the universe (*trilokī*) are the [very] fountain of its bliss

[1] Literally, to whom he has taught or solemnly set forth (*jagau*) the knowledge, as in the Bṛihadāraṇyaka Upanishad.

[2] Literally, one whose banner has the plough as an emblem.

(*māṅgalyā*), and who are, like the divine Dawn, adorable to the world. 10

Arundhatī—May the Light Supreme shine within thee! And may He also spread His holiness over thee (*punātu*), the Orb divine (*deva*) that blazes from beyond darkness [and dispels it]!

Janaka—Worthy Gṛishṭi, is it all well with this mother of that—that Shepherd of the people?[1]

Chamberlain, *aside*—Surely, he has reproved us quite bitterly. *Aloud.* Royal sage! When, taking offence at this very thing, the Queen [Kausalyā] has for so long a time declined the very sight of the moon-like face of her dear [son] Rāma, it is unkind of you to add to the grief of her who is already so much grieved. And as to our dear Rāma, it was a peculiar stroke of his misfortune that his subjects should, as is well known (*kila*), set agoing all around that foul calumny. And it was because those little minds disbelieved the Fire-ordeal that he did that cruel deed.

Janaka—What! And who is this Fire that he should essay to purify *our* daughter? Alas! Insulted as we already are by Rāmabhadra, here is a fresh insult, when people begin to talk like that!

Arundhatī, *heaving a sigh*—Exactly so. To talk of fire—fire! in connexion with Sītā is highly derogatory. Say merely 'Sītā' and all is said. Alas, my dear girl,—

> Thou art unto me a child, a pupil: be that as it may, the eminence of thy virtue compels my devotion for thee. Let alone the fact that thou art a child or a woman, thou art nevertheless adorable to the worlds: for, it is virtue—amongst those that are virtuous—that has a claim for respect, and *not* mere sex or age. 11

Kausalyā—Oh, I am bursting with my agonies! *Faints.*

Janaka—Alas! What is this?

Arundhatī—What else can it be, my Royal sage?

> That King [Daśaratha]—that bliss—those dear children—those [old] days—all this has flashed upon her memory at the sight of thee, her friend. And so, in her present dreadful plight, don't you see that this thy dear friend has really fainted? For, the hearts of matrons are tender like a flower. 12

Janaka—Alas, alas! I have proved altogether too cruel here, in that I see with rather unkindly eyes her whom I have met after such a long time, this dear wife of my dear friend [Daśaratha].

> A worthy connexion was he, a friend after my heart, my very heart in fact; he was an embodiment of joy to me, he was the

[1] Said in bitter irony.

whole purpose of my existence: my body, my soul, my whatever-else-dearer-than-these-there-may-be—was there anything that that great and illustrious King Daśaratha was not to me? **13**

And is this, alas, that same Kausalyā?—

Between her and her Lord, in [the confidence of] privacy, whatever occasion of displeasure there arose, it was to me that the husband and the wife severally communicated their complaints; and then, whether it was a case for forbearance or for anger, the issue rested entirely with me. Away rather with these memories that assail and consume my heart! **14**

Arundhatī—Alas, alas! With this long suspension of breath her heart has [almost] ceased to beat!

Janaka—Alas, my dear friend! *Sprinkles [her] with water from his kamaṇḍalu.*[1]

Chamberlain—Having at first, like a delightful bosom-friend, manifested unalloyed favours, Fate, terrible in the suddenness of its reverses, is next intensifying [by contrast] the anguish of the heart. **15**

Kausalyā, *regaining consciousness*—Alas my child, Jānakī, where art thou? I [still] remember thy face all suffused with the glory imparted to it by thy [recent] marriage sacraments, [thy face] with that pure smile playing upon it, and charming like a [full-blown] lotus. With limbs fair as the light of the shining moon, once more, my darling, do thou grace my lap. The great King [Daśaratha] would always say: "Of the mightier ancestors of the race of Raghu she may be a daughter-in-law; to us, however—such is our friendship for Janaka—she is just 'little daughter' [no more, but no less]."

Chamberlain—It was, just as the Queen has said:

Although the King [Daśaratha] had five children, it was [Rāma] the enemy of Subāhu[2] that was specially dear to him. So likewise, among his four daughters-in-law, Sītā was as much adored by him as was his own daughter, Śāntā. **16**

Janaka—Oh, my dear friend, thou great King, Daśaratha! So indeed thou art, in every way a delight to the heart: How canst thou be forgotten?

It is customary (*kila*) for the parents of the bride to pay court to the kinsfolk of the son-in-law; but with our connexion [through the marriage of Rāma and Sītā] all was reversed: it was me that thou wast assiduous to please! Such as thou hast been, Time

[1] An ascetic's gourd.

[2] A demon who molested Viśvāmitra's sacrifice, and who was killed by Rāma.

has snatched thee away, as also that cause of our connexion [Sītā]. Now in this world of life, in this dreary hell, accursed be the continuance of me, the sinful! **17**

Kausalyā—Dear Jānakī, what *can* I do? Fastened firm [to my body] with a hard and adamantine cement, this wretched life *will* not leave me, ill-fated that I am!

Arundhatī—Take heart, thou who art sprung from kings! It is at least necessary to allow your tears rest from time to time. And don't you further recall what, in Ṛishyaśṛiñga's hermitage, your family-preceptor[1] [Vasishṭha] said?—'That it was to be so, we had already divined; but it will all have a prosperous issue.'

Kausalyā—How [can that be] when I have already outlived my wishes?

Arundhatī—Do you then, O daughter of kings, regard that as an untruthful utterance? You must not, O noble Princess, think it false: it *must* come about.

The utterances of those Brahmans to whom has been revealed the Light [celestial]—let there be no doubt about them. For, upon their speech awaits the beneficent Lakshmī;[2] they never utter words that do not come true. **18**

A [confused] noise[3] *behind the curtain: all listen.*

Janaka—To-day being a holiday [in honour] of [distinguished] guests, it is the boys at sport that are raising this noise.

Kausalyā—It is very easy indeed, in childhood, to find joys! *Observing.* Aha! Who now is this [boy] in the midst of these [others]—he with his form (*añga*) supple and handsome and well-proportioned, and endowed with the grace of [our] dear Rāma: who is he that so delights even our sight?

Arundhatī, *Aside, with joyful tears*—This then must be the thing that Bhāgīrathī related to me: the secret that was as a nectar to my ears. We do not yet know, though, which of the two long-lived ones—Kuśa and Lava—he may be.

Janaka—Like a blue lotus-leaf dark and mellow [in complexion], marked with the round tufted locks [of a Kshatriya], and by his guileless charms adorning, as with an innate-grace, the circle of his school-mates—the sight of him all of a sudden gives an ambrosial collyrium to my eyes, as if [he were] that Joy of the [race of the] Raghus, my darling [Rāma] himself, become once again a child! Who may he be? **19**

[1] It is not usual for a wife to call her husband by his name. Cp. p. 63, l. 6, above.

[2] Goddess of wealth and prosperity.

[3] As if in confirmation of iv. 18.

Chamberlain—I think the youth must certainly be a Kshatriya student.

Janaka—Assuredly: for, he carries

> Upon his back, one on each side (*abhitas*), a pair of quivers, the heron-feathered [arrows] of which kiss his crest; his chest, bearing [yet] the ample marks of the holy ashes, is clad in the hide of a *ruru*-deer; a girdle of the *mūrvā*-grass holds together his madder-dyed lower garment; in his hand he has a rosary of *rudrākshas* and a bow, as well as another staff made of *pippala*. **20**

Exalted Arundhatī, what do you surmise? Whence is he?

Arundhatī—It is only to-day that we have come.

Janaka—Worthy Gṛishṭi, I have an intense curiosity; do you therefore go right to the exalted Vālmīki and inquire. Unto this child, likewise, say, 'Here are some old people desirous of seeing thee.'

Chamberlain—As you command. *Exit.*

Kausalyā—What do you think? Thus addressed, will he come?

Arundhatī—Can proper conduct be lacking in one whose form is so graceful?

Kausalyā—Lo! Having respectfully listened to Gṛishṭi's speech hasn't he dismissed the ascetic youths and isn't the dear lad in fact approaching hither?

Janaka, *observing him long and attentively*—Ah, how extraordinary all this!

> This his perfect nobleness [of mien], charming in its modest and youthful simplicity—[this perfection] which only the connoisseurs can comprehend but which passes the wits of the vulgar—it forcibly carries away my mind although [naturally] proof against such transports (*sammoha*), as would a tiny piece of magnet a mass of iron. **21**

Lava, *entering*—Ignorant as I am of their names and order of precedence and lineage, and so not knowing what propriety demands, how am I going to salute these people, worthy of a salutation though they undoubtedly are? *Reflecting.* This, however, the ancients have declared to be an unobjectionable mode [of address]. *Approaching them with modesty.* This is Lava, bowing his head unto you all in due succession.

Arundhatī *and* **Janaka**—Mayest thou live long, O blessed one!

Kausalyā—Long life, my darling!

Arundhatī—Come, dear! *Taking Lava in her lap, aside.* O bliss! Not only my lap but my life's desire also has been filled!

Kausalyā—Come to me also, a while, my darling! *Taking him in her lap.*

How strange! Not only in the build of his body, which is dark and resplendent like a half-opened blue lotus—nor again only in his voice, that has the prolonged resonance of the sonorous notes of a swan whose throat is mellowed (*kasāa*) by feeding on lotus filaments—does he take after our dear Rāma; even the very touch of his body, smooth like the interior of a full-grown lotus, has the same quality. Let me look at thy face a while, my darling! *Raises his chin and observes him closely; then with tears and as-if-trying-to-divine-some-hidden-secret* (*sākūtam*). And don't you also mark it, Royal sage? Narrowly observed, does he not [also] show resemblance to the moon-like face of [Sītā] my dear daughter-in-law?

Janaka—I mark it, friend, I mark it.

Kausalyā—Forsooth! My heart, as if in madness, dreams of things impossible, and wanders far, far astray!

Janaka—In this boy here is plainly visible [the contour] of my daughter as well as of [Rāma,] that eminent scion of Raghu: it is as if all perfectly mirrored in him—that very same form, that grandeur, that voice, that inborn modesty, and even that selfsame divine lustre. Alas, alas, Fate! Wherefore is it that my mind should now run waywardly into devious paths? **22**

Kausalyā—Darling, Hast thou a mother? Dost thou remember thy father?

Lava—No.

Kausalyā—Whose [son] art thou then?

Lava—The exalted Vālmīki's.

Kausalyā—Why, my darling! Say that [at least] which may be said.[1]

Lava—This is all I know.

[**Voice,**] *behind the curtain*—Hey ho, soldiers! This is what Prince Chandraketu commands: 'Let no one trespass on the ground sacred to (*abhyarṇa*) the hermitage!'

Arundhatī *and* **Janaka**—Ah! Following—as its guard—the track of the sacrificial horse, it is dear Chandraketu that we shall see to-day—What a happy day this!

Kausalyā—'The son of our dear Lakshmaṇa commands'—these words that I hear are [indeed] sweet like drops of nectar!

Lava—Noble Sir, who is he—this Chandraketu?

Janaka—Knowest thou Rāma and Lakshmaṇa, the sons of Daśaratha?

Lava—The same that are the heroes of the Rāmāyaṇa?

Janaka—The same.

Lava—Why, then of course I know them.

[1] Vālmīki, of course, never married.

Janaka—Of that Lakshmaṇa this Chandraketu is the son.

Lava—He is then the son of Ūrmilā, and a daughter's-son of the royal sage Janaka?

Arundhatī, *smiling*—Thou hast indeed evidenced thy thorough acquaintance with the story!

Janaka—If then thou dost claim to be so conversant with the story, let us put thee some questions: Tell us, first, how many children do the sons of Daśaratha have, how are they named, and of what [mothers] are they born?

Lava—This portion of the story, to this day, has never been heard either by us or by any one else.

Janaka—Is it that it has not been composed by the poet?

Lava—Has been composed, but not published. And a certain section from the same has been turned into a distinct type of work, full of sentiment, and adapted to dramatic representation. And that, written in his own hand, the exalted sage [Vālmīki] has sent over to sage Bharata, the author of the Aphorisms of Dramaturgy.[1]

Janaka—To what end?

Lava—That holy sage [Bharata], they say, is going to have it enacted by the heavenly nymphs.

Janaka—All this is, to us, extremely tantalizing!

Lava—Great, however, has been the care that the exalted Vālmīki bestowed upon it. For, to prevent [possible] mishap, he has sent our brother, bow in hand, as an escort of those of his pupils by whose hands he sent [the work] to the hermitage of Bharata.

Kausalyā—So, thou hast also a brother?

Lava—Yes: the noble Kuśa.

Kausalyā—Implying [by thy manner of mention] an elder brother?

Lava—Even so: the order of birth has—as is right (*kila*)—given him the seniority.

Janaka—You—my long-lived ones—are you then twins?

Lava—Exactly.

Janaka—Tell me, how does the [published] part of the story end?

Lava—Harassed by false rumours current among his subjects, the King [Rāma] banished Queen Sītā, born [though she was] from the [very]

[1] Literally, Author of the science of dancing and vocal and instrumental music—all the three being the elements of a drama. The original Aphorisms have not survived. The extant 'Nāṭya-śāstra' is probably a later digest, bearing to the original Aphorisms the same relation that the 'Kāmandakīya Nīti-śāstra' has to the newly discovered 'Kauṭilīya Artha-śāstra'.

sacrificial ground of the Gods. Her, nearing her travail, Lakshmaṇa abandoned all alone in the forest and returned [to Ayodhyā].

Kausalyā—Alas, my child! Thou whose face was lovable like the moon! In that forlorn plight, of what sudden and malignant sports of Fate has the flower of thy body been the victim?

Janaka—Alas, my daughter!

Assuredly, when that indignity fell upon thee, and the terrors of the wilderness, and the pains at the hour of childbirth; when on all sides troops of flesh-eating [Monsters] thronged about thee; then, stricken with terror, more than once must thy mind have turned to me as thy [natural] protector! **23**

Lava, *to Arundhatī*—Pray, Madam, who are these?

Arundhatī—This is Kausalyā, and this is Janaka.

Lava looks at them with sorrow, respect, and curiosity.

Janaka—Oh, the impudence of these citizens! Oh, the precipitancy of King Rāma's actions!

When over this dreaded fall of a thunderbolt in the form of this dire calamity I sit for ever brooding, is it not time [yet, I ask,] for my wrath to kindle-and-blaze forth with arrow or with curse? **24 a, b**

Kausalyā, *in fear*—Help, exalted [Arundhatī], help: Appease this angry royal sage.

Arundhatī—When high-souled persons are treated with indignity, this [viz. being victims to their wrath] is the natural expiation [of that offence]. [Janaka,] my King, Rāma is as a son to thee; and the subjects, contemptible though they be, have to be protected. **25**

Janaka—Peace then! Let neither [arrow nor curse] be used upon [Rāma] that scion of Raghu; for he is the treasure of a son unto me: And as to the subjects, they are for the most part a mere assemblage of Brahmans, of infants and of dotards, of decrepits and of females! **24 c, d**

Enter some excited boys.

Boys—Prince, O Prince! A strange species of animal—a horse, a horse—as the country-folks call it—why, we have just now seen one with our own eyes!

Lava—[A horse?] A horse is mentioned in that catalogue of beasts and in the treatises on warfare. Say, what is he like?

Boys—Listen:

Behind he carries a flowing tail, and this he's waving all the time.
He has a long neck, and hoofs he has—just four. Grass he eats,

and he drops lumps of dung, big as a mango. But why so much talk? He's on the move and will soon be far. Come, come, let us follow. **26**

They approach him and pull him by his hands and his garment.

Lava, *with mingled feelings of curiosity, constraint, and respect*—Behold, noble ones! Here am I being dragged [off from your presence] by these boys! *Moves about hastily.*

Arundhatī *and* **Janaka**—Thou mayest satisfy thy curiosity, child!

Kausalyā—Exalted [Arundhatī], I seem as if robbed [of something], now that he is out of sight. Let us then move from here and see the long-lived one, where he is going.

Arundhatī—That nimble child, with his very swift pace, has already shot far ahead: how is it possible to see him now?

Chamberlain, *entering*—The exalted Vālmīki replies, 'This matter, in good time, you will come to know.'

Janaka—It must then be something very mysterious! Exalted Arundhatī, friend Kausalyā, worthy Gṛishṭi, come, let us go in person and see the exalted son of Varuṇa [Vālmīki].

Exeunt older people.

Boys—Let the Prince now look upon this wonder.

Lava—Yes, I see it—understand it too. He is evidently a sacrificial horse.

Boys—How dost thou know?

Lava—Why, fools! Have you not also studied that section? Don't you know, 'There are cuirassiers, mace-bearers, and bow-men, numbering a hundred of each sort, to form the escort'? And this force here appears to answer the description. If you don't believe me—just ask.

Boys—Ho, Sirs! Tell us: Why [in the world] is this horse turned loose and [yet] guarded?

Lava, *enviously, to himself*—A horse-sacrifice is, for the world-conquering Kshatriyas, the great and glorious touchstone of their pre-eminence, calculated to abash all [opposing] warriors.

[Voice,] *behind the curtain*—

This horse here—he is as the banner or as the proclamation of the valour [of Rāma,] of that one supreme hero of the seven worlds, the foe unto the race of that ten-necked [Rāvaṇa]. **27**

Lava, *as if in wounded* [*pride*]—Oh, how they inflame my wrath—these words!

Boys—There is no use talking—the Prince *does* know.

Lava—Sirs! Is it because [you think] there is no Kshatriya in this world that you are proclaiming in this fashion?

[**Voice,**] *behind the curtain*—Fellow! To compare with our great King [Rāma] there *are* not any Kshatriyas.

Lava—Fie upon you, villains!

If they [your masters] are [great, as you say,] let them be. What need, however, of this your scarecrow [of a proclamation]? But, why waste words thus? Here am I now, seizing by force your 'banner' as you call it. **28**

Here, Boys! Hem [this horse] in, throw clods at him and compel him to turn back: Let the poor creature, for once, graze amongst the roebucks!

A Soldier, *entering, angry and overbearing*—Tush, rash boy! what didst thou say? Don't forget (*hi*) that these files of doughty and ruthless warriors brook not even a mere child's insolent words. And the Royal Prince Chandraketu, who knows how to chastise an enemy, is [away now], being attracted by a desire to see these mild and unfamiliar forests; but before he returns, do ye, and quickly, slip away through this shady thicket.

Boys—Have done with this horse, Prince! For, these columns of warriors with their flashing weapons seem to threaten thee! And our hermitage is far from here. Come then: let us flee with the bounding speed of deer.

Lava, *with a laugh*—So the weapons, you say, are really flashing, are they? *Stringing his bow:*

Then, [let this my bow] with its string lapping—like a tongue—the tapering, tooth-like bow-tips—[this bow] the sound of the twang of which is, like a belching, terrific and grim: [my bow,] imitating the yawns of the jaws in the cavernous mouth of Death as when He grins ready to swallow [the world]—let my bow now open its gaping maw! **29**

All walk about, as suits the occasion,[1] *and go out.*

[1] This would mean that Lava fights the soldier and drives him off the stage, himself in pursuit.

END OF ACT IV

CALLED

KAUSALYĀ AND JANAKA.

ACT V

[Voice,] *behind the curtain*—Ho, ho! Soldiers! 'Tis come, 'tis come—our succour!

For here he is in his chariot, Sumantra in haste urging forward its fleet and galloping steeds—its flagstaff of *kovidāra* violently shaken at each jolting—here is our Chandraketu coming hither upon the news of our fighting. **1**

Then enters in a chariot, with the charioteer Sumantra, Chandraketu, bow in hand and full of wild joy and excitement.

Chandraketu—Look, worthy Sumantra, look!

His handsome face flushed with just a tinge of glowing anger—the bow incessantly twanging at the tips—the five locks [on his head] all floating [to the winds], there, as he takes his stand in the van of the battle and rains a shower of arrows upon the battalions,—he is indeed a marvel (*kopi*), this son of a hero! **2**

How strange!

This lad from the hermitage, all alone, and scattering everywhere upon [my] army thousands of blazing shafts, impelled with a terrific twang and piercing the joints of the elephants' temples: He engages my interest as though he were some new, unknown scion of the race of Raghu. **3**

Sumantra—Long-lived one,—

As I look upon this boy who in his prowess excels Gods and Demons and who is so like [unto Rāma] in form, I am reminded of that Joy of the Raghus [our Rāma], when, bow in hand, he subdued the foes that disturbed the holy sacrifice of Kuśika's son [Viśvāmitra]. **4**

Chandraketu—That so many should exert themselves against him singly—for this I feel ashamed in my heart:

On one side is this solitary stripling; and here are [on the other] our forces clutching with their martial fingers these dense files of weapons and brandishing them wildly in the brunt of the battle—[some seated] in chariots ringing with the jingle of the tinkling golden bells, and [others mounted] upon rutting tuskers, pouring down, like clouds, actual torrents of ichor—all [arrayed on the other side and trying to] overwhelm him! 5

Sumantra—Prince, all of these, united, cannot possibly hold against him: much less, disunited!

Chandraketu—Make haste, worthy [Sumantra], make haste! For, this fellow here has commenced a great havoc amongst those whom I must shield—[our soldiery]. For,

As he sets his bow resounding, its twang, amplified by the stunning din of the war-drums, causes a furious aching in the ears of herds of elephants roaring even in the [distant] mountain recesses; and as he sends down rolling [or] hacks to pieces these countless heads, hideous to behold, the hero makes these grounds seem as if strewn over with morsels [of food] ejected by the terrific mouth of satiated Death! 6

Sumantra, *to himself*—How can I permit dear Chandraketu to engage in single combat with such [a fighter as this boy]? *Reflecting.* Or rather we have grown old in [the service of] Ikshvāku's family: What alternative is there when [a fair fight] has presented itself?

Chandraketu, *with feelings of amazement, shame, and confusion*—Oh, fie! My forces are being scattered on all sides!

Sumantra, *speeding the chariot*—Long-lived one, here now is this hero, come within range of thy call.

Chandraketu, *as if in forgetfulness*—Worthy [Sumantra], what name was given him by those who came to call [us]?

Sumantra—'Lava' they said.

Chandraketu—Ho, Lava of mighty arms! Why busiest thou thyself with these [mere] soldiers? Here am I: Come hither unto *me*: Let light be quenched in light. 7

Sumantra—Lo! Behold, Prince!

He has turned—this heroic youth—summoned by thee from his [work of] carnage amongst the army; as, at the roar of thunder, the valiant whelp of a lion [turns] from his [work of] slaughter amongst troops of elephants. 8

Then enters Lava with hurried and defiant strides.

Lava—Well done, Royal youth, well done! Thou verily art a [true] scion of Ikshvāku. Here then I am, just come to meet thee.

A great tumult behind the curtain.

Lava, *quickly turning back*—What! Once routed, do the leaders of the army return and obstruct my path, wishing again to engage me in combat? Fie on the wretches!

Unto the mighty flames of my wrath, flaring like those issuing from Vaḍavā's[1] mouth, as when some falling mountain[2] dashes upon it and disturbs it—let it serve as a morsel: this stunning confused din arising on all sides from the army and resembling a billow of ocean when it is lashed by the winds that portend the dissolution of the universe! **9**

Moves about excitedly.

Chandraketu—Ho, my young warrior,—

This thy extraordinary valour has endeared thee to me: thou art my friend therefore, and what is mine is even thine. Wherefore then dost thou deal destruction unto thy own dependants [this army]? Am not I, rather, the one on whom thou shouldst try thy mettle (*nikasha*), I, Chandraketu? **10**

Lava, *hastily turning, with joy*—Oh, how gracious and yet stern is the language of this hero of great prowess—this Prince of the Solar race! Let alone these [soldiers] then; I'll rather pay *him* my [warrior's] compliments.

Again a tumult behind the curtain.

Lava, *with wrath and disgust*—Ah! I am vexed-past-endurance (*kadarthita*) by these wretches that come in the way of a meeting between warriors! *Advances towards them.*

Chandraketu—Behold, worthy [Sumantra], it is a sight to see:

His attention riveted upon me in pride not unmingled with curiosity—the full-stretched bow in his hand, and my forces keeping close upon his rear—he is emulating the grace of some cloud decked with Indra's rainbow, and dragged by violent winds in two opposite directions. **11**

Sumantra—The Prince at least knows how to look upon him: we, however, are simply lost in amazement!

Chandraketu—O ye kings [and warriors],—

That you in countless numbers, with him who is here alone—you upon horses and elephants and chariots, with him who is on foot—you sheathed in armour, with him whose upper garment is just the holy deer-skin—you mature in age, with him tender in years and a lovable person—that you should thus gird up your loins to battle with such as he—fie, oh fie upon you, and upon us! **12**

Lava, *resentfully*—How? would he commiserate me? *Reflecting.* Well

[1] Submarine fire, which accounts for the non-increase in the volume of the ocean, in spite of the many rivers falling into it.

[2] When Indra began to clip with his thunderbolt the wings of the mountains, some of them threw themselves into the ocean for shelter. The legend is given in Maitrāyaṇī Saṁhitā, i. 10[13].

then: to prevent loss of time I will, with my *jṛimbhaka* missile, throw this army meanwhile into a stupor. *Remains meditating.*

Sumantra—Wherefore then, of a sudden, is all the hubbub in our army hushed?

Lava—Now we shall have a meeting all to ourselves (*sapragalbham*).

Sumantra, *excitedly*—Meseems, dear Prince, this young warrior has employed the *jṛimbhaka* missile.

Chandraketu—There is no doubt about it:

> Like some terrific blending as of darkness and of lightning, [the missile] renders ineffectual even a steadfast eye, now obscuring it and now giving it a free scope. And as if drawn in a picture is this army standing here without even winking! Verily it is the *jṛimbhaka* of unfailing potency that is at work here! **13**

Wonderful! wonderful!

> Black like the darkness massed in some recesses in the interior of the Nether regions—blazing in the radiance of their flames that are yellow like some hot and glowing brass—these *jṛimbhaka* missiles fill the skies, as if they were the peaks of the Vindhya mountains tossed up by those harsh and dreaded whirlwinds that rise at the end of the *kalpa*,[1] [peaks] with their caverns flaring with lightnings issuing from some clashing clouds! **14**

Sumantra—But from whom, I ask (*punaḥ*), has he had these *jṛimbhakas*?

Chandraketu—From [Vālmīki,] the exalted son of Varuṇa, we[2] think.

Sumantra—No, dear Prince, it is not thus in the case of missiles, and especially the *jṛimbhakas*; for,

> They are the creations of [sage] Kṛiśāśva, and from Kṛiśāśva they went to [Viśvāmitra] the son of Kuśika; then the tradition was imparted to our dear Rāma, with whom it rests. **15**

Chandraketu—But there may be even others, the 'Seers of Mantras' [so called], who, through the perfection of the light of their *sattva*, can 'see' things for themselves.

Sumantra—Be on thy guard, dear Prince: thy heroic opponent has returned.

The two Princes, *the one to the other*—Ha! how charming is this Prince to behold! *Observing each other in cordial affection:*

> Is it [merely] this chance encounter or is it the excellence of his qualities—is it some ancient and intimate friendship of an earlier birth—or is it some kinship between us that has remained

[1] Kalpa = 4,318,272,000 human years. At the end of a kalpa comes a dissolution of the universe.

[2] The 'we' is here to be noted. It shows that, confident of his own valour, Chandraketu was not at all dismayed by Lava's prowess.

unknown by the power of Fate, and inexplicable?—[I know not why, but] as I look upon him my heart becomes all attention.[1] 16

Sumantra—This, as a rule, is the way of all living beings, that some one should feel a spontaneous love for some one else. This popularly is known as 'astral friendship'[2] or 'love at sight'. And this love has been declared to be incomprehensible, one for the motives of which it is vain to seek:

When there is an attachment with no [apparent] cause there is no counteracting it; for, it is a thread of cordiality that knits together the inmost vitals. 17

The two Princes, *the one to the other*[1]—

Upon this form lovely like a polished jewel how can I let my arrows descend?—a form which, as it draws near, my body bristles all over with horripilations in my longing to embrace it. 18

But when he has displayed such fiery spirit, what alternative can there be but a weapon? And to what use can a weapon serve if such as he is not to be its target? And what will he himself say if I be averse to fight when the weapon is already taken in hand? [Oh,] the warriors' code of honour is indeed relentless and thwarts the [natural] course of affection. 19

Sumantra, *observing Lava attentively, with tears, to himself*—Why dost thou, my heart, thus wander astray?

What was the germ of our hopes, that by Fate has already been robbed[3]: upon a creeper cut at its root how can flowers appear? 20

Chandraketu—I would descend, worthy Sumantra, from my chariot.

Sumantra—Wherefore?

Chandraketu—Because, in the first place, this young hero will thereby have received the deference [due]; and further, worthy Sir, it will be in obedience to Kshatriya law. 'Men in chariots do not engage in fight men on foot'—such is the ruling of those that know the Shastras.

Sumantra, *to himself*—Ah! I am [now] really placed in a trying situation:

This course that is but just, how can a man like me object to it? And how likewise can he permit this deed that is rashness pure and simple? 21

Chandraketu—When, upon any dubious matter religious or secular, even my sires seek your advice—you, worthy Sir, who were the dear friend

[1] For the joint speeches see the Notes.

[2] An affinity due to a certain astrological conjunction of the stars of their nativity.

[3] In other words, Sītā, on whom rested the hopes of the continuance of the elder line of the Raghus, is no more. Cp. p. 62, n. 4.

of [Daśaratha] my sires' sire, what is it then that makes your worship hesitate?

Sumantra—Yes, my long-lived one, even so: thy sentiments are in strict accord with the law:

For, this is the rule on the battle-field; this is the eternal law: and this also is the heroic course of conduct pursued by the Lions of the [race of] Raghu. **22**

Chandraketu—Most apposite are your worship's words:

History, chronicles, the mandates of law, and also the traditions of the family of Raghu—these none but your honour knows [thoroughly]. **23**

Sumantra, *embracing him in affection and with tears*—

Not many, my dear child, [not many] have been the days since your father, the dear [Lakshmaṇa], vanquished even that vanquisher of Indra [Indrajit, son of Rāvaṇa]. And thou, the son of such a father, art also following the path of heroes. Happy it is indeed that Daśaratha's family has attained stability! **24**

Chandraketu, *with sorrow*—

When the head of the Raghu-family [Rāma] is yet without stability [in the form of issue], wherein consists the stability of our family? It is this grief that weighs upon our three other sires.[1] **25**

Sumantra—Alas! These words of Chandraketu, they pierce the vitals of my heart!

Lava—Forsooth! diverse feelings struggle in me for precedence:

As in the rise of the full moon the lotus-creeper finds its joy, even so does my sight [find its joy] in him: nevertheless it is fighting that this [my arm] desires—my arm which has fixed its love on this heavy bow, vocal with the string that resounds with a cruel twang, [my arm] with its wrist (*mukha*) marked by an open gaping scar.[2] **26**

Chandraketu, *alighting*—Worthy [Sumantra, this is] Chandraketu of the Solar race, saluting you.

Sumantra—May the holy, resplendent, and invulnerable lustre of a Kakutstha[3] be thine: May the Eternal God [Vishṇu, incarnate as] the Boar bless thee with happiness! **27**

Furthermore,—

May the Divine Sun uphold thee in thy combat—he who is the

[1] Literally, 'three other fathers' = his father Lakshmaṇa and his two uncles, Bharata and Śatrughna. The 'fourth father' would, of course, be Rāma.

[2] Due to contact with the bow-string.

[3] A famous ancestor of Rāma.

father of thy race! Unto thee may the son of Mitra and Varuṇa [Vasishṭha]—he who has been the *guru* of thy *gurus*—speak gladness! Of Indra and Vishṇu, of Fire-god and Wind-god, and of the [heavenly] Eagle, may the vigour be thy own! And may the twang of the bows of Rāma and Lakshmaṇa be [unto thee] the magic-spell that yields victory! **28**

Lava—Prince, thou dost certainly look extremely comely even as thou art—in thy chariot: enough, enough of this excess of courtesy.

Chandraketu—In that case, let the valiant one also grace another chariot.

Lava—Worthy [charioteer], take the Royal prince again upon his chariot.

Sumantra—Then do thou also assent to dear Chandraketu's wishes.

Lava—Why hesitate when it is a question of one's own equipage? We however are foresters, unused to going in chariots.

Sumantra—Thou knowest, noble youth, how [to speak] what pride and politeness demand! If, for once, the noble scion of Ikshvāku, [I mean] King Rāma, were to see thee as thou art, then would his heart melt for very love![1]

Lava—Yes, [worthy Sir]; we have heard that that Royal sage is kind-hearted. *Colouring slightly.*

Neither are we—by any means—of a sort to be jealous even of [holy] sacrifices; for, breathes there the man that would not, for King [Rāma's] virtues, accord him pre-eminence? Still, that speech of those guardians of the horse—it stirred me up by that arrogant defiance which it conveyed unto all Kshatriyas whatsoever. **29**

Chandraketu, *smiling*—Indeed! Is the eminence of even father [Rāma's] prowess something you cannot put up with?

Lava—Perhaps I can—I may—put up with it, perhaps not; but this I would ask. We have, to be sure, heard that the noble descendant of Raghu [Rāma] has subdued his own self. It is said he is not himself arrogant, nor is there arrogance in his subjects. Why then do his men utter a speech worthy only of a Rākshasa [demon]?—

For, that, declare the sages, is a speech worthy of a Rākshasa which flows from arrogance and intoxication: such [a speech] is the source of all feuds: it is the world's curse (*nirṛiti*). **30**

Thus they censure this kind of speech, the other they praise thus—

It yields desires and dispels misery; it begets fame and blunts malice (*dushkṛita*): such a speech [at once] truthful-and-agreeable

[1] Sumantra artfully introduces this reference to Rāma to ascertain if what he suspected (cf. v. 20, above) about the boy's parentage be true. Lava's answer sorely disappoints him.

(*sūnṛita*) is, say the wise, the parent of all blessings—a [veritable] cow![1] **31**

Sumantra—This youth, this pupil of the son of Varuṇa [Vālmīki], is indeed a pure soul: a glow of sacred learning suffuses all his utterances.

Lava—And then further, Chandraketu, you ask me, if the eminence of even father [Rāma's] prowess is something I cannot put up with: I ask, Are the qualities of a Kshatriya absolutely restricted in the matter of possessors?[2]

Sumantra—Thou certainly dost not know the Royal descendant of Ikshvāku [Rāma]. Desist now, desist and do not transgress the bounds:

Thou hast to be sure wrought havoc amongst the soldiery and proved thy prowess; but thou must not speak so lightly of [Rāma,] the vanquisher of the son of Jamadagni.[3] **32**

Lava, *with a laugh*—Worthy Sir, why all this tall talk about the King [simply] because he vanquished the son of Jamadagni?

For, it needs no proving that it is the valiance in words that belongs to the Brahmans; but as to the valiance in arm, that belongs to the Kshatriyas. The son of Jamadagni was a Brahman who [happened to] wield a weapon: for his having vanquished him what praise can the King [Rāma] claim? **33**

Chandraketu, *slightly provoked*—Have done, my worthy [Sumantra], no more bandying of words!—

This fellow apparently is some extraordinary *avatāra* of manliness, because not even [Paraśurāma,] the exalted descendant of Bhṛigu, is a hero to him! And he seems not to *know* even the holy exploits of father [Rāma]—exploits that have conferred upon the seven worlds [the gift of] eternal immunity from danger! **34**

Lava—Who indeed does not know the exploits—the greatness—of the Lord of the Raghus? If indeed one were only to have his say—but never mind!

They are old folks; their career must not be scrutinized; let them be: why discuss them? For, they are the world's great men, and their glory abates not even if they kill a woman—the wife of Sunda![4] And those three steps—I do not say in retreat![5]—which were taken [by Rāma] in that *mêlée* with [the

[1] And the praise could go no higher.

[2] That is, may not others, besides Rāma, possess the Kshatriya qualities?

[3] For Paraśurāma, the son of Jamadagni, see p. 20, note 6.

[4] Tāṭakā, see note 4 on page 19 above.

[5] Literally, 'with his face turned in a particular direction', which I need not specify. As Khara came rushing upon Rāma, the latter took a few steps backwards in order the more freely to use his bow.

demon] Khara, or that skill[1] exhibited in the murder of [Vālin] the son of Indra—the people are all conversant with that! **35**

Chandraketu—Fellow! In traducing father [Rāma] thou art going beyond all bounds: Wilt thou then be so defiant?

Lava—Aha! He is frowning upon *me*, is he?

Sumantra—All ablaze now is their wrath! For,—

The tremor produced by excitement has unloosened the knots of hair tied upon their forehead; their eyes, partaking slightly of the nature of a red lotus, redden spontaneously: and, by the sudden movements of the knitted eyebrows, their faces wear the beauty of the moon in which the spot is prominent, or of a lotus with the bees hovering around it. **36**

The two Princes—Let us then hence repair to a place suitable for combat.[2]

All go out.

END OF ACT V

CALLED

PRINCES IN COMBAT.

[1] Rāma struck Vālin, the King of the Monkeys, while the latter was engaged in fight with Sugrīva.

[2] The place, however, was already suitable for combat in that it is on this very place that Lava routed the soldiers a while ago. See, however, note 2 on page 11 above

ACT VI

Then enter in an aerial car a pair of air-sprites gaudily attired.

Male Sprite—Oh, how marvellous really are the valorous deeds of these two scions of the Solar race [Lava and Chandraketu] fiercely engaged in a sudden combat—deeds that inflame [all the more] their [blazing] Kshatriya lustre, so that even Gods and Demons seem to be quite lost in amazement! For, look, look here, my love!—

As they bend their bow, the tiny bells [upon it] tinkle like jingling bracelets, and it produces by its [vibrating] ends and by the twang of its tough string a terrific clamour; and as they discharge [a shower of] arrows, the crests on their head throb ceaselessly: it is a combat waxingly wondrous and striking the whole world down with terror! **1**

And as a portent of victory for both of them, here goes the deep boom of the celestial war-drum, rumbling like a roaring rain-cloud. **2**

Let us then start continually pouring upon these two heroes a thick coursing shower of flowers, mingled with a charming succession of the full-blown golden lotuses—[a shower] surcharged with comely dew-drops [glistening] upon the bunches of fresh and rubied buds [culled] from the garden of the Gods.

Female Sprite—Why then, all at once, does the sky appear yellow, as if with the flashing streaks of some sudden and mightily throbbing lightning?

Male Sprite—Can it then be that even to-day—

The Blue-red [God Śiva] is going to open the lid of the [third] eye in his forehead, [that eye] which dazzles like the flaring orb of the Sun when whirled[1] on Tvashṭṛi's whirling lathe? **3**

Reflecting. Ah, I see. It is Prince Chandraketu who has employed this Fiery missile, from which are shooting these streaks of fire. For, now—

[1] As happened when Tvashṭṛi, the divine architect, wanted to trim off a portion of the Sun's brilliancy, which proved too strong for Sañjnā, Tvashṭṛi's daughter, wedded to the Sun. For another explanation see Notes.

These countless aerial cars are flying [in all directions], their flags and chowries all singed and besmirched; while, upon the fringes of their [silken] pennons, these flames are producing, for a moment, the appearance of a tint of saffron! 4

Wonderful! It is already gaining ground everywhere—this puissant (*bhagavān*) fire from which are issuing sparks that fly crackling with the noise of the splinters of some wrathful thunderbolt—[fire] which is terrific in the [seething] mass of its tall and towering flames coursing rapidly! And fierce is its heat on every side. I shall, therefore, screen my dear [wife] with my body and withdraw to a [safe] distance. *Does so.*

Female Sprite—Oh, joy that this touch of my dear Lord's body, cool like some stainless pearl, and smooth and soft and tender,—as I in ecstasy had gently closed my rolling eyes—[this touch] has quite banished all my anguish!

Male Sprite—Why, what have I done here? Or rather—

Though doing nothing, by the very joy [of being together] we chase away all sorrow: Indeed it is a treasure indescribable when some one has some one to love.[1] 5

Female Sprite—How now? Why is the expanse of the sky being strewn over[2] with these clouds, decked with the fitful and incessant flashings of the sportive streaks of lightning, and sable like the throat of a youthful peacock?

Male Sprite—Why, this must certainly be the prowess of the Vāruṇa-missiles employed by Prince Lava. Lo! The showers of water descending one after another in thousands of streams have quite quenched the Fiery missile!

Female Sprite—I am glad, I am glad.

Male Sprite—But lo! Everything in excess is a fault; for now are all beings whatsoever thrown into [a fit of] trembling, quite overwhelmed by this impenetrable darkness which is rendered intense by the deep rumbling clouds as they are tossed up by the series of winds[3] that portend Dissolution—[beings] who seem as if weltering in the caverned jaws (*kaṇṭha*) of the dreaded [God of] Death, [jaws] wide gaping to swallow the universe in one morsel—or [they seem] as if lost in the belly of the Cosmic Spirit (*Nārāyaṇa*) when, at the end of the Yugas, all gates of egress being closed, He falls into His yogic sleep! Bravo, Prince Chandraketu, bravo! Most appositely hast thou sent forth the Wind-missile. For now—

[1] This verse = ii. 19, where it is spoken by Rāma. In the mouth of an inferior character it loses its dignity.

[2] 'Strewn over' and not 'overcast', for they were above the clouds.

[3] There are forty-nine of these winds that come into activity at a Dissolution of the universe.

This wind has dissolved all clouds, numerous though they were, into we-know-not-what (*kvāpi*), thus resembling the [highest] knowledge which dissolves [all] illusory-forms (*vivarta*) into the [fathomless] Brahma. 6

Female Sprite—But, my dear, who now is this [person], the fringe of whose upper garment is floating [to the winds] as he, in flurry, tosses up his hands, [this one here] who, even from afar, has by his sweet words forbidden the continuance of the combat and who is bringing [this] his excellent aerial car to the ground right between the two Princes?

Male Sprite, *observing*—This is the Lord of the Raghus [Rāma], returning from [his mission of] killing Śambūka:

Upon hearing the words uttered by this great personage [Rāma], Lava, out of deference to him, has withheld the discharge [of further missiles] and is appeased; Chandraketu is already paying his homage: may happiness attend the King [Rāma] by his being united with his [own] sons! 7

Come, let us hence. *Both go out.*

END OF INTERLUDE.

Then enter Rāma, and Lava, and Chandraketu [in the act of] making obeisance [to Rāma].

Rāma, *alighting from the Pushpaka*—

Moon (*chandra*) of the Solar race, my Chandraketu, come, quick, let me hold thee fast to my bosom! With thy body, cool like a lump of snow, let all the burnings of my heart be allayed! 8

Raising him up and embracing him with tears of affection. Has it all been prosperous with thee and the celestial weapons into which thou hast been initiated?

Chandraketu—All prosperous, [especially] by the happy acquisition of this sweet-looking and wonderfully valiant Lava. Let me request my honoured sire, therefore, to regard with the same affection with which you are wont to regard me, or even with more, this most eminent hero.

Rāma, *observing Lava*—Happily this my son's [Chandraketu's] friend has a form that is at once quite serene and charming:

He seems to be the very Science of Arms assuming a bodily form to protect the people; or is he the Code of Chivalry (*kshātra-dharma*) itself encased in a [human] body to safeguard the treasure of the Sacred Word? He is as if the aggregation of all powers, the sum total of all [good] qualities, or the accumulated store of all the holy products of the world—standing out in a visible form. **9**

Lava, *to himself*—This great personage, how serene is the sight of him and his prowess!

He is the one great source of confidence and friendship and devotion all at the same time: of some pre-eminent merit [of mine] he seems to be the [very] fruition, moving in a bodily form. **10**

Wonderful!

All enmity is at an end; a feeling of intense joy creeps over [my soul]; that [former] impudence has departed, I know not where: it is modesty that now sways me. Wherefore is it then that, at the sight of him, I have so suddenly lost control over myself? Or rather [it must be that] great men, like holy places, have some priceless and inexplicable efficacy. **11**

Rāma—Why then is it that this [boy], all of a sudden, alleviates my sorrows and, through some cause unknown, fills my inmost soul with affection? Or rather, that affection should at all be dependent upon any [assignable] cause is contrary [to all experience].

What binds things together is some inward mysterious tie: it is certainly not upon outward circumstances that affection rests. For, at the rise of the sun, the lotus [of itself] blooms, and so, when the moon rises, does the moon-gem (*chandrakānta*) ooze. **12**

Lava—Chandraketu, who is this great personage?

Chandraketu—My dear friend, it is the venerable father.

Lava—So likewise then must he be to me, strictly-speaking (*dharmataḥ*), since thou callest me thy dear friend. But there are, as I have learnt, four persons, the worthy heroes of the Rāmāyaṇa story, who claim from you this mode of appellation. So tell me [more] definitely.

Chandraketu—Understand then that he is my eldest sire.

Lava, *transported with joy*—What! The Lord of the Raghus [Rāma] in person! Blessings on the dawn of a day that has brought me the sight of this [divine] King! *After looking [at him] with eager curiosity and reverence.* Sire, this is Lava, the pupil of the son of Varuṇa [Vālmīki], saluting you.

Rāma—Come, long-lived one, come. *Embracing him affectionately.* Enough, my dear boy, enough of this excess of modesty. Let me fold thee again and again in a close embrace.

Soft and smooth and tender like the mellowed (*pariṇata*) interior of a full-blown lotus, and cool like the moon or like the juice of sandal—thy touch fills me with joy. **13**

Lava, *to himself*—Such is the causeless affection of this [great personage] towards me! And I, in my stupidity, conceived hostility even towards him, and carried my perverseness to the point of taking up arms against him! *Aloud.* Will the venerable father now pardon this Lava his childish folly?

Rāma—What is the fault that the dear one has committed?

Chandraketu—Hearing from the escorts of the horse the proclamation of Your Honour's valour, he has displayed his heroism.

Rāma—Why, this is just what adorns a Kshatriya.

For, a valorous man does not tolerate the encroaching valour of others: such is his proper nature inherent in his constitution and therefore not artificial; [and this explains] why it is that when the divine Sun shines incessantly with his rays, the fire-stone, as if in wounded pride, vomits flames. **14**

Chandraketu—Even an intolerance [of this sort] becomes graceful only in a [great] hero like him. For, let my revered father but see how the *jṛimbhaka* missile discharged by my dear friend has thrown all these forces into a dead stupor!

Rāma, *observing*—Dear Lava, withdraw the missile; and do thou also, Chandraketu, console thy forces that are stock-still in paralysing stupor.

Lava falls into a meditation.

Chandraketu—So as you command. *Exit.*

Lava—The missile is at rest.

Rāma—Dear [Lava], these [*jṛimbhaka*] missiles and the secret spells for employing and withdrawing them have a tradition of their own [without which they cannot be imparted]:

Brahmā (*Brahmán*) and others, in the interest of the Sacred Truth (*bráhman*), practised penances for over a thousand autumns. And then those Sires (*guru*) of old obtained a vision of these [missiles] as if these were the very fires of their own penances. **15**

Then the occult formulae relating to the study of these holy [missiles] the exalted Kṛiśāśva imparted to the son of Kuśika, [Viśvāmitra,] who had been his pupil for over a thousand years; and that exalted one [Viśvāmitra] [imparted them] to me. This then has been the previous succession [of teachers]. I would know therefore whence hast thou, noble youth, received the tradition?

Lava—The missiles revealed themselves spontaneously to both of us.

Rāma, *reflecting*—Nothing is impossible. It may be some peculiar greatness following as the result of the ripening of some pre-eminent merit. But, how '*both* of us'?

Lava—We are two brothers—twins.

Rāma—Where then is the other?

[**Voice**,] *behind the curtain*—Bhāṇḍāyana, Bhāṇḍāyana!

"That the long-lived Lava has had an affray with the army of the King"—is there any truth in this report? "Even so, dear friend," didst thou say? To-day then, in all the worlds, let the title 'supreme king' come to an end, and let the fires of the Kshatriya weapons be all quenched this day! **16**

Rāma—Who now may this be—he, of a complexion dark-blue like a sapphire, who even by the sound [of his voice] gives me a thrill of horripilation and makes me seem like a *kadamba* [tree] that, at the deep roar of an early and sable rain-cloud, instantly bursts forth into buds? **17**

Lava—This is he, my elder [brother], the noble Kuśa by name, [just] returned from Bharata's hermitage.[1]

Rāma, *in eagerness*—Hither, my dear boy, hither call him, the long-lived one.

Lava—Very well. *Walks about.*

Then enters Kuśa.

Kuśa, *twanging his bow in joyful assurance and pride*—

If it is with the scions of the Solar race, with those kings who have given their tribute of protection even unto [God] Indra, and who ever since the times of Manu—that exalted Son of the Sun-god—have ever, for consuming the high and the mighty, set ablaze their fires of Kshatriya valour—if it is with these that to-day I am to have a fight, then blessed is this my bow, the string of which is radiant with the fierce-shooting flames that flash from the fiery arms. **18**

Moves about in hauteur.

Rāma—A rare abundance of manliness has this lovable (*-ka*) young Kshatriya!

His eye, for even the mightiest of the mighty of the three worlds, shows a disdain as if for mere chaff; his stride, at once firm and proud, seems as though bending the earth low [in submission];

[1] See iv. 22[33 ff.] above, p. 69.

even in his tender-youth he carries the hauteur of a mountain—
Is it the Sentiment of Heroism or of Pride that, [incarnate in him,] is approaching me? 19

Lava, *approaching* [*Kuśa*]—Victory unto the noble one!

Kuśa—Well, long-lived [Lava], what is all this talk about the fight?

Lava—Ah, a mere trifle. Towards this one, let my noble brother, laying aside his haughty bearing, behave with respect.

Kuśa—And why?

Lava—Because it is the King, the Lord of the Raghus, that is standing there. He is affectionate towards us and is eager to meet you.

Kuśa, *reflecting*—Dost thou mean the hero of the Rāmāyaṇa story, the guardian of the treasures of the Sacred Word?

Lava—The same.

Kuśa—He certainly is a great man, and to see him is sanctifying and a thing to wish for! But how are *we* going to accost him, that is what I do not see.

Lava—In the mode prescribed for a *guru*: with reverence.

Kuśa—But how in the world can that be?

Lava—Here is Chandraketu, son of Ūrmilā, a youth exceedingly noble, who calls me his dear friend and offers me his friendship; so by virtue of that relation this Royal sage becomes, strictly speaking, our father.[1]

Kuśa—In that case, albeit a Kshatriya, we *may* show him deference without incurring any reproach [for lack of self-respect].

Both walk about.

Lava—Let my noble brother look upon this great personality: [Are not] his mien, his majesty, his serene-dignity sure indications of those countless and extraordinarily noble achievements?

Kuśa, *gazing attentively*—

How graceful is his form—how hallowing his majestic presence!
Rightly indeed has the poet of the Rāmāyaṇa [Vālmīki] transformed[2] the Goddess of Speech [into that poem]. 20

Approaching. Father, this is Kuśa, the pupil of the son of Varuṇa [Vālmīki], making his salutation.

Rāma—Come, thou long-lived one, come:

Here am I eager, in my affection, to embrace thee whose form-and-stature is lovely like a cloud filled with nectar. 21

Embraces him. To himself. Whose child then may this youth be? [He seems to be—]

1 The irony of the dramatic situation is obvious.

2 Compare ii. 5[2ff.] above.

Like the innermost essence of affection exuded from every particle of my body—as if the very substance of my soul, issuing from here and standing there visibly before me—besprinkled, as it were, with the very meltings of my heart when stirred up with an intense emotion of joy: him as I embrace, he seems to be, as it were, pouring a stream of ambrosial juice [upon me]. **22**

Lava—Father, upon our brows the hot-rayed [sun] is burning. Will you therefore deign to take a seat a while in the dense shade of this *Sāla* tree?

Rāma—Yes, if it is agreeable to my son.

They move about and sit down in the proper manner.[1]

Rāma, *to himself*—

Ha! Although they are deferential in their conduct, these postures in walking and standing and sitting, both of Kuśa and of Lava, they are things that bespeak their [future] sovereignty. **23**

These stately graces that seem inherently to belong to it: they set off a body that is handsome and waxes lovelier at every phase;—as do the pleasing rays the spotless jewel, or the drops of honey the full-blown lotus. **24**

I note further that they both possess in large measure the traits common to the princes of the [royal] race of Raghu:

A form dark-blue like the throat of some lusty pigeon, the shoulders broad like those of a young bull, the pose (*āśaya*) [very] elegant; a look dauntless like that of a reposing lion, and a voice deep-and-full like a festive drum! **25**

Observing [*more*] *closely.* Ah! It is not merely with mine that their form bears resemblance, but—

There are also those traits proper to the daughter of Janaka [Sītā]—all to be clearly made out here in these two boys: It is as if once again has come within the range of my sight that face of my beloved wife in all the glory of a fresh and full-blown lotus! **26**

Lovely with the lustre of teeth clear as pearls, here are their lips of the very same stamp, and also the same curve of the ear. The eyes, to be sure, are not blue;[2] but they have the same note of comeliness. **27**

Thoughtfully. And this is that same forest, inhabited by the son of Varuṇa [Vālmīki], where, I was told, the Queen was abandoned. And

[1] So as to reveal to Rāma their princely breeding.

[2] 'Not blue', but red, as a man's eyes should be, according to Sāmudrika-śāstra.

such here are the looks and the age and the prowess of these two [boys]. Now as to the missiles being self-revealed to them, let me see: Can it really be that the permission which, in the course of our viewing those pictures, I gave unto the missiles has had its effect? For, even in the case of the ancients, we never have heard of any missiles obtained without a [formal] handing over. There is also this my heart's extreme joy-and-sorrow that affords to my wavering mind [further] assurance. Often had I perceived that it was twins that the Queen would bring forth. *With tears*:

In those days gone by, when our love, once formed, had grown with the growth of familiarity, I was the first, with the practised feel of my hand, to discover, in the confidence of privacy—her eyes lowered nevertheless in her inborn bashfulness—that it was twins that were in store for her. It was some days later that she discovered it. **28** *Weeps.*

Shall I then, in some way or other, ask them [directly]?

Lava—What can this mean, Father?

Unto this face that is as a blessing to the world, with this shower of tears, you are lending the beauty of a white lotus glistening [lit. besprinkled] with dew-drops. **29**

Kuśa—But don't you see, my dear boy?—

Without his Queen, Sītā, to the Lord of the Raghus what thing is there that may not be painful? For, with the loss of one's beloved, the whole world, it is said, becomes a wilderness! On the one hand, that [extreme] degree of love, and here, on the other, is this separation that is endless! Why askest thou thus then, as if thou hadst never studied the Rāmāyaṇa? **30**

Rāma, *to himself*—Oh, they talk as if the matter did not concern them: no need therefore of asking any [direct] question. Thou wretched heart! What means this thy sudden transport of emotion? Not being able to contain within me the anguish of my heart, I am commiserated even by these boys! Well, I will change the topic. *Aloud.* There is current, my dear boys, a report about what they call '*Rāmāyaṇa*', a panegyric of the Solar race, the outpouring of the exalted Vālmīki's learning-and-eloquence (*Sarasvatī*). I wish, therefore, out of curiosity, to hear some part of it.

Kuśa—That entire story is [quite] familiar to us. Here, to begin with (*tāvat*), are these two stanzas,[1] coming in a chapter at the end of the '*Bālacharita*', that rise into my memory.

[1] The Calcutta recension of the Rāmāyaṇa gives these very stanzas near the end of the Bāla-kāṇḍa (Gorresio, i. 78^{13-15}); in the other recensions the readings differ. See Notes.

Rāma—Repeat [them], my dear boy.

Kuśa—"It was her nature that made Sītā dear unto Rāma's mighty heart; but she endeared herself all the more unto him by reason of her [good] qualities. **31**

So also was Rāma unto Sītā dearer than her very life: only their heart knows the extent of each other's affection." **32**

Rāma—Alas! Exceedingly cruel is this blow upon the very vitals of my heart! Ha, Queen! So indeed it then was! Oh, how tormenting are these affairs of the world—fraught[1] with capricious reverses [of fortune], extremely painful, and all terminating in void phantoms!

Where now is that joy which, springing from an absolute [mutual] confidence, knew no bounds? Where that mutual assiduousness [for each other's comfort], and where those fathomless charms of novelty? In pleasure or in pain where indeed [can I now find] that unison of hearts?—and yet this my cursed heart (*prāṇa*) does continue to beat and will not cease! **33**

Woe and alas!—

That period wherein were revealed to me, as in one flash, those [hundreds and] thousands of my dear [Sītā's] charms—of that period beset with painful memories, the memory recurs to me now. **34**

For then, little by little, each succeeding day leaving its mark upon them, the breasts of my fawn-eyed [Sītā] kept expanding slowly like a bud; and then also it was that, strengthened by the concord of our age and our love and our longings, the God of Love had his opportunity (*sphurati*) to rage freely in our hearts, but demurely in the outward-expression (*vapushi*). **35**

Lava—Here is another stanza[2] addressed by the Lord of the Raghus unto the Queen Sītā in the course of their pleasure-trip in the outskirts [*vana*] of the Chitrakūṭa [mountain] close by the [river] Mandākinī.—

"As if set purposely for thee, here in front is this slab of stone; all around it this *kesara* tree has rained as it were a rain of flowers!" **36**

Rāma, *with a bashful smile and a mixture of love and pathos*—Children are indeed artlessly-simple, especially if they be forest-bred. Alas, Queen! Dost thou remember what transports of unreserved endearments we did then have? Alas, alas!

[1] Or, devoid of all real relations, positive or negative.

[2] See Rāmāyaṇa, Bombay recension, the extra canto after ii. 95, stanzas 5–6.

[Thy face] bedewed with the cooling drops of sweat and radiant with thy moonlike forehead upon which thronged thy tresses as they blew to the breezes wafted gently from over the Mandākinī [river]—with thy cheeks glistening and [thy forehead] no longer marked with the [wonted] *kuṅkuma*-spot [1]—thy face gentle with the mild curve of thy unadorned ears: it is as if I were seeing it now vividly (*utprekshyate*) before me! **37**

Remains stock-still [in meditation], with pathos. Alas, alas indeed!

After a long, long meditation, when one creates [in fancy] and puts before him the image of his love, it is by no means the case that such [an image], although [the actual object be] far off, does not fill one with reassurance; but with the dissolution of that [product of] imagination, the whole world becomes [once more] a void wilderness, and thereafter, as if upon a heap of blazing husks, the heart seems to be broiling! **38**

[**Voice,**] *behind the curtain*—

Alarmed at the report of the boys' affray, Vasishṭha and Vālmīki and the [widowed] Queens of Daśaratha, Janaka along with Arundhatī: from the far distant hermitage they are in sooth all coming hither, very slowly—their frames tottering with age, and themselves slow with fatigue, but hurrying with their mind. **39**

Rāma—How, the exalted Arundhatī and Vasishṭha and the Queen-mothers and Janaka—are they all even here? Alas! How indeed can I meet them [now]? *Observing, and with pathos.* Ha! That father[-in-law] Janaka also should have come right hither—this is like the blow of a thunderbolt to me, ill-starred that I am!

After having seen that union of father [Daśaratha] with [my] father[-in-law Janaka] on that festive occasion of the marriage of their children—[a marriage] approved by Vasishṭha and others, all overjoyed at the desirableness of the connexion—after that, why am I not torn to a thousand shreds as I, following upon such a terrible disaster [to my wife], behold, in this his present plight, Janaka, this friend of my father? **40**

[**Voice,**] *behind the curtain*—Woe and alas!—

Upon seeing suddenly, in his present plight, the Lord of the Raghus [Rāma], shorn of all his glory save his innate-majesty, these sorrow-stricken Queen-mothers—after reviving Janaka who

[1] Saffron (*kuṅkuma*) forms the indispensable adornment of every married woman. In this case it was temporarily rubbed off. Respecting the incident as given in the Rāmāyaṇa, see the Notes.

was the first to fall into a swoon—are themselves going into a swoon! 41

Rāma—Alas, father! Alas, mothers!

Seeing that for her who was, of Janaka's and of Raghu's family, the all-in-all of auspiciousness, I showed no compassion,—vain is your [present] compassion for me! 42

I will go forthwith to attend upon them. *Rises.*

Kuśa *and* **Lava**—This way, this way, father!

All move about in pathetic flurry and exeunt.

END OF ACT VI

CALLED

PRINCES RECOGNIZED.

ACT VII

Then enters Lakshmaṇa.

Lakshmaṇa—Ho, my worthy Sirs! To-day the exalted Vālmīki, as ye know (*khalu*), has summoned, along with ourselves, [our] subjects from towns and districts, with all Brahmans and Kshatriyas; and he has also, by his own [spiritual] power, secured the presence of hosts of Gods and Demons, [Apes and other] animals, the Serpent-lords with their retinue: in fact, the whole assemblage of Beings movable and immovable. And I am directed by the noble [King, Rāma] as follows—" Dear Lakshmaṇa, the exalted Vālmīki has invited us to witness his own play that is to be enacted by heavenly nymphs. Go, therefore, to the banks of the Ganges, which is to be the place for the concert, and seat the audience properly."—I have accordingly assigned proper seats to all the assemblage of Beings mortal and immortal. And here, now,—

> Is the noble [King, Rāma] who, even while carrying on the life-and-functions (*āśrama*) of royalty, has to follow the rigorous course of a hermit's life: he is coming hither out of deference to [sage] Vālmīki. 1

Then enters Rāma.

Rāma—Dear Lakshmaṇa, have the distinguished spectators (*prāśnika*) taken their seats?

Lakshmaṇa—They have.

Rāma—And those two boys—Kuśa and Lava—let them have accorded to them a position similar to [that of] Prince Chandraketu.

Lakshmaṇa—Considering Your Lordship's affection for them, that is just what I have done. Here is spread out the Royal seat. *Both sit down.*

Rāma—Sirs, let the play begin.

Stage-manager, *entering*—The exalted son of Varuṇa, [Vālmīki,] truthful in his utterances, thus commands the world movable and immovable—" Here is what dawned upon us in our spiritual insight—a certain composition of ours pure-and-edifying and full of the Pathetic and the Marvellous sentiments. Do you, therefore, because of the importance of the issue [connected with it,] pay attention to the same."

Rāma—The meaning is, that sages possess a direct intuition of what is right (*dharma*). The knowledge of [such] exalted personages is uncoloured by passions, is a Repository of Truth,[1] is never known to fail. It must therefore be beyond [every possibility of] doubt.

[Voice,] *behind the curtain*—Alas, my noble Lord! Alas, dear Lakshmaṇa! Alone and undefended as I am, and with these pangs of childbirth upon me, in this [dreary] forest, the beasts of prey, desperate [with hunger], are longing to devour me! Therefore now, ill-starred that I am, I will throw myself into the Mandākinī [Ganges].

Lakshmaṇa, *to himself*—Woe and alas! This is something quite unexpected!

Stage-manager—The daughter of the All-sustaining [Earth], Queen
Sītā, being abandoned by the King in the great forest: she, with
travail coming upon her, is throwing herself into the divine
Ganges. 2 *Exit.*

Rāma, *excitedly*—Queen, my Queen! Just tarry [but] one instant!

Lakshmaṇa—My noble brother, this is a play!

Rāma—Alas, Queen! Thou dear companion in the wilderness of Daṇḍakā! This then has been the evil ripening of thy fate—and through Rāma!

Lakshmaṇa—Noble brother, let us, if you please, see how the play turns out.

Rāma—Here am I, ready and with a heart of adamant!

Then enters Sītā swooning and supported by Pṛithivī [the Earth] and Jāhnavī [the Ganges], who have each an infant in their lap.

Rāma—Brother, lend me thy support: I seem to be plunging into some unknown and untrodden [abyss of] gloom!

The two Goddesses [Pṛithivī and Bhāgīrathī]—

Take heart, [Sītā,] thou blessed daughter of [Janaka,] King of the
Videhas: Fortune is smiling upon thee. While in the waters
thou hast given birth to two sons that shall be the upholders of
Raghu's line. 3

Sītā, *recovering*—Oh, joy! I have given birth to [two] sons!—Ha, my noble Lord! *Swoons [again].*

Lakshmaṇa, *falling [at Rāma's feet]*—I say, my noble brother, Fortune is smiling upon us! The stock of Raghu has put forth glorious offshoots. *Observing.* Oh, how now? Overwhelmed by the flood of stirring tears, my noble brother has swooned quite away! *Fans [him].*

The two Goddesses—Cheer up, dear daughter, cheer up!

Sītā, *recovering*—Who may your Ladyship be—and you?

[1] A technical term of Yoga, for which see Notes.

Pṛithivī—This is the Guardian-divinity of your father-in-law's house—[the river] Bhāgīrathī.

Sītā—My homage unto thee, Exalted one!

Bhāgīrathī—Mayest thou attain all those blessings that thy [noble] character [richly] merits!

Lakshmaṇa—We are [by this expression of goodwill mightily] favoured.

Bhāgīrathī—This is the Exalted [Goddess], the All-sustaining [Earth]: thy mother.

Sītā—Alas, mother! That thou shouldst see me—and in such a plight!

Pṛithivī—Come, darling—Come [unto me], my daughter!

Embraces [Sītā] and faints.

Lakshmaṇa, *in joy*—So [happily] the noble Queen has been by Pṛithivī and Bhāgīrathī taken under their protection.

Rāma, *observing*—It is indeed good—but it harrows me so!

Bhāgīrathī—Is even the all-sustaining Goddess [Earth] thus affected? Then all-triumphant indeed is a mother's affection! Or rather [why do I say so?]—Nobody that has any feelings at all can escape this [affection, this] unending thread of the world-and-its-concerns (*saṁsāra*), this mysterious knot of infatuation. My child, thou daughter of the King of the Videhas! And thou Goddess [Earth] that art [thyself] the stay unto all creatures! Take heart [both of you]; be comforted.

Pṛithivī, *recovering*—Goddess [Bhāgīrathī]! Being mother to Sītā, how *can* I take heart?

> First there was her long abode among the Rākshasas [with Rāvaṇa], and, as a second [calamity], this her abandonment, most dreadful [even] to hear:

Bhāgīrathī—But what being indeed is there—when Fate is intent upon evolving its fruit—that can close the gates against it [Fate]? **4**

Pṛithivī—Bhāgīrathī, is this becoming—is this at all like dear Rāma?

> No regard whatever has he shown to this [my Sītā's] hand, clasped in her tender years by him in tender years—nor any [regard] for me, nor for Janaka, nor for the Fire[-ordeal], nor for [Sītā's] companionship [in the Daṇḍakā-forest], nor [finally] for the continuance of [his own race]! **5**

Sītā—Alas, my noble Lord! Of thee I am put in mind—

Pṛithivī—Forsooth! who now is thy *noble* Lord?

Sītā, *abashed, with tears*—So [be it then] as my mother says.

Rāma—Mother Pṛithivī, here am I, such [I confess, as thou sayest].

Bhāgīrathī—Exalted [Earth], thou Giver of all blessings! Thou art of this living world its very body [and soul]. Wherefore then, as if not cognizant [of facts], art thou wroth at [Rāma,] thy son-in-law?

> A dread infamy was gaining ground among the people; and as to that clearing [of Sītā] by the [ordeal of] fire, it took place in the [distant] Island of Lañkā [Ceylon]: how possibly could the people of this place give credence to it? And it has always been the precious heritage (*dhana*) of Ikshvāku's race to keep the entire people content. In this trying extremity, therefore, what [else] *could* my dear [Rāma] have done? **6**

Lakshmaṇa—Divinities indeed possess an unerring intuitive vision in regard to [the thoughts and motives of] all beings.

Bhāgīrathī—Nevertheless, here am I folding my hands in supplication [and craving thy grace and pardon for Rāma].

Rāma—Holy mother [Bhāgīrathī], continual has been thy favour towards [us] the descendants of Bhagīratha.

Pṛithivī—I am always favourably disposed towards you; but it was the vehemence of my affection, [terrific] sudden and hard to withstand, [that prompted those words of mine]. I am indeed not unaware of dear Rāma's love to Sītā:

> Constrained through Fate to abandon dear [Sītā], he [Rāma], with that [keen torment] consuming his mind, has been kept alive only by his own supernatural firmness (*sattva*), and by the [pre-eminent] merits of his subjects. **7**

Rāma—Indeed they have been full of tenderness for [me] their child—these my *gurus* [Pṛithivī and Bhāgīrathī].

Sītā, *weeping, with folded hands*—Let my mother [Earth] receive me in her bosom for eternal rest.

Rāma—What else could she ask?

Bhāgīrathī—God forbid! Mayest thou for thousands of years continue in [the bloom of] thy life!

Pṛithivī—Child, these thy dear sons need to be looked after.

Sītā—What have I to do with these, now that I am without my Lord?

Rāma—Thou art of adamant, my heart!

Bhāgīrathī—How—thy Lord[1] still alive—canst thou be without a Lord?

Sītā—Luckless as I am, what does my Lord's being alive signify for me?

The two Goddesses—Being, as thou art, the source of all blessings to the world, wherefore dost thou thus misprize thyself? Even we ourselves, in thy company, feel an augmentation of our purity. **8**

[1] The word for 'lord' or husband means also protector.

Lakshmaṇa—Did you hear that, my noble brother?

Rāma—The people—let *them* hear. *A tumult behind the curtain.*

Rāma—Something yet more marvellous [is coming]!

Sītā—Why is it that the whole firmament seems ablaze?

The two Goddesses—We know:

Those very missiles of which Kṛiśāśva, [Viśvāmitra] the son of Kuśika, and Rāma were in turn the masters,—those missiles that produce stupor—are appearing! 9

[**Voice,**] *behind the curtain*—All hail, Queen Sītā! It is before thy sons that we have to present ourselves; as was said—in the course of seeing those pictures—by the noble descendant of Raghu [Rāma]. 10

Sītā—So, happily, these are the Deities of the missiles: Ha, my noble Lord, thy favours continue unabated even now!

Lakshmaṇa—My noble brother had then said [unto Sītā], 'Assuredly now these will attend upon thy offspring.'[1]

The two Goddesses—Our homage unto you, ye mighty missiles! Blessed are we in this your favour: Be pleased to reveal yourselves whenever they [the boys] shall meditate upon you; and may these our dear sons prosper under your favour! 11

Rāma—These surging billows of grief—broken by the mingling [floods] of joy and wonder—they have really thrown me now into an inexplicable state of mind! 12

The two Goddesses—Rejoice, child! For now have thy sons become the equals of our dear Rāma.

Sītā—But who, exalted [Goddess], will now do for them the rites befitting a Kshatriya?

Rāma—This one now, the maintainer of that line of the Raghus which claims to be under Vasishṭha's protection; alas, even she—Sītā—is at a loss to find some one who shall give unto her sons the sacraments and befitting education! 13

Bhāgīrathī—My child, why this anxiety? For, as soon as they are weaned, I shall deliver them into the exalted Vālmīki's hands. He will do all that needs to be done for them as Kshatriyas:

As are the sages Vasishṭha and Āṅgirasa, even so is the [saintly] son of Varuṇa, [Vālmīki,] the *guru* of both the families, that of Janaka and that of Raghu. 14

Rāma—A happy thought this of the exalted [Bhāgīrathī].

Lakshmaṇa—Noble brother, to tell the truth, I am really led to surmise,

[1] See p. 19, above.

by these indications, that these [two infants] [represent] our Kuśa and Lava:

For they also [the real Kuśa and Lava] have the missiles manifest to them from their birth, and they have both received the sacraments at the hands of the saintly son of Varuṇa [Vālmīki]; they are heroes, and in age are [just] twelve years. **15**

Rāma—Dear [Lakshmaṇa], it is even for this very reason that my heart is adrift and I am lost in bewilderment.

Pṛithivī—Come, daughter, sanctify [with thy presence] my abode in Rasātala.[1]

Sītā—[Rather] let my mother [Earth] receive me in her bosom [for eternal rest]: I can no longer endure the vicissitudes of this world of mortals.

Rāma—What will the answer be now?

Pṛithivī—Child, follow my behest and look to the needs of thy sons until they are weaned. But after that—as shall seem good.

Bhāgīrathī—That is right.

Exeunt Ganges, Earth, and Sītā.

Rāma—How? Has the daughter of the King of the Videhas really found the rest eternal? Alas, Queen! Thou dear companion of my residence in the Daṇḍakā, thou divine embodiment of Virtue! Art thou then departed for the other world? *Faints.*

Lakshmaṇa—Help, help, Exalted Vālmīki! Is this your Poem's end-and-aim?[2]

[Voice,] *behind the curtain*—Let the concert[-instruments] be removed. Hark ye, all living beings—ye mortals movable and immovable! Behold the holy miracle that Vālmīki permits to happen.

Lakshmaṇa, *observing*—As if by some churning, the waters of the Ganges are in agitation; the skies are thronged with Gods and sages: and, oh wonder!—the noble [Sītā], along with the Goddesses Pṛithivī and Bhāgīrathī, is rising from the waters. **16**

[Voice,] *behind the curtain*—O Arundhatī, world-honoured! Deign to accept the greetings of us [two], Pṛithivī and Bhāgīrathī: into thy charge we here deliver this Sītā, her of holy life, our daughter. **17**

[1] Rasātala = Nether world. A distinction is apparently intended between 'staying with Pṛithivī in her abode' and 'being received into her bosom to rise up no more'. See Notes, however.

[2] Lakshmaṇa means, 'Was this your motive, Vālmīki, in inviting us to the play, namely, just to see Rāma faint?' There is perhaps also the suggestion, on the part of Bhavabhūti, that the tragic ending of the Rāmāyaṇa, as we have it, is not fitting for such a poem, and that it should end happily, as does the present play. See also Introduction, §21, and note.

Lakshmaṇa—Oh, joy and wonder! Behold, behold, my noble brother! *Observing.* Woe and alas! He has not even yet recovered his breath!

Then enter Arundhatī and Sītā.

Arundhatī—Haste, child, thou daughter of Videha's king! Away with this thy bashfulness! Come and revive my dear [Rāma] with thy hand, the touch of which is [so] dear [to him]. **18**

Sītā, *in flurry, touching Rāma*—Let my noble Lord revive, and compose himself.

Rāma, *reviving, in joy*—Oh, what can this be? *Observing, with joyful astonishment.* Is it possible? my Queen! *In confusion.* Oh, and mother Arundhatī—and Ṛishyaśṛiñga and Śāntā and all our other *gurus*, all beaming with joy!

Arundhatī—Dear [Rāma], here is the exalted Ganges, the Presiding-divinity of the house of Bhagīratha;[1] she is gracious [towards thee].

[**Voice**,] *behind the curtain*—Dear Rāma, Lord of the world, call to mind what thou saidst to me[2] when looking at the pictures: [Thou didst then say—] 'Be thou, therefore, O [divine] mother, towards this thy daughter-in-law, Sītā, ever cherishing kindly thoughts—even like unto Arundhatī [herself].' I have acquitted myself of my duty therein.

Arundhatī—And here is thy mother-in-law, the exalted giver of all blessings [the Earth].

[**Voice**,] *behind the curtain*—The long-lived one [Rāma] had said[3] formerly, when abandoning Sītā—'O holy [Earth, thou] Giver of all blessings! This thy virtuous daughter do thou regard with kindness—this daughter of Janaka!' So now I have, O Lord [of men], carried out thy words with regard to my daughter [Sītā].

Rāma—How! Guilty of grievous offence though Rāma has been, have the exalted [Goddesses really] shown him their favour [and sympathy]?

Salutes [them].

Arundhatī—Ye people from the city and from the country! Considering that Pṛithivī and Bhāgīrathī have now [in your presence] commended her and entrusted her to me, Arundhatī, and that formerly the holy Fire had attested to her spotless character and Brahmā and all other Gods applauded her—will you now accept [as your Queen] her, who is the dutiful daughter-in-law of the Solar race and who is sprung from the [very] sacrificial ground of the Gods? What do you, my worthy Sirs, think in regard to this?

[1] For Bhagīratha, see note 6, p. 21.

[2] See above, p. 22, near the top.

[3] See above, p. 29, near end.

Lakshmaṇa—Thus reproved by the noble Arundhatī, these our subjects, as also these assembled Beings, one and all, are saluting the noble [Queen], while the Guardians of the world and the seven sages are honouring her with a shower of blossoms.

Arundhatī—Lord of the world! My dear Rāma!—

This thy dear [and dutiful Sītā]: employ her now—as the rites demand—to participate in the religious offices connected with the sacrifice—her who is the holy [and living] original of that image of gold. **19**

Sītā, *to herself*—My noble Lord knows how to wipe off Sītā's sorrows.

Rāma—As the exalted [Arundhatī] commands.

Lakshmaṇa—Now have I gained the one wish of my heart!

Sītā—This is life to me!

Lakshmaṇa—Noble Queen, here salutes thee that shameless Lakshmaṇa.

Sītā—Just as thou art, dear [brother], long mayest thou live!

Arundhatī—Exalted Vālmīki, bring forward now, unto [our] dear Rāma, those two sons of Sītā, Kuśa and Lava. *Exit.*[1]

Rāma *and* **Lakshmaṇa**—Oh, joy! It *is* as we thought.

Sītā, *with tears, and agitated*—Where, where are my darlings?

Then enters Vālmīki [leading] Kuśa and Lava.

Vālmīki—Kuśa, Lava, my boys! This is the Lord of the Raghus—your father; this is Lakshmaṇa, your worthy uncle; this is Queen Sītā who gave you birth: this is the Royal sage Janaka, your mother's father.

Sītā, *observing, with joy and sorrow and amazement*—How! My father [Janaka—and here]!

Kuśa *and* **Lava**—Oh, father! Oh, mother! Oh, grandfather!

Rāma, *embracing [them] joyfully*—Why, my dear boys! It must be through our [special] merit that you have been restored unto us!

[1] There is no apparent reason for this *exit* unless it was the special object of the poet to leave Vālmīki, as the one highest personage then on the stage, to pronounce the concluding benediction. In a sense, it is proper that Vālmīki should pronounce the benediction, but it is a bit odd, particularly as the last stanza contains a flattering allusion to Vālmīki's own poem.

Now we know that Bhavabhūti was on most intimate terms (cp. Prologue to Mālatī-Mādhava) with the actors. The account Lava gives, in Act iv, of Vālmīki's preparation for the play within the play in Act vii sounds almost as a leaf from our poet's autobiography. We further know that in later times (cp. Rājaśekhara's Bāla-Rāmāyaṇa, Prologue, stanza 16) Bhavabhūti was regarded as an *avatar* of Vālmīki. May we, therefore, conclude that Bhavabhūti himself played the part of Vālmīki, and came in, just at the end, to make his courtesy to the audience and receive their plaudits?

Sītā—Come, dear Kuśa! Come, dear Lava! Give a long, long embrace to this your mother, who has [as it were] been born again.

Kuśa *and* **Lava,** *having done so*—We are blessed [to-day]!

Sītā—Exalted Sir, my obeisance!

Vālmīki—My dear child! Thus, oh thus [united to thy Lord and thy sons] mayest thou long continue!

Sītā—Oh, joy! Here now is my father, [our] family preceptors [Vasishṭha and Vālmīki], these honoured ladies [my mothers-in-law and the exalted Arundhatī], queen Śāntā with her husband [Ṛishyaśṛiṅga], as also these feet of my noble and gracious Lord, together with Lakshmaṇa and Kuśa and Lava: As I see all these together I am transported with joy!

Tumult behind the curtain.

Vālmīki, *rising and observing*—Having extirpated the demon Lavaṇa, this is [Śatrughna] the Lord of Mathurā approaching.[1]

Lakshmaṇa—Blessings bring blessings in their train.

Rāma—Although experiencing all this, I cannot yet believe it: this, however, is in the nature of all wished-for blessings![2]

Vālmīki—Say, my dear Rāma, what further good can I render thee?

Rāma—Beyond all this, can there be any further good? Let there be this, however—

> This story which—even like the Mother of all creation [Earth] or like the [river] Ganges—cleanses from [all] sins and augments [every] blessing; [this story] which is full of auspiciousness and which captivates the heart: may the wise hold in esteem this [same] story which is here put together in a dramatic form, and which is the composition (*vāṇī*) of a Poet[3] of matured genius and conversant with Brahma-in-the-form-of-the-Word! **20**

Exeunt all.

END OF ACT VII

CALLED

REUNION.

END OF THE PLAY.

[1] Cp. Notes to i. 50.

[2] Cp. Mālatī-Mādhava, vi. 9[15].

[3] Vālmīki; but there is also a secondary reference to Bhavabhūti himself.

HARVARD ORIENTAL SERIES

Harvard Oriental Series. Edited, with the coöperation of various scholars, by CHARLES ROCKWELL LANMAN, A.B. and LL.D. (Yale), LL.D. (Aberdeen), Wales Professor of Sanskrit at Harvard University; Honorary Member of the Asiatic Society of Bengal, the Société Asiatique, the Royal Asiatic Society of Great Britain and Ireland, and the Deutsche Morgenländische Gesellschaft; Member of the American Philosophical Society; Fellow of the American Academy of Arts and Sciences; Foreign Member of the Royal Bohemian Society of Sciences; Honorary Correspondent of the Archæological Department of the Government of India; Corresponding Member of the Institute of Bologna, of the Royal Society of Sciences at Göttingen, of the Imperial Russian Academy of Sciences, and of the Institute of France (Académie des Inscriptions et Belles-Lettres).

Published by the Harvard University Press, Cambridge, Massachusetts, U.S.A. To be bought, in America, of GINN & COMPANY, 29 Beacon Street, Boston, Mass.; in England, of GINN & Co., 9 St. Martin's Street, Leicester Square, London, W.C.; in Continental Europe, of O. Harrassowitz, Leipzig.—The price of volume 3 is $1.20. Price of volumes 7 and 8 (not sold separately) is $5. Price of volume 10 is $6. The price of each of the other volumes is $1.50. Volumes 18 and 19 are not sold separately.—One dollar ($1.00)=Marks 4.18=francs or lire 5.15=4 shillings and 2 pence=3 rupees.—Volume 10 is royal 4° (32 cm.); volumes 7 and 8 are super-royal 8° (28 cm.); the rest are royal 8° (26 cm.). All are now bound durably in full buckram with gilt top.

Volume 1. Jātaka-Mālā, Stories of Buddha's former incarnations, by Ārya Çūra. Edited in Sanskrit (Nāgarī letters) by Professor H. KERN, University of Leiden, Netherlands. 1891. Second issue, 1914. Pages, 270. (Translation by Speyer, London, 1895, Frowde.)

Volume 2. Sānkhya-Pravachana-Bhāshya, or Commentary on the exposition of the Sānkhya philosophy, by Vijñāna-Bhikshu. Edited in Sanskrit (Roman letters) by Professor R. GARBE, University of Tübingen, Germany. 1895. Pages, 210. (Translated by Garbe, Leipzig, 1889, Brockhaus.)

Volume 3. Buddhism in Translations. Passages selected from the Buddhist sacred books and translated from the original Pāli into English by HENRY CLARKE WARREN, late of Cambridge, Massachusetts. 1896. Sixth issue, 1915. Pages, 540. (Over 100 extracts from the sacred books of Buddhism, so arranged as to give a connected account of the legendary life of Buddha, of his monastic order, of his doctrines on karma and rebirth, and of his scheme of salvation. The work has been widely circulated and has been highly praised by competent authorities.)

Volume 4. Karpūra-Mañjarī. A drama by the Indian poet Rājaçekhara (900 A.D.). Critically edited in the original Prākrit (Nāgarī letters), with a glossarial index and an essay on the life and writings of the poet, by STEN KONOW, of the University of Christiania, Norway; and translated into English with notes by C. R. LANMAN. 1901. Pages, 318.

Volumes 5 and 6. Brihad-Devatā (attributed to Çāunaka), a summary of the deities and myths of the Rig-Veda. Critically edited in the original Sanskrit (Nāgarī letters), with an introduction and seven appendices (volume 5), and translated into English with critical and illustrative notes (volume 6), by Professor A. A. MACDONELL, University of Oxford. 1904. Pages, 234+350=584.

Volumes 7 and 8. Atharva-Veda. Translated, with a critical and exegetical commentary, by the late Professor W. D. WHITNEY, of Yale University; revised and brought nearer to completion and edited by C. R. LANMAN. 1905. Pages, 1212. (The work includes critical notes on the text, with various readings of European and Hindu mss.; readings of the Kashmirian version; notices of corresponding passages in the other Vedas, with report of variants; data of the scholiasts as to authorship and divinity and meter of each verse; extracts from the ancillary literature concerning ritual and exegesis; literal translation; elaborate critical and historical introduction.)

Volume 9. The Little Clay Cart (Mṛcchakaṭika), a Hindu drama attributed to King Shūdraka. Translated from the original Sanskrit and Prākrits into English prose and verse by A. W. RYDER, Instructor in Sanskrit in Harvard University. 1905. Pages, 207.

Volume 10. Vedic Concordance: being an alphabetic index to every line of every stanza of the published Vedic literature and to the liturgical formulas thereof, that is, an index (in Roman letters) to the Vedic mantras, together with an account of their variations in the different Vedic books. By Professor MAURICE BLOOMFIELD, of the Johns Hopkins University, Baltimore. 1906. Pages, 1102.

Volume 11. The Pañchatantra: a collection of ancient Hindu tales, in the recension (called Pañchākhyānaka, and dated 1199 A.D.) of the Jaina monk, Pūrṇabhadra, critically edited in the original Sanskrit (in Nāgarī letters; and, for the sake of beginners, with word-division) by Dr. JOHANNES HERTEL, Professor am königlichen Realgymnasium, Doebeln, Saxony. 1908. Pages, 344.

Volume 12. The Pañchatantra-text of Pūrṇabhadra: critical introduction and list of variants. By Professor HERTEL. 1912. Pages, 245. (Includes an index of stanzas.)

Volume 13. The Pañchatantra-text of Pūrṇabhadra, and its relation to texts of allied recensions as shown in **Parallel Specimens.** By Professor HERTEL. 1912. (Nineteen sheets, mounted on guards and issued in atlas-form. They give, in parallel columns, four typical specimens of the text of Pūrṇabhadra's Pañchatantra, in order to show the genetic relations in which the Sanskrit recensions of the Pañchatantra stand to one another, and the value of the manuscripts of the single recensions.)

Volume 14. The Pañchatantra: a collection of ancient Hindu tales, in its oldest recension, the Kashmirian, entitled **Tantrākhyāyika.** Sanskrit text, reprinted from the critical editio major by Professor HERTEL. Editio minor. 1915. Pages, 160.

Volume 15. Bhāravi's poem Kirātārjunīya or Arjuna's combat with the Kirāta. Translated from the original Sanskrit into German and explained by CARL CAPPELLER, Professor at the University of Jena. 1912. Pages, 231. (Introduction, notes, and various other useful additions.)

Volume 16. The Çakuntalā, a Hindu drama by Kālidāsa: the Bengālī recension critically edited in the original Sanskrit and Prākrits by RICHARD PISCHEL, late Professor of Sanskrit at the University of Berlin. (Nearly ready.)

Volume 17. The Yoga-system of Patañjali, or the ancient Hindu doctrine of concentration of mind: embracing the Mnemonic rules (Yoga-sūtras) of Patañjali, the Comment (Bhāshya) attributed to Vyāsa, and the Explanation (Tattva-vāiçāradī) of Vāchaspati-Miçra: translated from the original Sanskrit by JAMES HAUGHTON WOODS, Professor of Philosophy at Harvard University. 1914. Pages, 422.

Volumes 18 and 19. The Veda of the Black Yajus School, entitled Tāittirīya Sañhitā. Translated from the original Sanskrit prose and verse, with a running commentary. By ARTHUR BERRIEDALE KEITH, D.C.L. (Oxford), of the Inner Temple, Barrister-at-law, and of His Majesty's Colonial Office, sometime Acting Professor of Sanskrit at the University of Oxford, Author of 'Responsible Government in the Dominions'. Volume 18, kāṇḍas I–III; volume 19, kāṇḍas IV–VII. 1914. Pages, 464 + 374 = 838. Not sold separately.

Volume 20. Rig-Veda Repetitions. A statistical and critical and historical account of the repeated verses and distichs and stanzas of the Rig-Veda. By MAURICE BLOOMFIELD. (Nearly ready.)

Volumes 21 and 22 and 23. Rāma's Later History, or **Uttara-Rāma-Charita,** an ancient Hindu drama by Bhavabhūti. Critically edited in the original Sanskrit and Prākrit, with an introduction and English translation and notes and variants, &c. By SHRIPAD KRISHNA BELVALKAR, Graduate Student of Harvard University, Assistant to the Professor of Sanskrit at Deccan College, Poona, India. Volume 21, Introduction and Translation. 1915. Pages, 190. Volume 22, Text; Indexes of Stanzas, Metres, &c.; Prākrit Glossary. (Nearly ready.)—Volume 23, English notes and Variant readings; Appendixes. (The material for Volume 23 is now, in 1915, upon a steamship interned at a port of the Balearic Islands.)

Printed in the United States
42611LVS00003B/98